THE SCOTT AND LAURIE OKI SERIES IN ASIAN AMERICAN STUDIES

THE UNSUNG GREAT

Stories of Extraordinary Japanese Americans

GREG ROBINSON

UNIVERSITY OF WASHINGTON PRESS

Seattle

The Unsung Great was supported by a grant from the Scott and Laurie Oki Endowment for Books in Asian American Studies.

Design by Katrina Noble
Composed in Arno Pro, typeface designed by Robert Slimbach

Cover photos: (clockwise from top left) Mary Oyama Mittwer and Sam Nagata. War Relocation Authority portrait, Bancroft Library, University of California, Berkeley; Jokichi Takamine. Courtesy of Science History Institute; Sono Osato dancing. Courtesy of the Mitchell Library, State Library of New South Wales; Aiko Herzig-Yoshinaga, circa 1945. Courtesy of Herzig-Yoshinaga family; John Okada, Broadway High School (Seattle) graduation portrait, 1941. Personal collection of Joanne Mock; Yoichi Okamoto, the official White House photographer, taking a picture of himself in the mirror at the LBJ Ranch in Stonewall, Texas; President Johnson seated at left. Courtesy of Lyndon B. Johnson Presidential Library.

24   23   22   21   20   5   4   3   2   1

Printed and bound in the United States of America

UNIVERSITY OF WASHINGTON PRESS
uwapress.uw.edu

LIBRARY OF CONGRESS CONTROL NUMBER: 2020932708

In loving memory of Jean-Francis Clermont-Legros (1977–2020)

CONTENTS

THE UNSUNG GREAT

Introduction

AN OUTSIDER LOOK AT JAPANESE AMERICANS

I AM PROUD TO PRESENT *THE UNSUNG GREAT*, A NEW COLLECTION of my short pieces on Japanese American history and culture. Over the past fifteen years, in addition to writing scholarly books and articles, I have worked as a journalist and columnist, turning out historically themed newspaper articles and blog posts on a regular basis. The bulk of the pieces featured here were originally published in "The Great Unknown and the Unknown Great," my column for the San Francisco–based newspaper *Nichi Bei Weekly*, or posted on *Discover Nikkei*, the blog of the Japanese American National Museum. The rest of the pieces appeared in other venues or are presented here for the first time.

The appearance of a new book, as always, gives rise to a series of emotions in me. First, there is the joy and paternal pride I always feel at seeing my work between covers—there is something magical about being the author of a book! In this case, there is also the excitement of revisiting my past writings and in a few cases inserting material that did not fit into the original columns or that I have uncovered since. One special pleasure of my line of work is receiving messages from readers. I am especially gratified to hear from relatives of my subjects who have learned more about their families through my research, and who in turn fill me in on aspects of those lives about which I was unaware.

As I explained in the opening pages of my first collection, *The Great Unknown: Japanese American Sketches* (University Press of Colorado, 2016), the primary purpose of my short pieces is to enlighten and intrigue readers by telling tales of fascinating but unknown people and things. Because the stories are intended for a general readership and designed for easy reading, I have limited the number of notes, though I include a general bibliography. Nonetheless, beyond being entertaining—as if that was not reason enough to do them!—my stories serve a serious purpose. My goal is to challenge conventional and outmoded ideas of Japanese Americans by focusing on unsung areas of the group's history.

For one thing, popular memory and general histories of Nikkei (ethnic Japanese) tend to center on West Coast communities. While I certainly give due attention to the region, I take a broader, nationwide view. By the same token, the mass of scholarship on Japanese Americans covers Issei (Japanese immigrants) and Nisei (American-born citizens of Japanese ancestry) in the period before World War II, or the wartime confinement experience (often, if imprecisely, known as the "Japanese American internment"). Without neglecting these eras, I also concentrate on the years after World War II, a period that has received much less attention in historical literature.

Each chapter in this collection revolves around a different theme. The first chapter is devoted to the mixed-race Japanese American families that formed in the decades before World War II. I start with an overall discussion of the subject. I was surprised to learn that during that period, despite the presence of laws in many states against interracial marriage, and despite widespread social stigma against sexual relationships between whites and ethnic Japanese, an impressive number of such couples formed, and they gave birth to a visible population of hapa (mixed-race) children. Many of these early hapa distinguished themselves as creative writers, artists, entertainers, businesspeople, and academics. What is more, whether because of their ability to operate outside of ethnic communities, their cosmopolitan outlook, or their own feeling of being marginal, a visible fraction of them engaged in political activism and formed ties with members of other minority groups. A highlight of this chapter is the story of the multigenerational

Takamine clan of scientists and doctors. Another is the diverse, far-flung Ohnick/Onuki clan.

Chapter 2 covers Japanese American literature. It reveals in particular the diversity of Nisei writing, which included poetry, short stories, children's literature, and novels, including mystery stories. One highlight of this chapter is a new essay on the creation of *John Okada: The Life and Rediscovered Work of the Author of "No-No Boy"* (University of Washington Press, 2018), which I coedited with Frank Abe and Floyd Cheung, and which won an American Book Award in 2019. Another illuminating piece studies the reviews that greeted the original 1957 edition of Okada's groundbreaking novel *No-No Boy*.

Chapters 3 and 4 are devoted to stories involving the World War II era. The first chapter recounts the diverse lives of Japanese Americans amid war and mass confinement. For example, the brothers Tsuyoshi and Toru Matsumoto, a pair of Issei Christians, both faced internment as dangerous aliens, then subsequently supported the American war effort. Yet the circumstances of their lives remained radically different. Chapter 4 takes up the stories of a series of non-Japanese people who worked to support Japanese Americans during their confinement. One highlight of this chapter is the piece on relations with Chinese Americans. Although popular images of Chinese Americans have stressed their support for China in its struggle against the Japanese occupation, numerous individuals offered support to their confined Nikkei friends, neighbors, and spouses.

Chapter 5 explores different forms of political activism among the Nisei and their struggles for civil rights. Whether in running for office, campaigning, legislative lobbying, court cases, or advocacy, Japanese Americans and their allies were active in the public sphere throughout the twentieth century. One noteworthy piece from this chapter studies the contributions of Loren Miller, an African American civil rights attorney and outstanding supporter of Japanese Americans. Conversely, the chapter on Ben Kuroki and Clifford Uyeda reveals the strong attraction of conservative politics to Nisei in the 1960s.

Chapter 6 deals with creativity among the Nikkei. Since their origins, Japanese communities in the United States have been marked by the presence of artists, designers, photographers, filmmakers, and performing artists. While they have had to struggle for patronage and visibility, their contributions have enriched the larger society. What is especially interesting to discover is that a similar spirit of invention and innovation is true of scientists. Newton Wesley's development of the contact lens not only gave birth to a giant industry but also saved his own failing sight. Eugenie Clark, the "shark lady," transformed public consciousness about sharks and developed a commercially successful shark repellant.

Chapter 7 centers on the queer history of Japanese Americans. Ever since I began writing for the *Nichi Bei* newspapers in 2007, I have done an annual "Queer History" column. These writings trace the evolution of attitudes toward different forms of sexuality among Japanese Americans and explore LGBT Nikkei voices. Because the topic of homosexuality was long taboo within Japanese communities (as in the larger society), locating sources of information on the past is difficult, and interpreting them can be tricky. Perhaps as a result, my essays on this theme have been especially praised but have simultaneously led to complaints and hate mail. One highlight of this section is my discussion (originally a book review) of *Two Spirits, One Heart*, Marsha Aizumi's memoir of her experience with her transgender son.

Chapter 8 features columns on Japanese Americans outside the West Coast. I cover individuals and groups in such far-flung places as Chicago, Boston, upstate New York, Alabama, Tennessee, and Louisiana. Considering that Issei and Nisei were a quite small population group and remained marginalized in differing degrees due to their racial and religious identity, it is amazing to note the dispersal of Nikkei lives even before 1970. As an epilogue, I feature my piece on nunc pro tunc, which reveals the role of the late Toni Robinson in helping form me as a historian of Japanese Americans.

CHAPTER ONE

Mixed-Race Japanese Americans

FAMILY STORIES

Hapa Japanese America: An Overview

Japanese Americans in the twenty-first century represent an increasingly exogamous group. Recent statistics reveal rates of intermarriage around 50 percent among individuals of Japanese ancestry in the United States, leading to a significant birth rate of hapa (mixed-race) children of these marriages. The coming of age of this new multiracial generation has led various writers to speculate on the reshaping of the traditional ethnic group. There have even been occasional prognostications about the disappearance of the ethnic community. Strangely, however, the past history of interracial marriage and mixed-race Japanese Americans has remained largely obscure in such discussions.

Scholars, as well as popular commentators, have tended to assume that before recent decades mixed unions and their offspring were a rare and marginal phenomenon. There are some rational grounds for such a belief. While the idea of "miscegenation" between whites and ethnic Japanese did not trigger the level of panic among elite white Americans—in the South or elsewhere—that black-white sexual relations did, there was palpable opposition to interracial unions (as well as to the social leveling implied) during the early twentieth century. Indeed, during this period every state on the West Coast and in the mountain region except New Mexico and Washington had laws forbidding Asians to marry whites, and so did some Southern states. In the territory of Hawaiʻi, where white-Japanese unions were not barred, they were stigmatized.

In some cases, race-baiting West Coast journalists and politicians brandished intermarriage as a threat to justify racist exclusion of Chinese immigrants and later Japanese. Most notably, during the 1920s West Coast farmers and businessmen angry over economic competition from Issei trumpeted the menace of intermarriage in lobbying for immigration restriction. Not everybody agreed with this. Popular columnist Walter Lippmann deplored the insertion of race-based appeals into an economic argument for exclusion: "The Japanese ask the right to settle in California. Clearly it makes a whole lot of difference whether you conceive the demand as a desire to grow fruit or to marry the white man's daughter." Still, even Franklin D. Roosevelt, a liberal easterner who campaigned for better relations between Japan and the United States, expressed agreement with West Coast whites that legal bars to entry of Japanese, as well as discriminatory laws to prevent Japanese aliens from owning property, were justified because they preserved white "racial purity" against intermarriage and the menace of mixed-race children. "Anyone who has travelled in the Far East," FDR wrote in a newspaper column in 1925, "knows that the mingling of Asiatic blood with European or American blood produces, in nine cases out of ten, the most unfortunate results."

To be sure, there was a strong gender-based factor in relation to intermarriage, as romances between Asian men and white women were far more taboo than those between white men and Asian women, especially in Asia. A curious point concerns the first well-known fictional image of a mixed-race Japanese American, the baby named "Trouble" in John Luther Long's story "Madame Butterfly" and its subsequent theatrical and operatic adaptations. Born in Japan of the union of a white American sailor and the Japanese woman he abandons, Trouble is claimed by the returning father and his new white American wife, who seek to take him to the United States. In none of the versions of the story does Trouble's mixed ancestry make him undesirable to his white family, nor is there any sense that he would face difficulties over it once in America.

In any case, despite the legal and social obstacles to white-Asian marriages, they occurred in significant numbers. The incomplete WRA roster of Japanese American West Coast residents "relocated" during World War II, maintained at the National Archives, lists 192 Nikkei of mixed white and Japanese ancestry, plus another 183 listed as "Japanese and other" (a category that included those with African American, Hispanic, Chinese, and Filipino ancestry, as well as a group of inmates from Alaska who were partly Inuit). Such unions were even more common in the cosmopolitan urban Northeast and Midwest, where ethnic Japanese populations did not trigger the same level of hostility as on the West Coast. While there is no accurate accounting of their numbers, we have impressionistic accounts of their existence. According to one Nikkei community survey in New York taken during the mid-1930s, at least one-third of its members—and possibly as many as half—had non-Japanese partners.[1]

Not only was white-Asian intermarriage legal in the East, Issei there also had extra incentive to find non-Japanese spouses. Unlike on the West Coast and Hawai'i, many of these immigrants were educated young male professionals who integrated easily into mainstream society and thereby more easily met white women (frequently from working-class or ethnic backgrounds), with whom they had children. Their great distance from Japan made returning home to find a Japanese bride or sending for a "picture bride" less practical.

Furthermore, a review of the lives of early mixed-race Japanese Americans reveals a panoply of often exceptional individuals, who left their mark in fields as diverse as literature, visual and performance arts, sports, business, and political activism. Beyond the individuals whose lives are chronicled in this book, one could easily make up an additional list of notable figures that would include the Nisei writers Kathleen Tamagawa and Milton Ozaki (as well as the Issei poet and critic Sadakichi Hartmann); artists Isamu Noguchi and Earle Goodenow (Kyohei Inukai); dancers Ailes Gilmour and Marian Saki; actress Lotus Long (née Pearl Shibata); and activists Fred Makino, Yone U. Stafford, and Toshi Ohta Seeger. Another aspect of mixed-race Japanese American history that I find equally remarkable is the development of hapa clans that produced multiple family members of note. The rest of this chapter is devoted to some intriguing examples of these.

Takamine Family

One extraordinary hapa American saga is that of the Takamines. The family patriarch, chemist Jokichi Takamine Sr., was arguably the most famous Nikkei in the United States, if not the Western world, at the time of his death in 1922. However, his celebrity has diminished over time, while the name Takamine has become better known as a brand of guitars (whose name stems from Japan's Mount Takamine, not the Takamine family). More importantly, the story of Jokichi Takamine's descendants, who continued to produce leaders in health sciences and business over generations, remains largely unstudied.

Jokichi Takamine Sr. was born on November 3, 1854, in Takaoka, Japan. His father was Seiichi Takamine, a doctor of the Kaga domain (today's Toyama and Ishikawa prefectures). He was educated in science, first in Japan at Kobu Daigakko (now University of Tokyo) and then for one year at University of Glasgow and Anderson's College in Scotland, where he was sent by the Japanese government. In 1883 he returned home to Japan and was hired by Japan's Department of Agriculture and Commerce. The following year, the young scientist was dispatched by the Japanese government to serve as co-commissioner of the Japanese pavilion at the World Cotton Centennial in New Orleans. (Among the exhibits at the pavilion was the Japanese plant *kuzu*—thus did the kudzu vine make its entry into the United States.) While at the fair, Takamine studied fertilizers and was impressed by the use of phosphates in soil. He stayed on afterward in New Orleans at a local boardinghouse owned by Ebenezer Hitch, a Union army

Jokichi Takamine. Courtesy of Science History Institute.

veteran, and fell in love with Hitch's daughter Caroline. The two were married, and after a honeymoon studying phosphates the two moved to Japan, settling in the Tokyo region, where Takamine founded the Tokyo Artificial Fertilizer Company. Meanwhile the couple had two sons, Jokichi Jr. and Eben Takashi (named for his maternal grandfather).

After a few years in Japan, the Takamine family migrated to the United States in 1890 and settled in Chicago. There Takamine started experimenting with koji, a culture made from a fungus, grown on rice or wheat bran, whose enzymes break down starch molecules, and which aids fermentation of sake and soybeans. Takamine adapted koji for use as a substitute for malt in distilling whiskey. After moving to Peoria, Illinois, home of the Whiskey Trust, Takamine was able to develop a new whiskey using the cheaper process, although he developed serious liver disease soon after and was forced to return to Chicago for surgery. In 1894 he founded the Takamine Ferment Company. Under the sponsorship of the drug giant Parke-Davis, he patented an artificial enzyme, which he dubbed Taka-Diastase, and licensed it to Parke-Davis as a digestive aid, for treatment of dyspepsia.

The product was such a success that in 1897 Takamine moved with his family to New York. There, using his profits from Taka-Diastase, he established an independent research facility, the Takamine laboratory, on East 103rd Street. In 1899 he was granted a doctorate in Chemical Engineering from the Imperial University in Tokyo (in 1906 he would be granted a second doctorate in pharmacology). With assistance from a young Japanese chemist, Keizo Uenaka, Takamine began research into glandular secretions. In 1900 he succeeded in reducing secretions of the adrenal gland to crystalline form which would be used to raise the blood pressure of humans via injection. Takamine dubbed the product "adrenalin" (now adrenaline) and secured a patent. While the originality of Takamine's work was challenged by chemist John Jacob Abel of Johns Hopkins University, who had previously developed epinephrine into a powder, Takamine's patents were ultimately upheld in federal court in 1911.

With the proceeds from his twin discoveries, Takamine became a rich man. He largely withdrew from scientific research and concentrated on business affairs, in 1913 founding the Sankyo Pharmaceutical Company in Japan (today Daiichi Sankyo) and became its first president. He also expanded his original company into the International Takamine Ferment Company. In 1915 he moved the Takamine Laboratory to Clifton, New Jersey.

Takamine used his wealth to provide himself a comfortable life. In addition to taking an apartment on New York's opulent Riverside Drive, he built a summer estate, Merriewold, on two thousand acres near Passaic, New Jersey. He took over Ho-o-Den, the Japanese pavilion that had been built for the Louisiana Purchase Exhibition, the 1904 St. Louis World's Fair. Once the fair closed, Takamine had the pavilion dismantled and shipped from St. Louis to Merriewold, where it was installed in a twenty-five-acre Japanese garden.

Takamine also spent much time leading Japanese community activities, and he dedicated himself to improving US-Japanese relations. In 1906 he became first president of the Nippon Club, a social and business fraternity for Japanese immigrants in New York, and helped found the Nippon Jin Kai (Japanese Association). In 1910 Takamine arranged for the mayor of Tokyo to offer Japanese cherry trees to Washington, DC as a symbol of Japanese-American friendship. After the initial plants, about two thousand, were rejected as diseased Takamine ordered a new shipment, and isolated them in greenhouses until they were approved. The cherry trees were planted along the Tidal Basin, where some of them today remain a leading tourist attraction of the nation's capital. Takamine suffered for many years from liver disease. In mid-1922, while he was already ailing, he converted to Catholicism. In July he died, leaving the bulk of his fortune to Caroline and his sons and their wives. Caroline soon after married Charles Beach, who rapidly exhausted much of the family fortune. The Takamine children, however, would continue work in health science research.

The first was Jokichi Jr., who attended Horace Mann School and Yale University, then studied chemistry in Germany and at the Pasteur Institute in Paris. After returning to the United States, he entered business with his father, directing the Takamine Laboratory. He married Hilda Petrie, and in the succeeding years had two children, Caroline and Jokichi III. Following his father's death, Jokichi Jr. assumed control of all of the family businesses, including the International Takamine Ferment Company and the firm of Takamine & Darby. In addition, he served as a director of the Bankers Petroleum Company and director of the Clifton Piece Dye Works.

In 1930, while staying at New York's Hotel Roosevelt, Jokichi Jr. fell from a fourteenth-story window and died at the age of forty-one. His grieving mother was convinced that Jokichi had been murdered by Prohibition-era gangsters pressuring him to reveal his whiskey fermentation process. However, following an official investigation, authorities determined that the death had been accidental, revealing that Jokichi had spent the evening carousing in nightclubs, had entered the hotel in a state of intoxication, and had been in the company of a young woman who was not his wife.

Following Jokichi Jr.'s death, Eben Takamine became the head of the family. Born in 1890, he had likewise attended Yale University. Not long after his graduation, he married Ethel Johnson and went into business as a manufacturer and importer of machinery. In the years following his father's death, Eben's life shifted. In 1925 he and his wife divorced, and he left New York to live in Arizona for a time. In 1928 he eloped to Maryland to marry Odette Jean, a former showgirl with the Ziegfeld Follies.

With his brother's death, Eben was thrown into managing the family businesses, and he helped expand them during the Great Depression. On

December 7, 1941, following Tokyo's attack on Pearl Harbor, the Takamine Laboratories plant was surrounded by a police guard that prevented employees from entering. Due to his birth in Japan, Eben was unable to become a US citizen, despite his mother's citizenship. He may have feared that the business would be closed. In the event, however, the company remained intact and contributed to the war effort by developing penicillinase, an enzyme used to assay the new antibiotic "wonder drug" penicillin. In 1943 Eben married his third wife, Catherine MacMahon, an English woman. Ten years later, in 1953, he died at sixty-three, just weeks after he finally became a US citizen under the 1952 McCarran-Walter Act. His widow sold off the family businesses, which were subsequently dispersed. The Takamine Laboratory was bought by Miles Laboratories. Catherine later financed the creation of the Takamine Garden, a Japanese garden featuring a pond and Japanese maples, in San Francisco's Golden Gate Park.

A third-generation family member engaged in health science was Jokichi "Joe" Takamine III. Born in 1924, he was only five when his father, Jokichi Jr., died, and he was brought up by his mother. After attending Williams College, Joe received his MD from New York University Medical School in 1953. Following a residence at Lenox Hill Hospital, he moved to Los Angeles. There he made addiction medicine his specialty. "Addiction is the most untreated treatable disease in America," he once said, "The message we want to get out to families is that there is hope—people not only can survive, they can recover and lead whole lives." Takamine served as a medical director at various California hospitals, in addition to his private practice. He also served as chairman of the American Medical Association Task Force on Alcoholism and was a member of the American Medical Association Task Force on Drugs. His most notable position was at St. John's Hospital and Health Center in Santa Monica, where he ran the twenty-one-day detox program. Among his patients were notable entertainment industry figures such as Dennis Wilson of the Beach Boys and Slipknot's Paul Gray. Buzz Aldrin, the astronaut, later recalled that he met the lean, sandy-haired doctor of internal medicine when he was admitted to St. John's to treat his alcoholism. Takamine told him, "You may not be responsible for your disease, but you sure should be responsible for your recovery—and that is your choice. There is only one reason for relapse. You want to . . . and you choose so to do." In support of his work on addiction, in 1986 Takamine produced a video, *Conquering Cocaine.*

In 2007 Joe Takamine was honored by Phoenix House, a treatment and prevention organization, for his dedication to the field of substance abuse. He was likewise recognized for his service to the community by the National Council on Alcoholism and Drug Dependency and was a recipient of the National Drug Abuse Medicine Award. He was certified in 1990 by the American Society of Addiction Medicine. He died in 2013.

Hirose Family

One of the pleasures of working on this book has been the joy of running across unfamiliar names, looking into their stories, and uncovering interesting information that makes the history we study richer and more complex. A case in point is that of George and Arthur Hirose, hapa brothers from New York. George was notable both as a religious singer and a Broadway stalwart. Arthur became an executive and leader in the field of advertising. Both their unusual careers stand in bold contradiction to received notions about the outsider status of prewar Japanese Americans in general, and the isolation facing mixed-race individuals in particular.

The Hirose brothers were born in New York City. Their father, Yoshisuke Hirose, a Japanese of samurai heritage, came to the United States during the Meiji period (1868–1912). He was sent to New York as a Baptist missionary to serve Japanese residents, especially sailors. According to descendants, he arrived knowing Japanese, Hebrew, Greek, Latin, and English. He studied at Beloit College in Wisconsin before enrolling in theological studies at Wheaton College in Illinois. Yoshisuke (known as Yosh or John) worked himself through school, partly through lecture tours on Japan he gave in midwestern towns, and partly with support from the Congregationalist church of Sterling, Illinois. While at Wheaton he met and fell in love with a fellow student, Barbara Gebhardt, who was studying to be a missionary.

After graduation, Yoshisuke moved to New York, where he directed the Prospect Street Mission (later known as the Japanese Christian Institute) in Brooklyn. There Barbara joined him, and the two were married in March 1898. George McGregor Hirose, their first child, was born in 1899, while Arthur came along two years later.

At the time of his marriage, Yoshisuke had spoken about his intention to return to Japan as a missionary and his wish to minister to Japanese in New York and open a school for their children. In 1906 Reverend Hirose was listed in a *New York Sun* article as the pastor of a Japanese mission at 330 East Fifty-Seventh Street. What happened to him after that is not clear—according to descendants, he returned to Japan. In any event, according to the 1915 New York State census, Barbara and the two boys were living without him in Manhattan by that year—George was listed as an "entry clerk" and brother Arthur as a schoolboy. Soon after, the family moved to the suburb of Mount Vernon, New York, where Barbara would live for some years.

While George remained in Mount Vernon and supported his mother for a time, in the late 1920s he married Naoe Kondo, a New Jersey–born Nisei, and moved to Manhattan. During the 1920s George worked as a salesman and manager, ultimately for a shoe company. Meanwhile he was drawn to work with Tom Noonan, the "Bishop of Chinatown," who operated a Baptist rescue mission on Doyers Street and conducted weekly radio services, *Cathedral of the Air*, from an old Chinese theater. Noonan engaged George as one of the regular stable of singers who performed on his program.

By 1924 Hirose was winning popular attention as a "Japanese baritone." A reviewer in the *New York Herald Tribune* celebrated Hirose as "one of the best baritones we have heard." Perhaps conscious of ethnic stereotyping, in his publicity George laid emphasis on his "manly style" and "clearness of tone." By 1930 he was sufficiently well known that he did concert tours, singing in Schenectady, New York, Hartford, Connecticut, and Ocean City, Maryland. A review of a Hirose concert in Farmville, Virginia, in late 1933 noted that George's size and the powerful vibrancy of his voice were impressive for a Japanese. Though the review complained of lack of warmth and excessive vibrato, the reviewer praised his stage presence and ability to "put over" a song.

In addition to singing in concert halls, Hirose began a series of "spiritual concerts" in churches and established a tradition of singing Palm Sunday and Easter services. In 1932 he sang the baritone part in the Easter section of Gounod's "Redemption" at the Park Avenue Church in New York City. The following year George appeared at Tom Noonan's mission to sing Methodist hymns—he shared the program with Goldie Mae Steiner, who was billed as "the only colored woman cantor in America." This concert may have inaugurated a pattern: the following year, he performed a sacred song concert at an African American church, Mt. Olivet Baptist, and then appeared with African American performers in an interracial concert at Calvary Baptist Church. During this same period, he spent three years as baritone soloist at the Central Congregational Church in Brooklyn. In 1938 he was featured on a radio program in Los Angeles, in which he sang Japanese songs. He also taught singing, both in his own studio and as head of the vocal department of the Purcell School of Music in Montclair, New Jersey.

Tom Noonan's death in August 1935 seems to have marked an important shift for George from concert and radio singing to theater, though he had been engaged in stage work for some years already. In January 1927 he was selected for the cast of *Ching-A-Ling*, an "Oriental Revue" that featured Chinese and Japanese in comic roles, plus a bevy of Asian chorus girls. The renowned modern dancer Michio Ito was the show's choreographer and star, and Yeichi Nimura, later famous as a dance teacher, made his stage debut as a dancer. The show opened in Wilmington, Delaware. By the time it reached Broadway later that year, under the name *Tokyo Blues*, it had been taken over by showman John Murray Anderson, and its stars were the youthful vaudeville players "The Three Meyakos" (in real life Esther, Florence, and George Kudara, three mixed-race Nisei from Buffalo).

Although Hirose was listed as engaged for a show called *Battleship Gertie* in 1934, his next Broadway appearance came in September 1935, just after Tom Noonan's death, when he was cast as Baron Ishiwara in the Theatre Guild production of *If This Be Treason*, a play by Unitarian minister John Haynes Holmes. The play only ran for two months but gained wide publicity due to its pacifist message. (After Japan launches a surprise attack on the United States and seizes Manila, the president of the United States resists all calls to declare war and instead flies to Japan to negotiate, thereby inspiring the Japanese people to rise up and throw out the militarists.) In April 1936, Hirose made use of his vocal gifts when he was cast as Pish-Tush in a short-lived Broadway production of Gilbert and Sullivan's *The Mikado*. *New York Times* reviewer Brooks Atkinson praised George's voice but found his acting too humorless for a light operetta. Naoe meanwhile acted in such productions as George S. Kaufman's *First Lady*, opposite Jane Cowl.

In 1936 George and Naoe traveled to Japan, where they stayed just over a year. According to newspaper stories, George appeared at the popular Tokyo theater Nippon Gekijo for thirty consecutive weeks. Upon his return he settled for six months in Los Angeles, where he worked as a singing teacher and dramatic coach and sang a concert at Union Church. His big break came when he was cast as Ichiro Kato (again a Japanese part) in the 1939 George Abbott musical comedy *See My Lawyer*, starring Milton Berle. It ran for 224 performances. In 1940, he was featured on the program of a musicale at the Japanese Garden of the Ritz-Carlton Hotel, singing selections from composer Claude Lapham's "Oriental" opera *Sakura*.

The outbreak of war with Japan and resulting anti-Japanese sentiment in the United States cut into George's career, and he was absent from performing for a generation. In later years he played a bit part in the 1965 Japanese monster movie *Gamera* and portrayed Charlie Chan in a series of TV commercials for shirts. He made a few more stage appearances, including in an unsuccessful Broadway show, *13 Daughters* (1961), starring Don Ameche, and performed as Dr. Li in summer stock tours of the Rogers and Hammerstein musical *Flower Drum Song*. (George was listed as a cast member in an out-of-town preview of the Anthony Newley–Leslie Bricusse revue *The Roar of the Greasepaint, the Smell of the Crowd*, but he was not in the final New York cast). Naoe played three years in the Broadway production of John Patrick's *The Teahouse of the August Moon*. George Hirose died in New York in August 1974.

While George Hirose devoted himself to the stage and concert singing, his younger brother Arthur built a distinguished career in advertising and was a member of the founding generation of market researchers. Arthur Pierson Hirose was born in New York on May 24, 1901. In his youth, he was an Eagle Scout, and, according to family lore, as a teenager he worked as a "spear carrier" at the Metropolitan Opera. After completing high school, he attended New York University but seems not to have earned a degree. Instead, he took a job as an editor at *McCall's* and *Redbook*. There he met Marguerite Byrnes, a white woman two years his senior and a fellow editor. The two married in 1921 and had one daughter, Nancy Pierson Hirose.

Soon after his marriage, Arthur Hirose was hired by the well-known McGraw-Hill Publishing Company. There he served both as an editor and as manager of the sales promotion and market analysis departments. In addition, he remained an active organizer of the marketing field. In 1933 he was elected secretary-treasurer of the New York chapter of the American Marketing Society. In 1937 he became secretary-treasurer of the Market Research Council, and in September 1939 he was elected president of the council and served a one-year term. Sometime later he was named national treasurer of the American Marketing Association.

In 1934 Hirose left McGraw-Hill and was hired back by *McCall's*, as director of market research. To supplement his income and increase his public profile, he began writing. His first productions were a regular series of features for *Better Homes and Gardens*. "Let's Discuss Your Plumbing," appeared in October 1934. "Hot Water All the Times," followed in February 1935, and "Soft Water," the following month. He also published a letter in the *New Yorker* and contributed an entry to *Encyclopedia Britannica*. In mid-1935 his visibility reached a height when he was invited by the *New York Times* to review a trade show on "The New Electric Home." In the article, Hirose spoke about the changes that would be brought to homes by newly developed electric appliances such as the kitchen garbage disposal, plus that new wonder, home air conditioning. He explained that these new machines would help women with housework, then concluded by extolling the advantages for their husbands: "To men will come a release from practically all the laborious household jobs that now face them before they leave in the morning and after they return in the evening."

Despite the Depression, the Hirose family seems to have prospered. They bought a house in the New York suburb of Teaneck, New Jersey. Beginning in 1935, the couple took yearly trips to Europe, plus one to Singapore and Sri Lanka (then Ceylon) in 1935. In 1940 Hirose took a holiday in Guatemala.

With the revival of the US economy following the outbreak of war in Europe, Hirose's services were increasingly in demand. His speeches began to be cited in the *New York Times* and other publications. In October 1940 he was invited to address the Association of Gas Appliance and Equipment Manufacturers at its Atlantic City conference. He told the meeting that sales of gas refrigerators and ranges that year would be at a ten-year high.

In 1941 Arthur Hirose won the coveted research medal at the Annual Advertising Awards sponsored by the trade magazine *Advertising and Selling*. In response, in September 1941 *McCall's* promoted him to director of promotion. (An article noting his appointment, complete with portrait photo, ran in the *New York Times*.) As director, Hirose produced marketing surveys with questionnaires and solicited the help of *McCall's* readers. The information he received was summarized in a group of articles in *Advertising and Selling*.

After the Pearl Harbor attack in December 1941, he threw himself into a more public role. At first his chief interest was aiding the war effort. In June 1942 Hirose told the American Marketing Association that all advertising in wartime had to justify itself and concluded by listing various ways that advertising could help build support for the war. Soon after, the federal Office of Price Administration appointed Hirose a consultant, and in summer 1943 the War Advertising Council appointed him as volunteer research coordinator. His mission was to help the council devise advertising to promote the war effort.

As time went on, Hirose shifted his attention to postwar planning. Starting in mid-1943, he gave a series of well-publicized talks to trade groups. He told a meeting of the Associated Printing Salesmen that women consumers had grown more sophisticated and knowledgeable as a result of their wartime experience, and he said that postwar marketers would have to be savvier in attracting them. Hirose explained that the market for automated equipment, notably, would skyrocket. "The woman who has run an automatic machine and worked in an air-conditioned factory will not be content to do her housework manually or shovel coal." He similarly warned gas stove manufacturers that they would have to advertise heavily in postwar months to stave off competition from electric ranges. In a speech to the New York Employing Printers Association, he stated that unless government "unduly restricted" private enterprise after the war, the nation would have the largest market ever for advertising and promotional printing. His talk evolved into his article "Market Research as a Practical Help in Reconversion Problems," which appeared in the trade review *Journal of Marketing* in 1945. In the article he declared that market researchers had the job of aiding postwar production by selecting new products or revamping old ones for production, and determining markets and distribution for them. In April 1944 he made a public address regarding postwar prospects for the home furnishing industry. He suggested that wartime brides and "new money girls" would be the largest consumers of home furnishings in the postwar era.

In the fall of 1944, Hirose was named director of promotion and research at *Newsweek*. He sold his Teaneck house and moved to an apartment at 21 East Ninth Street in Manhattan. (It would be interesting to know whether Hirose ever rubbed shoulders with Nisei artist Miné Okubo, who resettled from the Topaz camp to New York in early 1944 and moved into a studio two doors down at 17 East Ninth Street.) It seemed as if Hirose's career was peaking. Just a few weeks after starting at *Newsweek*, however, he undertook a speaking tour of the Midwest (presumably to discuss postwar marketing plans). While in Chicago he contracted a cold but insisted in keeping his speaking engagements. On the way home he grew so sick that he was taken off the train at Harrisburg, Pennsylvania, and hospitalized. On December 9 he died of pneumonia at Harrisburg General Hospital.

Hirose's death prompted an obituary with photo in the *New York Times* (which made no mention of his father or his Japanese heritage) and a range of tributes in advertising and marketing industry journals. An official resolution of the American Marketing Association acknowledged his death and commemorated his career. While Hirose was not much discussed in Japanese American media during his lifetime, *Pacific Citizen* editor Larry Tajiri mentioned him in a column for the magazine *NOW* on outstanding Japanese Americans of mixed ancestry.

Without denying Arthur Hirose's solid achievements, perhaps the most extraordinary thing about him in retrospect is just how normal he seems: a successful young executive rising in his field before his untimely death. Yet his life becomes more intriguing when we reflect that his was an age in which job discrimination against Japanese Americans was rampant, especially on the West Coast, a time when few if any Nisei were hired as executives by mainstream firms. George Hirose, working on the New York stage, was restricted to playing Asians. Yet his brother Arthur (who was listed as white in the 1920 and 1930 federal census, which did not have a categories for people of mixed Asian and non-Asian heritage) was able to integrate and find a slot for himself in the corporate world despite his Japanese name and ancestry, which he never concealed.

Ohnick Family

One remarkable Japanese American family is the Ohnicks, a mixed-race clan whose adventures span continents.

The patriarch of the Ohnicks was Hachiro Onuki. Born in Japan circa 1849, the oldest of four children, he grew up in the mountains near Nikko. According to legend, as a five-year old he saw Commodore Matthew Perry's famous "black ships" sail into Japanese harbors in 1854. There were no schools near the Onuki family's house, and Hachiro's father engaged a Russian to tutor his family. In addition to Russian, the young Hachiro learned at least a smattering of English from his tutor.

In 1875 a US Navy ship came to Japan to purchase "various items of Japanese manufacture and culture" to be displayed the following year at the Japanese pavilion at the Centennial Exhibition, a world's fair taking place in Philadelphia. (The Japanese pavilion, Tokyo's first official entry in any international exhibitions, helped introduce many Americans and other westerners to Japanese art and culture). The American sailors faced difficulties in communicating with the Japanese to obtain the artifacts. Summoned as an interpreter by a Tokyo merchant, Hachiro grew friendly with the sailors, showed them around town, and helped negotiate sales. While the sailors had no funds to pay for his services, they offered in exchange to transport him to the United States to care for the cargo and then to return him to Japan on their next voyage. According to legend, Hachiro was at first reluctant, but once he learned that the exhibition would feature modern lighting, which could be turned on by the push of a button, he agreed to travel to America.

The ship took several months to cross the Pacific, then sail around South America, and proceed up the Atlantic Coast. After landing in Boston, where he was entertained by some of the sailors' families, Hachiro traveled on to Philadelphia, where he attended the Centennial Exhibition. After completing his task of unloading the cargo, Hachiro was supposed to return to Japan. However, as he was in no hurry to leave the United States, he agreed with his shipmates that he would make an overland crossing by rail to San Francisco, then eventually catch his ship following its voyage back around South America. While en route to California, he fell in with a pair of white prospectors who were heading to the West to mine for gold or silver. Hachiro agreed to join them. In the process, they persuaded him to Americanize his name to Hutchlon Ohnick (or just H. Ohnick).

After trying their luck at gold mining in Carson City, Nevada, the trio turned south to Arizona. In August 1878 Ohnick opened a restaurant, Bon Ton, in Prescott, Arizona. A local paper, the *Weekly Arizona Miner*, carried an advertisement from Ohnick offering a meal for fifty cents or full board for a week for seven dollars. Ohnick stated, "Guests will find my tables supplied with all the delicacies of the season done up in first-class style." A writer for the paper stated, "Judging by the experience of the tables, the most fastidious epicure would have no cause for complaint. The proprietor, H. Ohnick, has extensive experience in catering to the appetite, and will no doubt please the Prescott public."

The Bon Ton seems not to have succeeded, though, as by 1880 Ohnick had settled in Tombstone, Arizona (which would soon after become legendary for Wyatt Earp and the gunfight at the OK Corral). According to one source, Ohnick applied to work in the local silver mines but was refused employment because of his short stature and thin body, and he instead worked as a teamster hauling wood and water for the mine's mess hall. He also seems to have started a new career as a financier and to have had a litigious tendency, as several lawsuits in which he was a claimant were filed in the following years. An article from 1886 mentions that "the Jap Ohnick" had seized mules, harnesses, and wagons from C. S. Banham, boss of the Cananea copper mines in Sonora, after Banham failed to repay a loan.

According to another newspaper story, Ohnick, while working at a mine in Tombstone, had inadvertently cut wood on federal land, prompting a government lawsuit against the mine owners. After two representatives of the mining firm arrived in Tombstone to defend the owners, they befriended Ohnick, who served as chief witness in court. In the end, the mining company won the lawsuit. Ohnick's new friends advised him to move to Phoenix and seek new opportunities there.

Once settled in Phoenix, then a small town, Ohnick made his start by farming and selling drinking water. Soon he branched out into starting a streetcar line. After finding white partners—possibly the same mining company officials he had met in Tombstone—in 1886 he founded the city's first gas and electricity utility, the Phoenix Illuminating Gas and Electric Company (later known as Arizona Public Service) and requested a franchise from the Phoenix City Council. It was a daring proposal, especially as the very first electric utility company, Thomas Edison's New York Edison Company, had begun operations only four years before. However, the contract was granted, and in 1887 the company introduced the first gas-powered streetlights in Phoenix.

Following his success, Ohnick became a naturalized US citizen, served on the city's board of education, and was a 32nd Degree Scottish Rite Mason. In 1888 Ohnick married Katherine Shannon, a twenty-two-year-old American woman. Family legend has it that the two met when Ohnick went to her family's Phoenix home to install electric lighting. Within six or seven years the Ohnicks had four children: Helen, Ben, Tom, and Marion.

During the depression of the early 1890s, the Phoenix Light and Power Company endured serious problems and wound up under control of a receiver. In 1894 Ohnick resigned from the company and brought suit for salary payments owed him. Mrs. Ohnick sued the company as well, over loans she stated that she had made. After receiving an eighty-acre ranch and country house outside Phoenix as settlement for an investment in a failed bank, Ohnick started a truck farm, Garden City Farms, and hired Chinese laborers from San Francisco to operate it. The farm did not prosper, and

Ohnick eventually sold the land. In the years that followed, he worked as an electrician and opened a gardening business.

In 1898, following the death of his mother in Japan, Ohnick decided to take the family on a trip to Hawai'i (then newly annexed by the US government) and then Japan. He, his wife, and their children traveled to Seattle to embark on the transpacific liner. However, in the end, Mrs. Ohnick elected to remain in Seattle with the children, and Ohnick made the trip alone. While he had planned to stay only a short time in Japan, shipping from Asia was interrupted by the Boxer Rebellion in China, and Ohnick was stranded in Japan for several months.

In 1901, after returning to Arizona (where he stood trial for breaking a canal check gate, was found guilty, and was fined $20) Ohnick rejoined his family in Seattle. Taking two other Seattle Issei as partners, Ohnick founded the Oriental American Bank there and served as its business manager. He meanwhile worked in real estate and labor contracting. In 1907, after leaving the bank, he was appointed president and treasurer of a labor union and attempted to obtain labor contracts and fair wages for Japanese workers. The fledgling union was hampered not only by opposition from white employers but also from Japanese labor contractors, and it did not survive. After leaving the union, Ohnick experimented with sending red Holstein cattle to Japan for breeding stock purposes. He later formed another bank, the Specie Bank. In 1910 he applied to become a notary public. However, even though Ohnick produced his naturalization papers, Washington governor M. E. Hay (acting on advice from the state's attorney general) refused to grant him the notary license on the grounds that Japanese immigrants were ineligible for citizenship.

Little information is available on Ohnick's later years. According to one source, in 1912 Ohnick suffered a paralytic stroke and was left unable to work. He sold his interest in the Specie Bank to a Mr. Furuya. According to another source, while Ohnick had been a moderately wealthy man, he lost the family money in a bad investment and was left without a dollar. Regardless, he moved to Southern California, where his daughter Helen lived, and frequented various hot springs. He died in Long Beach, California, in 1921.

The children of the Ohnick family pursued various life paths. Son Tom Ohnick moved to Los Angeles, where he worked in the lumber business, married an Irish-American woman, and had two children. He died shortly after the outbreak of the Pacific War. The two Ohnick daughters achieved renown in the 1910s as a vaudeville team touring in the Northwest, notably as headliners at the Lyric Theatre in Spokane. Helen played the piano while Marion sang. Sometime around 1917, Helen retired from the stage, moved to Los Angeles, and found work with an insurance firm. In later years she continued to reside in Los Angeles, where she served as secretary of the Japan America Society of Southern California. (Perhaps because of family connections or a non-Asian physical appearance, none of the Ohnicks was removed from the West Coast following Executive Order 9066, President Roosevelt's February 1942 authorization of military concentration camps.)

After sister Helen left the stage, Marion made a career in show business, touring in vaudeville on the Orpheum Circuit and singing under the stage name Haruko Onuki (later Haru Onuki). In 1916 she moved to New York and joined the cast of a successful Broadway musical, *The Big Show*, where she introduced the hit song "Poor Butterfly," based on the character of Madame Butterfly. In 1918 she was featured in a show at New York's Royal Theatre with comedian Chic Sale. In 1919–20 she traveled to England and performed in music halls in London and Manchester. After returning to the United States, she performed at the Hillstreet Theatre in Los Angeles in 1922. The next year she starred in a production of Gilbert and Sullivan's *The Mikado* in Baltimore. In 1925 she played in vaudeville programs at the Hippodrome in New York and the Stanley Theatre in Philadelphia and sang ballads at the Washington, DC nightclub Le Paradis. In 1927 she performed at the Orpheum Theatre in Los Angeles. In 1928 she returned to England and played in British music halls.

Throughout her career, Onuki was racialized, both in her roles and in reviews, which emphasized her "daintiness" and her Japanese identity. When she performed in Los Angeles in a kimono, the *Los Angeles Times* referred to her as "that delectable morsel of Japanese femininity." Onuki played her image as an exotic to the hilt. Although at first she made clear in interviews that she had been born in Seattle (and her white mother accompanied her on her tours), as time went on she took on a Japanese identity. In her promotional materials she stated that she had worked as a geisha in Tokyo before being discovered and said that she had personally chosen her costume wardrobe from shops in Japan. She performed in benefit concerts to raise money for the Tokyo-based women's school Tsuda College after it was damaged in the great 1923 Kanto earthquake.

In addition to her vaudeville career, sometime around 1919 Onuki turned to opera singing. First she was listed as a featured soprano with the Society of American Singers. Soon after, she launched a singing career with the San Carlo Opera Company, performing what would become her signature role with the company, Cio-Cio-san (Butterfly) in Puccini's opera *Madama Butterfly*. She first sang the role at the Curran Theatre in San Francisco and the Majestic Theatre in Los Angeles, where she created a sensation. No doubt as a result, she resolved to travel to Europe to train for an operatic career. In 1923 she again toured the country with the San Carlo, performing *Butterfly*. When she opened at Poli's Theatre in Washington, DC, a *Washington Post* critic praised her "infinite artistic sense" and the "many sweet notes in her register." The following year she sang Butterfly in New Orleans, where Japanese soprano Tamaki Miura had previously caused a sensation. Local critic Noel Straus asserted that Onuki was "an ideal Butterfly for the eye, if not for the ear." He noted that her performance was disappointing from a strictly vocal point of view but admitted, "So fascinating was [her] expressive pantomime . . . and so charming her personality, that she held the attention riveted on her interpretation, thus making amends for many other shortcomings in the presentation."

Although a performance of *Butterfly* with the San Carlo at the Century Theatre was advertised in 1923, Onuki's official New York opera debut seems to have come in September 1926. Her performance then was greeted with mixed reviews. The *New York Times* critic praised her "striking entrance" which gave "exotic flavour" to the opera, adding that her dramatic talent won her the interest and sympathy of the audience. However, he stated flatly that her voice was "not quite heavy enough for the dramatic demands of the role." In the event, she sang the role of Butterfly a last time with the San Carlo on a British tour in 1928, then left the company. Her place was soon taken by Japan-born soprano Hizi Koyke, who would sing Butterfly regularly and would become the San Carlo's most popular star over the generation that followed. Onuki played a final vaudeville performance at the Warner theaters in Los Angeles in 1930, then left the stage entirely.

Following her retirement, Onuki gained some notoriety through court appearances. In the mid-1920s she had begun dating cartoonist Robert Ripley (she appeared in one of his "Ripley's Believe it or Not" cartoons as a Japanese prima donna who took a full day to fix her hair). In 1932 she sued Ripley in the New York Supreme Court for $500,000 for breach of promise, claiming that he had proposed marriage to her. At the request of Ripley's attorneys the suit was transferred to the federal district court on grounds of "diversity of citizenship" (meaning that Onuki was a California resident, which she denied). There is no further record of the lawsuit in the press afterward, so presumably it was ultimately settled or dismissed. In the years that followed, Onuki remained in New York City. According to one source, she moved in Los Angeles in the 1950s and sold real estate. Whatever the case, she died in New York in 1965.

It was oldest son Benjamin Shannon Ohnick who achieved the Ohnick family's greatest renown. Born in Phoenix in 1890, Benjamin spent his teen years in Seattle. After attending Lincoln High School, where he distinguished himself as a football player, he entered the University of Washington. While in college he played end on UW's 1909 and 1910 football teams under the famous football coach Gil Dobie. He subsequently went on to study at UW's law school. In 1913 he opened his law office in Seattle. From the beginning, he was engaged in community affairs. Articles of incorporation for the Reliance Hospital Association were drawn up on December 28, 1912, and filed for record with the Secretary of State on January 6, 1913, and Ohnick was one of the first trustees of the association, along with Hoshin Fujii and Selma Anderson. (Selma Anderson was a former Christian missionary who converted to Buddhism and was an early member of the Buddhist Mission in Seattle.) In 1917, after the United States entered World War I, Benjamin Ohnick enlisted as a private in the US Army and was stationed at nearby Camp Lewis for the duration. Following the end of the war he returned to Seattle and resumed his law practice. Sometime during these years he met and married a secretary in the firm, a white woman named Ina. The couple had three children.

Despite his education and record, Benjamin Ohnick faced prejudice because of his Japanese ancestry. At least in part as a result, in 1922 the Ohnicks were attracted to move to the Philippines, then a US colony. Once in Manila, Benjamin Ohnick gained renown for winning a million-dollar lawsuit for a client. Sometime after that he became vice president of the conglomerate Marsman & Company, which developed into one of the largest mining companies in the world and had extensive holdings in the islands, including a drug company, an airline, and trading firms.

Throughout the 1930s, the Ohnicks split their time between Seattle and Manila, commuting across the Pacific on the Boeing Clipper flying boats. They bought a waterfront house in Seattle at 7326 Bowlyn Place and sent their three children to local schools. Their daughter Barbara attended law school in Seattle and later became an assistant attorney general in Washington State.

The Ohnicks attracted attention in Seattle's society pages. An article from 1940 in the *Seattle Times* noted: "Mr. and Mrs. Benjamin Ohnick and family of Seattle and Manila fly through the air with the greatest of ease. The Ohnicks have a beautiful home in the Uplands where they spend several months each year, Mrs. Ohnick generally leaving here in September and returning from Manila in the early spring."

By the time the Pacific War broke out in December 1941, Benjamin Ohnick had become one of the wealthiest men in the Philippines. However, he narrowly escaped death on December 10, 1941, when the Japanese air force bombed Manila. Once the Japanese overran the Philippines in the spring of 1942, he became a marked man. In March 1942, Ben and Ina Ohnick were taken prisoners by the Japanese and were held in the Santo Tomas Internment Camp in Manila.

"Santo Tomas was livable for two years," Ina later stated. "After that, there was a policy of deliberate starvation. The food was reduced each day. When I say food, I mean rice. Only rice. There were 800 women and children and two bathrooms. Never do I want to hear talk among women about dieting." Ben lost sixty pounds during his ordeal. The Ohnicks were liberated from prison in 1945 after US forces landed in the Philippines. In an interesting turn of events, their son Van Ohnick, who had joined the US Army Signal Corps, participated in the rescue operation that freed his parents. Following their liberation, the three of them were photographed outside Santo Tomas, their arms around each other, grinning at their reunion. Ina Ohnick returned to Seattle in May 1945. Ben stayed on part-time in Manila in hopes of reestablishing his business interests in the Philippines, then returned to Seattle for good in 1950. In Seattle he was active in Masonic activities and served with the American Legion (for a time on the Legion's national executive committee). In the words of his daughter Barbara, "They survived, but he never recovered his health." Worn out from his wartime ordeal, Benjamin Ohnick died in 1951 at age sixty.

Thomson Family

I came recently upon the intriguing story of the Thomson family, a set of siblings born of a British father and Japanese mother. While William T. Thomson, the eldest son, wrote at length of his origins and early life in a fictionalized family memoir, which was self-published under the title *The World of Bamboo*, his own intriguing later years are less documented, and some mysteries remain.

The Thomson family story starts with the patriarch, Bernard Hilary Thomson, born in 1875 in Tunbridge Wells, England, the son of a long line of ministers and teachers (his father, Rev. John Radford Thomson, was a lecturer in moral philosophy at University of London as well as a Congregationalist clergyman). Rather than go into either field, however, the young Bernard opted to become a sailor. At age fourteen he enrolled in an officer's training program run by the Royal Navy. Following graduation, he and a buddy, Rodney, signed on as sailors on a British merchant vessel and visited India and Java. On the last leg of one voyage, during an ocean storm, and a giant wave dashed Bernard against a spar, breaking his knee and leaving him with a permanent limp. During another voyage, he got into a fight with another sailor and was hit in the left eye, leaving him a detached retina. He soon lost all sight in that eye.

Bernard returned to England and thought of giving up sailing. Instead he decided to emigrate to South Africa, where his stepmother's brother had built a large horse ranch. Although he enjoyed life on the ranch, he did not stay long. His old friend Rodney came to visit and lured him to the city of Johannesburg. Soon after, the Boer War broke out. Bernard enlisted in the British army and was wounded in action. Once he had healed sufficiently, Bernard was sent back to England to complete his recovery. After arriving there, he was visited by a soldier named O'Connell whom he had met in South Africa. O'Connell had once worked as an opium smuggler in China, and he now invited Bernard to come work in the China trade as a navigator on a freighter, a dangerous but lucrative job.

As Bernard later recounted the story, he moved to East Asia and started smuggling contraband with O'Connell. However, on one of his first voyages, their ship was attacked and sunk by pirates off of the China coast. O'Connell was taken prisoner, and Bernard was left for dead. Though badly wounded, he managed to find a dinghy and climb in, but the dinghy contained neither food nor oars. He floated in the dinghy for several days and finally lost consciousness. Miraculously the boat floated to the coast of the Ryukyu Islands, where it was discovered by a local fisherman, who carried Bernard home. The fisherman and his wife nursed Bernard back to health. After a short time, Bernard wrote to the British consul in Kobe, explaining his penniless and stranded state. The consul advanced him money to pay his benefactors and to travel to Kobe.

After arriving in Kobe, Bernard was hired to edit the city's evening English-language newspaper (he narrowly missed getting a job with the morning newspaper *Kobe Chronicle*, whose previous editor was renowned writer Lafcadio Hearn). When the evening paper folded two years later, Bernard found a job teaching English at a high school in nearby Osaka. During this time, Bernard met Kei Sato, a young woman student in his evening adult class. Bernard fell in love and eventually asked her father for her hand. Kei's father was astounded by the proposal but finally accepted.

Bernard again changed jobs following his marriage. The directors of the Miyako Hotel, a deluxe hotel in nearby Kyoto that welcomed foreigners, hired him to write a travel guide to Kyoto that would serve as advertising for them, and also to edit a house magazine, the *Miyako*. The couple moved to Kyoto, where Kei attended classes at Doshisha University. Soon, however, the couple began having children. The first was a daughter, Yuriko. The first son, who was given the name Taro, arrived in 1909. To supplement the family's income, Bernard took a teaching position at schools in Hachiman and Hikone, using the Japanese name Hideo Sato. The family moved to the small town of Gujo Hachiman, where five more children were born in the years that followed. Kei converted to Christianity and attended church with her husband.

The Thomson children grew up in a unique set of circumstances. They lived in a standard Japanese house, with an *ofuro* (Japanese bath) and a Japanese garden. They ate breakfast and lunch Japanese-style, sitting on the floor and using chopsticks. However, behind the garden was a separate building that served as Bernard's retreat. It contained Western furniture, including a dining table and chairs, where the children would eat a dinner of Western-style food, using knife and fork. Their day was similarly divided linguistically. They went every day to Japanese school to learn read and write Japanese language, and as they went through the village, prostitutes would shout *Kawaii ainoko!* (Cute half-breed!), and boys at school would call them *keto* (foreigners). Between themselves and with their mother, the Thomson children spoke only Japanese. However, three days a week they would report after school to their father's cabin for English lessons with him.

Despite Bernard's genuine love for Japanese art and folk culture, he became increasingly anxious about life in Japan. First, though he had been initially welcomed, he was disturbed by the social prejudice against interracial marriages and the impact of that on his wife and his growing children. Meanwhile he grew fearful as World War I dawned and Japan grew increasingly military-minded and nationalistic. After refusing to accept military orders to quarter Japanese soldiers in his house in Hachiman, he was arrested and briefly held by local authorities, then forced to accept soldiers in the house. Bernard foresaw that Japan would end up going to war against the West and that his sons would be drafted into the military, so he decided to leave. He considered returning to England but was convinced that his family would not gain acceptance there.

In 1918 his father, Reverend Thomson, died, and Bernard received a small inheritance. He decided to use the money to take the family to California, which he could just barely afford. Bernard felt the children would have the best chance of acceptance in California, despite anti-Asian prejudice there. Although Kei was pregnant with their sixth child, and her family strongly opposed her leaving Japan, she agreed to follow her husband. A local missionary arranged with his brother, Gerald Walters, a California ranch owner, to employ the family once they arrived. Thus, in April 1919, shortly after the end of World War I, the Thomson family migrated to the United States. Although they arrived during the period of the "Gentlemen's Agreement," when only select categories of Japanese were permitted to enter the United States, the entire family was permitted to accompany Bernard into the country. (Apparently Kei's devotion to caring for ill passengers en route facilitated friendly processing by immigration authorities and her rapid admission into the country).

After arriving in the United States, the Thomson family took up residence in a house in Casitas Springs, on the Walters ranch. It was the beginning of a period of great hardship. Bernard, who was middle-aged, had a crippled leg, and had never learned to drive cars or farm machinery, was forced to adjust to life as a farmhand. Kei, who had always relied on maids to do her shopping and cooking, had to learn to prepare meals and bake bread. The children walked or rode to the nearest school, two miles away. After several months, Walters laid off Bernard. The family moved to a small two-room house at a lemon grove in nearby Ventura. There the Thomson adults worked long hours as menial laborers, picking and sorting lemons.

Fortunately, after about a year of such work, Bernard was able to contact an old acquaintance from his Miyako Hotel days and parlay his experience and language skills into a job as a travel agent and cruise director with the Raymond-Whitcomb travel agency in San Francisco. The 1920 census lists Bernard as a guide to "tourists—Japan."

The Thomson family members dedicated themselves to becoming Americans, though they lived around other Japanese and retained certain of their Japanese customs. The Thomson children—who ranged in age from twelve-year-old Yuriko and ten-year-old Taro to Mariko (eight), Joe (six), Bruce (five), and baby Tom—had rather distinct experiences in their new country. The younger children, born at a time when their father was growing disillusioned with Japan, had received Western names at birth and learned English as their mother tongue. However, the older children spoke English poorly at first and were teased at school for the British accent they had absorbed from their father. After being set back a few grades to master English, they soon adopted it as their primary language and returned to the grade level of their age peers. They eventually Americanized their names to Lily and William, while Mariko called herself Marie.

Within a few years, Bernard became a naturalized US citizen. He none-theless remained proud of his English heritage—according to one source, he continued to order all his suits, ties, and other clothing from a Saville Row tailor. Conversely, Kei and the children, as members of the "Japanese race," remained legally "ineligible to citizenship." (This issue would arise once more in later years, as we will see.) They faced a significant degree of racial prejudice from the dominant white population—even as their proud British father looked down on other ethnic minorities.

After four years with Raymond-Whitcomb, Bernard was hired as a tour conductor and cruise leader by the prestigious Thomas Cook Travel Agency and worked with the Cunard Steamship Company. With the increased income from this new job, the Thomson family was able to move to a house on Everett Street in a more affluent (and whiter) area of Alameda. Bernard remained on the road for his work almost year-round, absent for up to six months at a time on cruise ships. As a result, the children were raised largely by their mother, who proved a patient and indulgent parent. Although William described his mother as remaining a "Buddhist at heart," Kei dealt with her solitude by joining a local Japanese Christian church, read the Bible faithfully, and embraced Christian doctrine, forbidding her children to watch movies that were not religious. As the children grew older and had less need for care, she became engaged in teaching Japanese lan-guage classes at the Buddhist temple in Oakland. She also cultivated silk-worms and did calligraphy.

The Great Depression hit the Thomson family hard. Bernard lost his job and was forced to take a job selling ducks door to door, which left him humiliated and increasingly aloof. Kei helped out by doing sewing and light housework for a white family. (By 1930, according to that year's census, Kei was the owner of a cleaning business). Lily contributed a portion of her earnings as a stenographer, and the younger children did odd jobs to earn money. Kei, who had always felt guilt over leaving Japan and abandoning her Japanese family, carefully saved up money from her Japanese teaching for a final trip. She left in March 1935. By the time she arrived in Japan, she was already ill with stomach cancer, and she was apparently sufficiently aware of her mortality that she bought a gravestone in Japan. Upon her return to California, she was in such poor health that she was maintained in quarantine and almost not permitted back into the country. Within months, she died of cancer. She was barely fifty years old.

Kei's passing deeply struck the children. One month after her death, Bernard was hired back by Thomas Cook, amid an improving economy. He resumed touring, leaving the children to care for each other. During one of his cruises, he met a wealthy white woman, Adela Collins. The two soon married, and Bernard moved to her ranch in Los Gatos, California. He never returned to the house in Alameda. The rapid remarriage and move estranged Bernard from his bewildered children, who all felt deserted (but especially Lily, who had vowed to become an "old maid" and devote her life to caring for him). The younger generation of Thomsons also did not get along well with Adela, who was apparently old-fashioned and clearly uncomfortable in the presence of her half-Japanese stepchildren. William, at least, interpreted the remarriage as Bernard's having closed the door on a past of privation and shut himself off from the stigma of association with a Japanese family.

Eventually Bernard managed to achieve a kind of "uneasy truce" with his children, as William described it, though they seldom saw him and he remained (as always) emotionally distant. He continued his work in the tour business, and his marriage with Adela was reportedly a happy one. After she died, Bernard moved back to Alameda and lived near his sons Joe and Bruce. He died in 1966 and was buried in a vault with Kei in Alameda.

The six Thomson children all went on to successful careers in different fields. Lily (Yuriko), the eldest, set the pattern for the family. A star student at Alameda High School, Lily was named valedictorian of her class. Rather than attend University of California, for which she was well qualified, she instead elected to attend business school and in time became a secretary for an importing firm. Her earnings helped support the family through the depths of the Great Depression. Eventually Lily got married and moved to Los Angeles with her husband and took work as a legal secretary.

Marie, the second daughter, left home at the start of high school and moved in with a young woman attorney named DeReamer, for whom she did housework and cooking. Precisely what kind of relationship developed between them is unclear, but, when Marie decided to become a nurse, DeReamer paid her tuition, and the two women continued living together. After finishing nursing school, Marie worked as a nurse in San Francisco at Saint Francis Hospital, then moved to Indianapolis, married, and worked as a nurse there.

All four Thomson sons attended the University of California, Berkeley. After college, Joe worked as an insurance underwriter and put himself through law school in the evenings. Bruce, forced to leave school after an attack of tuberculosis, went into business. Tom majored in chemistry at UC Berkeley and then went on to study for a doctorate. The Pearl Harbor attack and the outbreak of war between Japan and the United States affected family life, even though none of the Thomson siblings on the West Coast was confined under Executive Order 9066. They do not even seem to have applied for an exemption; they were simply left undisturbed. Despite their Japanese ancestry, their English family name and appearance helped them to blend in.

The Thomson siblings did find ways to support the US war effort. Joe felt a particular need to demonstrate his loyalty by volunteering for service, as his three brothers were all barred from the military on health grounds. In June 1942 Joe enlisted in the US Army. He applied for officer candidate school but was blackballed because of his Japanese ancestry. Instead he served as a noncom and was ultimately shipped to the Pacific, where he saw action in Palau, specifically on Angaur. At the end of the war, Joe (by then promoted to warrant officer) was assigned to Japan. Upon his return to California, he finished law school and set up a practice in Alameda. Bruce, whose health remained frail, worked in manufacturing and real estate. Tom earned a doctorate in chemistry at Kansas State (his choice presumably influenced by his eldest brother, who taught there for several years). Tom later spent a career as professor of chemistry, first in Colorado and later at Arizona State University.

William Thomson, known as Bill, would end up as the most renowned of the Thomson siblings. From his early years, despite being an indifferent student, he showed himself to be mechanically inclined. At Alameda High School, which had a well-known vocational education program, he not only took vocational courses but also bought two ancient Model T cars and overhauled the engines at the school body shop. The Depression struck after Bill finished high school. Unable to find acceptable work, he decided to continue his studies. Because of his poor academic record, his high school advisors proposed that he enroll at San Mateo Junior College. He entered San Mateo and took a job at the college as a lab assistant. A friendly Christian minister named Hall offered Bill free lodging in his house.

After two years at San Mateo, Bill was accepted as an engineering student at UC Berkeley, from which he received his BS in engineering in 1933, then went on for an MS degree. (During this time Bill took a leave to undergo surgery to repair a detached retina, which had likely been caused by hits sustained during boxing matches, and he regained partial vision in the damaged eye). In 1935 he was hired as a lecturer–teaching assistant at UC Davis. He later recounted that the campus was a cosmopolitan community of scholars with no discernable racial prejudice, and for the first time he felt freed from the feelings of inferiority he had developed as a Japanese American. After a year at Davis, however, he was awarded a fellowship by the University of California and returned to Berkeley to complete his doctorate.

Following his graduation from Berkeley in 1937, Bill was hired by Kansas State College (as it was then called). He spent four years there as an assistant professor. To supplement his income, during his last year he spent the summer working at the Boeing Aircraft Company in Seattle. While at Boeing, he met Tricia Crawford, who worked as a cashier at the company cafeteria. Although William had never had a serious girlfriend before, he asked Tricia on a date, and the two discovered that they got on well. In a different way, Bill's interest in the Northwest was reflected in a landmark set of papers he produced on the demise of the nearby Tacoma Narrows Bridge. The bridge, which had attracted notoriety for the ways its roadways twisted in the wind (and had thus been dubbed "Galloping Gertie") had finally shaken itself to pieces during a heavy wind in November 1940. Bill was able to use vibration theory to explain the disaster: the periodic frequency of the winds matched the bridge's structural frequency, and the winds lashing the bridge brought on turbulence-induced vibration and torsion of the structure. (Bill's conclusions were later enshrined in a textbook, *Theory of Vibrations with Applications*, which was widely adopted in engineering courses and went through several editions.)

On the strength of his papers, Bill was recruited by the College of Engineering at the elite Cornell University. He began teaching at Cornell in fall 1941. Soon after, war broke out between the United States and Japan. Feeling anxious about the future, Bill left Ithaca at Christmas vacation and drove cross-country to propose to Tricia, who accepted. As 1942 dawned, and Japanese Americans on the West Coast were subjected to mass roundup, Bill began to feel further anxious uncertainty over his Japanese ancestry. His worries were heightened after a firm in New York City, who whom he had been recommended as a consultant, declined his services after discovering his ancestry. Thus Bill began inquiries as to his citizenship and rights. He wrote to the American Civil Liberties Union for assistance in clarifying or petitioning for his US citizenship. In 1943 Bill was hired by the California Institute of Technology in Pasadena to do war work. He later did war-related work for the Ryan Aeronautical Company in San Diego.

After the end of the war, Bill resigned from Cornell and took a job at the University of Wisconsin. After publishing articles and his first two technical books, he was granted the status of full professor. Although he was comfortable in Wisconsin and by then had two (later three) small children, he was flattered when invited to help develop a new engineering school at UCLA. He arrived at UCLA in 1951 and would remain there for nearly twenty years. In addition to teaching, he made extra money from Rand Corporation, whom he advised on missile research. In 1957 Bill was awarded a Fulbright to study at Kyoto University and went there for a year with his wife and family. He was able to tour the town where had lived as a boy and even ran into one of his father's former students. Ultimately he moved on to UC Santa Barbara, where he finished his career. William Tyrrell Thomson (at some point he had officially changed his name from Taro) died in 1998, at the age of eighty-nine.

Sono Osato and Timothy Osato

The dancer-actress Sono Osato was not just a uniquely visible Japanese American face in 1940s America but also an exemplar of progressive politics and good citizenship.

Born in Omaha on August 29, 1919, Sono Osato was the eldest of three children of Shoji Osato, a Japanese immigrant who worked for an Omaha newspaper and later ran a photo studio, and Frances Fitzpatrick, an Irish and French-Canadian mother. (Since interracial marriage was then illegal in Nebraska, the young couple had married secretly in Iowa.) The pair were socially ostracized after their marriage. Not long after Sono's birth, Frances left to make a career in Hollywood, then returned to Omaha. In the next years she and Osato had two more children, Teru and Timothy.

In 1927 Frances left her husband again and took her children to Europe. It was while on a trip to Monte Carlo that the young Sono saw her first performance of the Ballets Russes. In 1929 the family returned to the United States and settled in Chicago. There Sono studied ballet with Adolph Bolm and Berenice Holmes. In 1934, after Holmes secured an audition for her, she was accepted into the Ballets Russes de Monte-Carlo, directed by Wassily de Basil. She toured Europe and the United States with the company for the next six years, leaving her family behind. She mostly performed in the ensemble, with occasional solos. In order to fit in, she wore makeup to disguise her Asian features (she was told to adopt a Russian name but refused). For a time she became the lover of Roman Jasinski, one of the company's stars, who also served as her mentor.

By late 1940, both her talent and great beauty had flowered. She became a featured artist with the company (by then billing itself as the "original Ballet Russes") and won plaudits for her role as the Siren in George

Sono Osato dancing. Courtesy of the Mitchell Library, State Library of New South Wales.

Balanchine's ballet *The Prodigal Son*. However, tired of appearing in the chorus, with no credit or extra money for the lead roles she was given, Osato left the company in early 1941. She soon joined Ballet Theatre (today called American Ballet Theatre) as a lead dancer, and she stayed with the company for two years. Among her most memorable performances with Ballet Theatre were roles in two works by Antony Tudor—*Pillar of Fire* and *Romeo and Juliet* (1943). In the latter ballet she played Rosaline, a role developed specifically for her.

Osato's life was overturned by the outbreak of war in December 1941. Her father, Shoji, who had worked for the Japanese consulate in Chicago and the Japanese-run South Manchuria Railway, was arrested as a dangerous alien and interned for ten months by the US Justice Department. For a time, Sono danced under her mother's maiden name, Fitzpatrick, to defuse anti-Japanese hysteria. Furthermore, during 1942 she was barred from joining her colleagues on a transcontinental tour that wound up on the Pacific Coast, due to the restrictions against people of Japanese ancestry imposed by the Western Defense Command. During this period, Osato's sister, Teru, a student at Bennington College, costarred in William Bales's modern dance work *Es Mujer*.

In mid-1943, Sono Osato left the Ballet Theatre company. By that time, she had married Victor Elmaleh, a young architect and real estate developer. She intended to start a family. However, both her love of performing and the couple's parlous financial situation led her to resume her career. Nora Kaye, the Ballet Theatre's lead dancer, suggested that Osato write to Agnes de Mille, who was choreographing a Broadway show, *One Touch of Venus* (1943), with book by Ogden Nash and S. J. Perelman and music by Kurt Weill. Osato was hired, and the comic solo that de Mille eventually created for her launched her as a theatrical star. Osato won one of *Billboard* magazine's Donaldson Awards for the role. After nine months in *Venus*, she was engaged to create the non-singing dance role of Ivy (Miss Turnstiles) in Leonard Bernstein, Betty Comden, and Adolph Green's hit musical *On the Town* (1944), featuring choreography by Jerome Robbins. She remained with the show for a year. In 1945 Osato signed to play the lead in an upcoming American adaptation of the French stage hit *Undine*, by Jean Giraudoux, but she withdrew during rehearsals.

During the period, Osato remained actively involved with progressive political movements. She was present in Broadway delegations to Washington against the poll tax and for lowering the voting age from twenty-one (as it was then) to eighteen so that soldiers risking their lives could have voting rights. She also opposed the Franco regime in Spain. In 1945 she spoke at a rally sponsored by the Spanish Refugee Appeal. When conservative actor Frank Fay charged that the rally was "anti-Catholic" and that the participants were Communists, Osato and four colleagues brought grievance charges against him with the Actors' Equity union. In 1946 she gave a dance exhibition for striking CIO workers at the General Electric plant in Schenectady, New York.

Osato also became absorbed in supporting racial minorities. She served on the board of La Casa de Puerto Rico, a community center in East Harlem, appeared at fund-raisers for the National Urban League, and taught a free ballet class for African American youth in Harlem—her class was featured in a spread in New York's left-leaning daily *PM*. She also associated herself with the antifascist civil rights organization Japanese American Committee for Democracy (JACD). In the fall of 1944 she cosponsored a JACD rally to reelect President Franklin D. Roosevelt. In a statement read at the rally, she proclaimed: "I am voting for President Roosevelt as our greatest leader in the fight for racial equality and world peace. My brother and yours are fighting fascism abroad. It is our urgent duty to fight it here by reelecting President Roosevelt."

As a visible Japanese American figure, Osato carried a large burden of symbolism. Her success proved that Nikkei were assimilable, and her public activities were widely hailed in both mainstream and African American journals as examples of the good citizenship of the Nisei. (Ironically, African American sociologist Horace Cayton, who worked with numerous Nisei, related in his memoir *Long Old Road* seeing *On the Town* on V-J Day and being offended that Osato, as a "half-Japanese," was dancing and performing with white Americans even after the United States had dropped two atomic bombs on Japan.)

In 1947 Osato went to Hollywood. However, she was limited on racial grounds in the selection of parts offered her and faced blacklisting because of her politics. In the end, she appeared in just a single film, *The Kissing Bandit* (1948), with Frank Sinatra and Kathryn Grayson. She returned to New York and had two children in the following years. She continued to work sporadically on the stage and on television. In 1948 she performed in *Ballet Ballads*, a theatrical/dance piece created by Jerome Moross and John Latouche and produced by the Experimental Theatre at American National Theater and Academy in New York. In 1950 she appeared on comedian Fred Allen's TV variety show, and the next year she performed on Broadway in a production of Ibsen's *Peer Gynt*, opposite John Garfield.

In 1955 Osato attempted a return to the musical stage, in writer Mel Brooks's short-lived off-Broadway revue *Once over Lightly*. The same year she performed with the Ballet Theatre as a guest artist in *Pillar of Fire* and *Romeo and Juliet*, the two Antony Tudor roles she had premiered a decade earlier, and took the lead in Agnes de Mille's ballet *Tally-Ho*. She then gradually retired from performing. In later years, she worked as an installation artist and held exhibitions. Her memoir, *Distant Dances* (1980), won critical praise for its candid account of her life and career. In 2005 she endowed the

Sono Osato Scholarship Program in Graduate Studies at Career Transition for Dancers, which offers retraining grants for retired dancers entering second careers. She died in December 2018 at the age of ninety-nine.

The career of Sono Osato's younger brother, Timothy, also merits discussion. Born in Chicago on January 1, 1925, Tim was originally named Mitsuru Osato, but his mother's handwriting was so dreadful that it came out "Mitsrune" on his birth certificate. In the end, the Osatos changed the boy's name to Tim. Sono Osato, who had a conflicted relationship with her mother, later claimed that Tim was Frances's favorite. Tim was separated from his father at an early age and moved with his mother and sisters to France, where he spent his early years. Tim's fluency in French would mark his later career. The young half-Japanese boy attracted some attention. In 1931 he was the subject of a portrait by the noted post-impressionist artist Léonard Foujita (born Fujita Tsuguharu).

After a few years in France, Tim returned with his mother and sister Teru to Chicago, where he was reunited with his father. The young Tim became an avid reader of history books and quickly achieved renown for his phenomenal knowledge and memory for facts. As a result, during 1939–40 he was featured as a regular on the celebrated Wednesday-evening radio program *The Quiz Kids*, serving as an expert in history. In addition, Tim grew interested in painting and attended the Frances W. Parker School, a private prep school in Chicago. During this time he became enamored of his classmate Joan Mitchell, later a renowned Abstract Expressionist painter—though Mitchell's parents disapproved of her friendship with a Japanese American. According to Mitchell's biographer Patricia Albers, Osato was attractive not only for his striking good looks and brains but also for his dreamy and mercurial temperament. When Mitchell threw a party, Tim and a friend together put on a daredevil show, hanging off Mitchell's tenth floor balcony, "just to show they could."

Like his sister Sono, Tim found his life turned upside down by Pearl Harbor. In the period that followed, his father, as noted above, was interned as a dangerous enemy alien. Fatherless, Tim was conflicted over the Japanese side of his ancestry. In 1943 Tim joined the newly formed all–Japanese American combat unit, the 442nd Regimental Combat Team, and was placed in the Cannon Company. His proud sister Sono, noting that he was the first Japanese American enlistee from the Chicago area, invited him to visit her in New York and brought him backstage. After going through basic training at Camp Shelby, Mississippi, Tim was sent with the unit to Europe, where he earned a Bronze Star.

Osato's experience with the 442nd persuaded him to choose the military as a career. Once the war was over, however, he took a leave and enrolled at Yale University on the GI Bill. There he joined the varsity fencing team. During this time, he and Joan Mitchell met again and became lovers. While they soon split up, and each married other people, Osato remained (according to Mitchell's later husband Barney Rosset) the true love of her life.

After earning a bachelor's degree at Yale cum laude, Osato enrolled at Columbia University. His master's thesis, "Nationalism and the Reforms in French Primary Education, 1879–1882," was completed in 1950, the year after he married poet Ruth Ludlow. In 1950, during the Korean War, he returned to combat duty with the Third Division, and in 1951 he was awarded the Silver Star. After returning to the United States, he received his doctorate from Harvard. In 1952, at the young age of twenty-seven, he was engaged as professor of history at the US Military Academy at West Point, where he specialized in Far Eastern history. (For a time, he left his wife, who was pregnant with a second child, and resumed his affair with Joan Mitchell, and even after he returned to his family he insisted on hanging a painting of Mitchell's in his home). In 1954 Tim visited Indochina to observe the Indochina War. Upon his return, he prepared a set of lectures, illustrated by color slides. During this time he also helped care for his mother, who died soon after.

By 1963 Tim had been promoted to major and engaged as professor of political science at the Air Force Academy in Colorado Springs. In 1965, together with Louis Gelas, he published a translation of French scholar Lionel M. Chassin's *The Communist Conquest of China*. Coming at the dawn of the Cultural Revolution and serving as a guide to Mao's victory, the book was widely reviewed and cited. Two years later he was assigned to the historical project of the Army Air Defense Command and produced a pair of studies on air defense. "Militia Missilemen," on the Army National Guard in Air Defense, was later published by the Office of Military History. (The other project, "ARADCOM's Florida Defenses in the Aftermath of the Cuban Missile Crisis 1963–1968," written with Sherryl Straup, remained unpublished.) In 1968 Osato, by then promoted to lieutenant colonel, began a series of lectures at l'École Supérieure de Guerre (during which time he once again entered briefly into an affair with Joan Mitchell). From there he was transferred to Vietnam and served in the Vietnam War.

In the 1970s Tim Osato retired from the US military. According to his daughter, he was a man of "dashed dreams and frustrated everything." He died of a self-inflicted gunshot wound in Pittsburgh in October 1979. Osato is buried in Arlington National Cemetery. His life is a record of great talent and virtuosity but also unrealized promise. How much of his self-destructiveness was founded in the limitations imposed by prejudice and marginalization as a half-Japanese person is undeterminable. Tooru Kanazawa's 1994 book *Close Support*, an oral history of the Cannon Company of the 442nd Regimental Combat Team, featured illustrations by Osato.

CHAPTER TWO

Literature

How *John Okada* Was Born

With the publication of the book *John Okada: The Life and Rediscovered Work of the Author of "No-No Boy"* (University of Washington Press, 2018), my coeditors and I shed light on a remarkable man and artist and came to terms with his life and message.

In 1971, weeks after novelist John Okada's death at age forty-seven, a group of young Asian American writers rediscovered and began championing his 1957 novel *No-No Boy*, which had lain largely neglected until then. These young writers, including Frank Chin, Jeffery Chan, Shawn Wong and Lawson Fusao Inada, published an excerpt from the novel in *Aiiieeeee!*, their anthology of Asian American literature, and arranged publication of a reprint edition through CARP (the Combined Asian American Resources Project). Meanwhile scholar Stephen H. Sumida and actor-activist Frank Abe each began a decades-long concentration on studying Okada's life and work. Abe, in particular, interviewed numerous family members, accumulated biographical details, and began work on a documentary film about Okada entitled *In Search of "No-No Boy."* However, by his own admission, he had trouble with the project and ultimately left off work on it.

John Okada, Broadway High School (Seattle) graduation portrait, 1941. Personal collection of Joanne Mock.

My own involvement with Okada came about through a rather concentrated series of events. In early 2007 I visited Seattle to do research for my book *A Tragedy of Democracy*. One of my main sources of information was articles in bygone Japanese American newspapers. At the Seattle Public Library I found bound collections of the postwar English-language Nisei newspaper *Northwest Times*. These collections started in 1950 and ran until 1955, when the paper folded. I had never heard of this newspaper or seen it cited. I found it to be a gold mine of material, from the columns of famed resister Gordon Hirabayashi to the editorials of editor Budd Fukei. During that visit I stayed at the house of my dear friend Chizu Omori. I had heard of Frank Abe's work, and when I expressed interest in meeting him, Chizu organized a dinner party. During that dinner Frank talked eloquently about his fascination with John Okada. Meanwhile Chizu suggested that I might contribute to the *Nichi Bei Times*, for which she wrote her column "Rabbit Ramblings." Thanks in part to Chizu's recommendation, the intrepid *Nichi Bei* editor Kenji Taguma hired me to write a regular column on intriguing but unknown parts of Japanese American history.

Fast-forward a year. I had a sabbatical leave in early 2008, and I decided to spend the month of February in Vancouver doing research (and gorging myself on good Japanese food). Vancouver being striking distance from Seattle, I headed south to attend the Day of Remembrance ceremonies at the University of Washington and to do some research for my new column. I found that the UW libraries held microfilm of earlier volumes of *Northwest Times*. On looking through the first issues, dated January 1947, I discovered a one-act play and several short stories written by John Okada (described in a headnote as being a UW student). Once back in Vancouver, I wrote to Frank Abe, attaching a sample, and asked whether he was aware of these writings. His response was enthusiastic: "This is amazing. I am going to talk to Okada's family about how they would like to proceed with re-introducing this material to the public. Okada scholars are going to go nuts. Steve Sumida and Shawn Wong will go nuts when they hear this. Thanks for thinking of me at the library. I owe you dinner next time you make a lightning visit to Seattle." Frank mentioned that John's brother Roy remembered a one-act play performed on campus—Roy had been enlisted in playing a small part—but could remember little of it.

Fortified by Frank's interest, I sent him another piece I had found. While doing research at the University of British Columbia, I had found a little-known Nisei newspaper from Toronto, the *Continental Times*. In its pages from 1957 I had found a long review of the original edition of *No-No Boy*. Again Frank was rapid and enthusiastic in his reply. He explained that the text of this review was so positive that the publisher had excerpted it for use as part of the book's publicity package, but he said that the source of the review had remained obscure: "OH MY GOD. I thought I would never ever see this, being such (to me) an obscure paper. Thank you! . . . For 30 years all most of us have ever seen is the blurb published on the back of the first edition CARP paperback reprint of *No-No Boy*. Whatever article it was excerpted from was lost in someone's file. So I had the attached excerpt, but never the full review."

Once I had turned up all these unknown works by and about Okada, I became convinced that they should be published and the whole received story of Okada reexamined. I turned to Frank, as the great expert on Okada, and suggested that we collaborate. After a good deal of back and forth, and

Frank checking with the Okada family, we decided that we would compile an anthology that would contain the newly rediscovered works, some biographical background, plus essays. The ensemble would work on the general model of *Miné Okubo: Following Her Own Road*, a collection that I had just completed with my friend Elena Tajima Creef and a team of collaborators. Even as that collection served as a companion volume to Okubo's book *Citizen 13360*, we thought we could produce a work that illuminated Okada's *No-No Boy*. Okubo's and Okada's books had been published by the University of Washington Press, so the press was a natural for such anthologies, and I was delighted to work with them both times. Several of the original team of Okada supporters agreed to participate in our anthology volume, and I was glad to join forces with them.

Still, the process of editing the book proved more involved than we thought. First, Frank and I were both extremely busy, with demanding day jobs. In addition to my teaching and administrative work in Montreal, from 2009 to 2012 I published three full-length books, plus writing articles and my *Nichi Bei* columns. As a result, Frank and I had almost no contact, except when I came through Seattle. Frank and I nevertheless continued to look for more sources. In John Okada's War Relocation Authority (WRA) file, Frank discovered mention of a poem by Okada. He managed to find the issue of the UW student paper where it had run (anonymously) as well as the Seattle newspaper that had reprinted it. While doing work at Stanford University libraries, I discovered an online database that listed an article by Okada in an obscure military procurement journal and was subsequently able to lay my hands on the journal issue with the article. Frank suggested that I might see if there were other articles in that same journal written under the name John Hillfield, Okada's sometime pseudonym ("Hillfield" being an approximate translation of "Okada"). I checked it out, and we hit pay dirt again. Frank also had the idea to look through the Frank Chin papers at UC Santa Barbara, and these contained copies of Okada's correspondence with his original publishers, Tuttle. Through online research, notably in the *Hoji Shinbun* and Densho databases, we came across snippets on Okada, plus reviews of the original edition of *No-No Boy* in newspapers, some obscure, from Asia and North America. As we assembled the data, we discussed interpretation and meaning, in a kind of continuing seminar by correspondence.

One particular problem we faced was how to analyze the newly discovered Okada writings and put them in context. Frank was not a literary expert, nor was I, and I doubted that I could do the works justice. I finally suggested that we turn to my friend and collaborator Floyd Cheung, professor of English literature at Smith College. It turned out that Floyd had done his own research long before on Okada's career at University of Washington, studying the transcripts of the courses Okada took as well as checking out his professors' careers, but had never made use of his findings. After receiving our invitation, Floyd wrote an amazing essay on Okada's writings. What is more, his overall suggestions were so brilliant that Frank and I agreed that he should join us as another coeditor. Floyd was very modest about his contribution and told me and Frank how much he enjoyed seeing us circulate documents and discuss interpretation: "It's such a pleasure to have this front-row seat to your collegiality."

The next problem was that Frank wanted to shed more light on the places mentioned in Okada's book, the physical community he had written about. We discussed this, and I wrote to him: "I think that while the location of the novel is clearly Seattle—and your tour of the sites of the novel is quite interesting—the 'place' of the book is at least as much the heart of Japanese America as it is Seattle or any particular area. The postwar years remain the black hole in Japanese American history, and the story of the damage the camps wrought on the Nisei is certainly one that needs to be told."

A final problem was the stringent word count requirements of the final volume. In order to get the promised contract, we had to trim down the manuscript by some 40 percent. I felt deeply the loss of the excised material, especially my own. I had written a major piece on the history of internment camp literature that situated Okada's achievement in the larger history of Japanese American literature. In the end, I cut something like half of it to fit (though I was able to incorporate part of the cut material into a separate project). I also had produced an essay examining the reviews of the initial publication of *No-No Boy*. This was removed from the final book, though it too was ultimately published elsewhere (and is reproduced below).

> The book John Okada: The Life and Rediscovered Work of the Author of "No-No Boy" was published in 2018, and its success has been a great gratification to me. I was especially proud when my coeditors and I received word in August 2019 that it had won a Before Columbus Foundation American Book Award.

First Impressions: Early Reviews of John Okada's *No-No Boy*

John Okada's landmark novel *No-No Boy* tells the story of Ichiro, a Nisei World War II draft resister who refused to fight for the government that had confined his family, and his difficult reintegration into his shattered community following his release from prison at the end of the war. First published in the United States and Japan by Charles E. Tuttle in 1957, it failed to attract a large readership. It was rediscovered and championed in the 1970s by a group of young writers and ultimately was recognized as a classic work of Asian American literature. Part of the legend surrounding *No-No Boy* is the idea that its initial publication was deliberately ignored and its author silenced by conservative Nisei, who wished to efface the wartime experience and role of dissenters, and that as a result the book failed to catch on.

In fact, reviews of the initial edition appeared in diverse publications in four countries. No reviews appeared in the English sections of daily or weekly Japanese American newspapers, but such silence also reflects the reality that in those years the Nisei press (including the nationally distributed journal *Pacific Citizen*) lacked literary pages and did not publish *any* book reviews. The initial reviews that did appear offer illuminating evidence as to how the work was understood at the time and hint at the prevailing climate regarding the wartime Japanese American experience.

Critics were starkly divided over Okada's literary skills and his portrait of the racial prejudice and internal conflict that Japanese communities experienced. A separate issue was the manner in which reviewers failed to recognize the distinction between the Nisei draft resisters and the "no-nos," inmates who gave unsatisfactory answers on the loyalty questionnaires in camp and were segregated at the Tule Lake camp in California. (This was in part Okada's responsibility, as the subject of his novel was the first group, while the title—likely imposed by his publisher—referred to the second.)

The first reviews of *No-No Boy* appeared in Japan's English-language press during May and June 1957, presumably in response to review copies sent from Tuttle's Tokyo office. These critics tended to minimize Okada's craft, even as they recognized his achievement in jump-starting Japanese American literature by focusing attention on the wartime events. For example, a review in the June 2, 1957, issue of *Mainichi Shimbun* by "B. L. M." asserted that the book was more "tractate" than literature. "This is a story with a purpose, a purpose so insisted upon, and so repeatedly, that it overwhelms the plot and the characters." Similarly, in the May 24, 1957, issue of *Japan Times,* an anonymous reviewer (likely Ken Yasuda, a poet and former Tule Lake inmate who was a Tuttle author) proclaimed, "By no means can Okada's novel be classed side by side with the best in literature. Its importance, however, is more historical. Being a first, the book marks a turning point in the efforts of the Nisei for expression through writing." The reviewer concluded that *No-No Boy* presaged a bright future for Nisei literature.

One rather unusual review appeared in the May 12, 1957, edition of *Yomiuri Japan News.* Its author was T. John Fujii, a Japan-born journalist who had grown up in Alameda before migrating to Singapore during the 1930s to work for a pro-Tokyo newspaper, then settling in Japan. Fujii, perhaps giving vent to his own demons, complained that Okada's work was "soap-box oratory" on the subject of racial discrimination. "One wonders why the Japanese-American society is filled with such bitterness when they have inherited the heritage of America. This is the adjustment of many minority groups. It's no worse than Saroyan's Armenians, Steinbeck's Mexicans and Faulkner or Tennessee Williams' 'southern trash.'" Despite Fujii's time in the United States and his continuing to write primarily in English, he did not seem to associate himself with Americans. In contrast to the Nisei, whom he presented rather disdainfully as a "lost generation" in a country that refused to accept them, he pointed to those like himself who had given up on America, returned to Japan, and settled easily into being Japanese. "Few of these individuals will admit any regrets, if they have any, at this late stage."

Contrasting strongly with Fujii's review was one that appeared in the *Asahi Evening News* by French journalist Alfred Smoular, a wartime resister and survivor of Auschwitz who moved to Japan after the war as head of the Tokyo bureau of Agence France-Presse. In his analysis, Smoular stated that the novel had no conclusion, apart from a faint note of hope, and that it should thus be considered more a document than a novel. Smoular likewise underlined the peculiarly Japanese-American nature of the story. "While it is not certain that all Americans were . . . aware of the question which is the subject of 'no-no boy,' it would be difficult to understand it, socially and psychologically, out of its national background. For many European readers, for instance, the hero of the novel would have had valid reasons for refusing to be drafted with his parents in camp and he would not have been psychologically confused."

Another intriguing review ran in the US Army's *Pacific Stars and Stripes* (a newspaper whose Tokyo edition was edited by Nisei journalist Yoshiko Tajiri Roberts). Considering the newspaper's military audience, reviewer Richard Larah provided a surprisingly sympathetic account of the work. Rather than condemning out of hand the tale of a draft evader's resistance, Larah instead praised the author's craft and approved his discussion of injustice: "A powerful novel, *No-No Boy* presents the entire subject of racial prejudice in America in a dramatic manner." Almost simultaneous with Larah's review was one in the Hong Kong–based English daily *South China Morning Post*. The *Post*'s reviewer, "K. C. W.," lauded Okada as a potential spokesman for the Nisei group and underlined the hopeful vision for a racially inclusive future that he located in Okada's conclusion.

The first North American review of the book appeared in July—not in the Toronto-based Japanese Canadian weekly *Continental Times*. Writing for an audience that included people who had experienced mass confinement in British Columbia, the reviewer—a Canadian Nisei man by inference—expressed admiration for Okada's literary style and presentation. "Although the author seems to have selected an unusual theme in which to portray the central figure of his story and leaves the reader with many questions unanswered, a situation which favors a dramatic approach to a realistic one, he has done commendably well in enlarging upon that theme. As a work of fiction, the book is immensely readable, which after all is a good test of any writing." The reviewer closed on a wistful note, deploring the lack of literature regarding the Japanese American and Japanese Canadian wartime experience. (In that respect the review proved prophetic—even as Okada's *No-No Boy* was rediscovered during the 1970s, Japanese Canadian author Joy Kogawa's landmark novel *Obasan* appeared.)

No-No Boy was published in the United States in September 1957. That same month it received a pair of reviews in notable American publications. First, the *Saturday Review* featured a critique by Earl Miner, a UCLA professor and scholar of Japanese literature. More than other reviewers, Miner clearly recognized that the book's action took place against a background of official injustice—he referred starkly to the Japanese Americans "whom we herded into concentration camps"—and he clearly picked up on Okada's audacious goal of providing an analysis of America itself as both hero and villain of the piece. Yet Miner's evaluation of Okada's novel as a work of literature was uneven. He appreciated the novel's structure and referred to it as "absorbing" but also stated (with a somewhat patronizing tone) that it descended into "strained melodrama." Miner ironically described *No-No Boy* as the best of its class and an advance in the literature, not knowing that it would also be not only the first but also the last novel on wartime confinement to appear for a generation.

Meanwhile *No-No Boy* was reviewed by Nisei writer Alan Yamada in the Catholic literary magazine *Jubilee*. Yamada admired the tone and Okada's overall message, though he questioned the author's prose style: "Okada writes with the raw fury of James T. Farrell about his angry group of 'Japs' and 'Americans' and the tensions they experience among whites, Chinese-Americans and Negroes. Though his writing is often awkward and confused, you know that these are real people who fill his novel and that they have something to say about the way life has treated them."

As mentioned, the Nisei press did not feature any formal reviews of *No-No Boy*, though there were various references to it. For instance, the *North American Post*, a Japanese-language newspaper in Okada's home town of Seattle, ran a brief article in September 1957 that offered a straight-forward summary of the novel, with this explanatory note: "The stories about Yamada and the other characters' struggles are based on real events around the Japanese community. The title 'No-no' is representative of those who resisted the war and were denied by society." Meanwhile a pair of articles mentioning the book in passing appeared in the *Post's* short-lived English section.

The only significant print analysis that the original edition of *No-No Boy* received was an account in columnist Bill Hosokawa's biweekly column "The Frying Pan" in the September 27, 1957, issue of *Pacific Citizen*. Getting reviewed in this column would have been considered a plum for Okada, as Hosokawa was a Japanese American Citizens League (JACL) stalwart and onetime editor-in-chief of the *Heart Mountain Sentinel*, published at the Heart Mountain Relocation Center in Wyoming. Hosokawa (who errone-ously described the novel's protagonist Ichiro as a Tule Lake "segregee") was clear in his disdain for "no-nos" yet offered measured, sincere praise for "the understanding and insight" Okada brought to his material. "Okada as a writer is at his best when handling dialogue, the part of the craft which many consider the most difficult. Nisei will recognize the authenticity of the idioms Okada's characters use, as well as his descriptions of the familiar Issei and Nisei mannerisms that make them come alive."

Two curious features of Hosokawa's piece are worth noting. First, Hoso-kawa made the shocking (perhaps rhetorical) statement that in the twelve years since the end of World War II he had never once met or talked with a no-no boy or draft resister about his experience. This points to the con-tinuing division and hostility in postwar Nisei circles that the government's wartime actions—and the decisions that Nisei were pressed to make in response—left on community members. Meanwhile, even as he praised Okada's authentic characterizations of Seattle community lingo and man-nerisms, Hosokawa (by then living in Denver) oddly concealed his own status as a Seattle-born and Seattle-raised Nisei. He seemed unable to acknowledge that Okada (eight years his junior) hailed from the same city and attended the same college.

Okada's novel, according to Tuttle's later testimony, did not sell well, and both the book and its author were soon dropped as subjects of media coverage. It is impossible to know how much, if any, importance the mixed reviews had on the public reception of *No-No Boy*. What is notable for our purposes is what the early reviews demonstrate, that readers from the outset found Okada's work thought-provoking and challenging.

Sanae Kawaguchi and Mitsu Yamamoto

Throughout much of the twentieth century, one unique feature of the West Coast Japanese community press was the New Year's supplement. These special holiday issues contained several additional pages in both English and Japanese, with feature articles highlighting the previous year's news stories and photos, plus various literature and art by Nisei. Indeed, in the postwar decades the New Year's supplements were often the only occasion during the entire year when Nisei newspapers featured fiction and poetry. The two historic Japanese American newspapers from Los Angeles, *Rafu Shimpo* and *Kashu Mainichi*, each featured holiday issues. The celebrated author Hisaye Yamamoto contributed stories and essays to *Rafu Shimpo*'s holiday issue into the 1980s, even as artist Miné Okubo produced New Year's drawings for *Kashu Mainichi* for over a generation. In the spirit of this tradition, I am glad to use my new year's column to shine light on Sanae Kawaguchi and Mitsu Yamamoto, two versatile Nisei literary artists based in New York who made their mark in the postwar era.

Sanae Kawaguchi was born in Southern California in 1931. Her Issei father, Sakujiro Kawaguchi, had labored as a young man on the railroads in the US West before taking up farming. Her mother, Fuki Endow Kawaguchi, in addition to her farmwork, was an avid Japanese poet and diarist.

After Sanae's birth, the family moved to Japan for a period, before deciding to return to the United States. Sanae spent her childhood with her parents and two older sisters on the family farm near Los Angeles.

The Kawaguchi family's life was interrupted by the outbreak of war. In the wake of Executive Order 9066, they were forced to entrust their land to a white agent. Sakujiro Kawaguchi, having secured a promise of sponsorship from old railroading buddies in Utah, organized an auto caravan with a few other families. In March 1942, during the brief period of so-called "voluntary evacuation," the Kawaguchis left the West Coast excluded zone. Although the family escaped mass confinement and the psychological trauma of camp by migrating, Sanae later recalled, life for them in wartime Utah was arduous. The entire family was forced to labor in the fields as itinerant farmhands. Because of difficulties finding living quarters, they lived in a tent, then an abandoned log cabin, and ultimately a chicken coop, carrying water for washing from a well. Fuki Kawaguchi was often too ill to work and was eventually bedridden for an extended period. The young Sanae's schooling was intermittent during those years. After exclusion was lifted, the Kawaguchis returned to Los Angeles, but Sakujiro's farm had been sold to new owners, and he was unable to get back his stake and was forced to seek work as a gardener. Sanae found life as a Nisei teenager in postwar Los Angeles oppressive. After going through high school, she left home. Joining forces with a fellow student, she hit the road and migrated to the East Coast.

Once arrived in New York, Kawaguchi swiftly made a new life for herself in the city's artistic circles. She took up modern dance and was accepted by the renowned modern dancer Martha Graham as a student. She studied with Graham's company for several years before being forced to retire due to an injury. She meanwhile worked as an independent performer and choreographer. In 1956 she joined the national tour of John Patrick's play *Teahouse of the August Moon*. She staged a performance of composer Marvin David Levy's *Sotoba Komachi*, a one-act opera based on Japanese Noh drama, in New York in July 1957, and she worked as a hostess at the Hawaiian Room, a Manhattan nightspot.

In addition to her performing interests, Kawaguchi was attracted to art and literature, especially Japanese. She credited her mother with inspiring her to appreciate the arts of her ancestral land and training her to speak Japanese fluently. During the mid-1950s Sanae began work on a children's book that would draw from her acquired knowledge of Japanese folk culture. Beyond entertainment, her goal was to promote international understanding at a time—barely a decade after World War II—when Japan remained little-known and suspect among many Americans. The result was *Taro's Festival Day*. The slim work told a tale of a Japanese boy's adventures during the *Kodomo no hi* (Children's Day) holiday, including his special meal and his catching of dragonflies. Kawaguchi added to the text a set of brightly colored illustrations that merged modern American graphics with classical Japanese art forms and scenes of traditional rural life. The book's lively charm attracted the distinguished, Boston-based Little, Brown, publisher of Lafcadio Hearn's works in the late nineteenth and early twentieth century, and the company offered Sanae a contract.

The first edition of *Taro's Festival Day* hit bookstore shelves in summer 1957. Its appearance attracted a spurt of media attention. While it was not the very first children's book by a Nisei author from a mainstream press— Yoshiko Uchida's book of Japanese folktales, *The Dancing Kettle* (1949) had appeared almost a decade earlier—the author's youth and the fact that she had produced her own illustrations were especially noteworthy. Journalist Lee Mortimer referred to Sanae in his syndicated "New York Confidential" column as "cutest author and illustrator of children's books in town."

The book's sales led Little, Brown, to commission a new work from Kawaguchi. Her second book, *The Insect Concert*, like its predecessor, was set in a timeless Japan. This time the story concerned a boy and girl, Yuki and Yoko, who find a golden cricket and put him in a cage so that he can play with the insect musicians. When they discover that the cricket is unhappy in his cage, they feel obliged to release him. However, on the night of the full moon, when the insects come together to play in the temple garden, the golden cricket returns. He rubs his legs together and fills the audience with joy with his beautiful song. While *The Insect Concert* did not sell as well as *Taro's Festival Day*, it was a more whimsical and inventive book. The historian must wonder whether author George Selden was influenced by Sanae's work when devising his own cricket virtuoso for his children's book *The Cricket in Times Square*, published two years later.

After completing her second book, Sanae Kawaguchi changed the direction of her career. She married John Moorehead, who had been the stage manager for *The Teahouse of the August Moon*. The couple had two children. In the following years, even as she raised her children, Sanae produced educational filmstrips (including illustrations for Asian American books), put on performances for young people through the federal arts program Project Reach, lived and worked for a period in Japan, and later operated a bed and breakfast in New York City. In 2006 she returned to publishing, after a nearly fifty-year absence, with the self-published young adult novel *A Time of Innocence*, a fictionalized portrait of her family's wartime exile from the West Coast and life in Utah. In 2013 she put out her first adult novel, the sensual romance *The Secret of the Zen Garden*. Set in postwar Japan, it tells the story of an older woman's awakening to life through an unexpected, forbidden love.

Another versatile author was the late Mitsu Yamamoto, who mixed classic literature with pop writing. Yamamoto was born Mitsie Ethel Yamamoto in Vermilion, Ohio, in 1920, the only surviving child of a Japanese immigrant father, Sannosuke Yamamoto, and a Swedish mother, Hilda Nildson (sometimes spelled "Nildsson"). In 1926 the family moved to Philadelphia, where Sannosuke Yamamoto partnered with Richard Okamoto in a silk-importing firm. In 1939 Mitsu enrolled at the College of Liberal Arts for Women at the University of Pennsylvania. After the start of World War II, her father was engaged to teach Japanese language to US Marine Corps recruits at Penn. Sannosuke was subsequently hired as an "informant" (i.e., research consultant) by the university's linguistics department. He meanwhile worked with Dr. Richard D. Abraham on a Japanese dictionary for the military, which was published in 1944 as *Japanese for Military and Civilian Use*. (The two later collaborated on a textbook, *Conversational Japanese: The Easy Method*, which went through several editions and is still in print).

Perhaps as a result of her father's defense work, and what she herself later termed her "white-bread appearance," Mitsu was permitted to enroll in the graduate school after receiving her BA in 1943, and she took classes in English literature, despite Penn's blanket (but unannounced) wartime policy of excluding Japanese American students. While at Penn, she met a fellow graduate student, George L. Anderson, and the two were married in

1945. Meanwhile she enrolled as a student in Dropsie College, a Philadelphia-based center for Jewish and Hebrew Studies, as "Mitsie Y. Anderson." In 1946 George Anderson was hired as an instructor at University of Maryland, and Mitsu accompanied him. She later moved to New York, where she studied at Columbia University during the 1950s.

It is not known precisely when Yamamoto began writing. However, in 1956 a one-act play of hers won a prize in the Fourth Collegiate Playwriting Contest, sponsored by the Samuel French Company. (It may have been *Pride Goeth*, which she copyrighted under the name "Mitsu Yamamoto" and as "Mitsie Y. Anderson" in 1962.) In November 1957 her short story "The Good News" appeared in the *New Yorker*. It recounted the tale of two women who meet when they are roommates in a hospital.

Although Yamamoto did not publish further in the *New Yorker*, "The Good News" was the first of a series of her stories that appeared in national magazines in the following years. For example, her story "In Any Language" appeared in *Redbook* in 1962, three of her pieces were featured in the *PTA Magazine*, and a mystery story of hers, "The Blue Rug," ran in the magazine *Alfred Hitchcock Presents* in 1973.

Perhaps most notably, two of Yamamoto's fantasy stories, "Miss Kemper Comes Home in the Dark" and "Karen Stixx and Her Jigsaw Puzzle," appeared in the *Saturday Evening Post* in 1972 and 1973. In the first, a woman is attacked on the street by a mugger and curious consequences result from her defending herself. This was later included in the anthology *Best Detective Stories of the Year, 1973*. The second was a Faust story of sorts, in which a mysterious stranger offers an unhappily married man a new life in exchange for a special service. She also published a nonfiction book for children, *Bridges to Fear: A Collection of Strange but True Stories* (1977).

Yamamoto likewise worked as an editor and critic. She produced abridged children's versions of classic novels such as Jack London's *The Call of the Wild*, Robert Louis Stevenson's *Dr. Jekyll and Mister Hyde*, and Charles Dickens's *Great Expectations*, plus the Bible. And she wrote book reviews for *Library Journal*. One pithy statement (perhaps revealing of her own identity) came in her August 1974 review of the pioneering Asian American literary anthology *Aiiieeeee!* These writers, she wrote, "pronounce themselves a unique American minority, Asian Americans —not Asians, not

Americans, not an uneasy combination of both. Overlong and overwrought prefaces repeat this valid identification while tossing around words like 'yellow goons,' 'racist henchmen,' and 'manhood.' Apart from this consciousness-raising, what? Mainly fiction and drama, with a rich, varied content not often matched by a like expression."

Yamamoto died in New York in 2006.

A personal aside: I had contact with both of these women. I was introduced to Sanae Kawaguchi Moorehead through a mutual friend in 1998, when I first began studying Japanese Americans. We met for lunch and hit it off so much that we ended up staying together talking all afternoon. We have remained warm friends ever since, and we collaborated on an annotated extract from her mother Fuki Endow Kawaguchi's unpublished diaries. Conversely, in August 1999 I contacted Yamamoto in connection with research I was doing on Japanese Americans at University of Pennsylvania during World War II. She generously sent a letter with copies that she had received of her government security forms, as well as other information. I then did a follow-up telephone interview with her. Though I was not aware of her writing career, she sounded so interesting that at the end of our phone chat I offered to take her out to lunch. She considered the invitation for a long moment, then said "I think not" and declined with thanks. I will always regret missing my chance to meet her.

Mary Oyama Mittwer and Henry Mittwer

One astounding aspect of Japanese American life is the number of accomplished families—clans that produced multiple members who made names for themselves in different fields. I recently had occasion to research the Tajiri family, which produced in one generation the journalists Larry and Yoshiko Tajiri, photographer Vince Tajiri, and sculptor Shinkichi Tajiri, plus career soldier James Tajiri. There is also the wondrous Yasui family of

Mary Oyama Mittwer, War Relocation Authority portrait. Bancroft Library, University of California, Berkeley.

Hood River, Oregon. Min Yasui, the most famous of the lot due to his wartime challenge to Executive Order 9066, became a lawyer and community activist. His siblings included two physicians (Robert and Homer), a public health nurse (Yuka), a teacher (Michi), two farmer-businessmen (Masao and Ray), and a peace activist (Roku). The siblings of the Uno family included the journalists Kazumaro Buddy Uno and Robert Uno, World War II veterans Howard, Stanley, and Ernest Uno, and activists Edison Uno and Amy Uno Ishii. Almost as striking were the siblings of the Oyama family of Sacramento. Apart from Robert, a chick sexer who died young in a car accident, there were Wesley Oyama, a successful businessman in postwar Japan; George "Clem" Oyama, Wesley's partner and a renowned inventor and horticulturist; Joe Oyama, a prolific journalist and longtime store owner and community leader in New York; and artist Lillie Oyama, the wife of physician-poet Yasuo Sasaki. The doyenne of this group of siblings was Mary Oyama Mittwer, known to her friends as Molly. Although her name had all but faded from view by the time of her death in 1994, she was in some ways the most intriguing of the bunch.

Mary Teiko Oyama was born in Fairfield, California, on June 19, 1907, and grew up in Sacramento. Her father Katsuji was a calligrapher. Her mother Miyo, a remarkably independent Issei woman, started a cosmetics manufacturing business and later traveled around selling her products in different regions of California. The young Molly was intensely literary. Her sister recounted how Katsuji Oyama would try to take books away from his daughter, to no avail, worrying that she was too thin and would contract

henry mittwer contemporary furnishings
pasadena . california

a new line of low cost
contemporary tables
designed with a structural
approach. all units
incorporate a slab covered
in durable linoleum.*
in a choice of six colors
on a black or white base.
slabs also available in
birch or black walnut veneer.

Catalog page from Henry Mittwer's furniture studio, circa 1951. Courtesy of the Mittwer family.

tuberculosis if she did not stop reading and start exercising. After graduating from Sacramento High School in 1925, Molly attended the San Francisco National Training School (a Methodist school for training missionaries) and then enrolled briefly at the University of Southern California. In 1933 she spent a stint in Seattle working for the Young Progressives, a political action group, then settled in Los Angeles. In 1937 she married Fred Mittwer, the Tokyo-born son of a German father and Japanese mother who worked as a linotypist with *Rafu Shimpo*. The couple soon had two children. They bought a house in the East Los Angeles neighborhood of Boyle Heights.

During the 1930s Molly distinguished herself as a poet and contributor to the fledgling Nisei press. Most notably, in 1935 she took up writing an advice column in the San Francisco journal *New World Sun*, under the pen name "Deirdre." She provided her readers with advice on matters such as interracial dating, resisting parental pressure for an arranged marriage, and struggles between family and career. As Valerie Matsumoto has shown, Mittwer worked to help Nisei (especially women) to navigate safely the customs of the white world, while keeping up parental and community standards. Molly meanwhile produced a stream of poems, stories, and articles for other Nisei journals and newspapers. In 1935 she founded a Nisei literary group called The Writers and helped put together their magazine, *Leaves*. (In addition to Japanese American writers, it featured the Korean American writer Ellen Thun). After three issues had appeared, in 1936 Molly made an agreement with Eddie Shimano, then a student at Cornell College in Iowa, to have The Writers contribute material to *Gyo-Sho*, the Nisei literary magazine he was putting together. Molly's own contribution, "Coming of Age," was a short story about a young woman casting her first vote in an election. She later collaborated with Carl Kondo and Yasuo Sasaki in forming a successor circle, the Nisei Writers Group. In the fall of 1941 she began a new column in *Rafu Shimpo*, "Daily Letter."

In addition to her own writing, Molly became an promoter of literature and social reform, a distinctive role that would become her specialty. During the late 1930s she made her house into a salon for discussion of art and ideas and organized private readings. In 1939 she hosted a lecture, on modern art, by the Japan-born poet and critic Sadakichi Hartmann, who was by then largely forgotten. She put together soirées to bring intellectual Nisei into contact with Italian-American novelist John Fante, muckraking journalist Carey McWilliams, and immigrant advocate Louis Adamic. Molly urged her fellow Nisei to make friends with people from other groups and published articles deploring anti-Semitism in the Japanese community. Her first mainstream publication was a letter in the *Los Angeles Times* in 1938 scoring the selling of "boycott Japan" buttons at Korean dancer Sai Shoki's recital—Molly extolled in somewhat naive terms the friendship between Koreans and Japanese. Historian Alfred McCoy has charged that Mary Oyama Mittwer worked as "Agent B-31" for the army intelligence wing G-2, reporting on Japanese espionage during 1940–41 (he rather unfairly blames her for fomenting popular misunderstanding of Japanese Americans through her reports on Japanese subversion.)

Mary Oyama Mittwer's life, like that of most Nisei, was changed by the outbreak of war. Fred Mittwer, who had been working as a radio operator for Japanese newspapers, lost his job following Pearl Harbor. In the face of widespread suspicion and race-based hostility, Fred was unable to find another job. Ripped from their home during the spring of 1942 by Executive Order 9066, the Mittwer family was confined first at Santa Anita, with most of the Oyamas, and then at Heart Mountain.

Beyond causing her own exile and confinement, the wartime events made a powerful impact on Molly's writing. First she concentrated on bringing the plight of the Nisei to a larger readership and seeking help from outside allies. She published a pair of articles in the New York–based pro-immigrant quarterly *Common Ground*, a project of the Common Council for American Unity. "After Pearl Harbor," which appeared in the Spring 1942 issue, was a sketch of the misfortunes that the coming of war had wrought on the Japanese community. She followed up soon after with "This Isn't Japan," an incisive sketch of conditions at Santa Anita. Once at Heart Mountain, Molly worked as an editor for the inmate newspaper, *Heart Mountain Sentinel*. In November 1942 she began a regular column, "Heart Mountain Breezes," in the *Powell Tribune*, a local weekly newspaper. In the wake of this activity, Molly was commissioned by the popular weekly magazine *Liberty* (which had been rabidly anti-Nisei in the prewar years) to write an article on the predicament of the inmates. Her contribution, published in the fall of 1943, "My Only Crime Is My Face," was among the first writings by a West Coast Nisei to appear outside of the ethnic press. It pointed out the Americanness of the Nisei and lamented the injustice of their confinement for "looking like the enemy." In January 1943 the Mittwers were able to leave Heart Mountain and resettle in Denver. Fred found a job working in the food processing industry. Molly continued to correspond with the *Sentinel*'s readers even after leaving the camp.

Molly's experience with official racism sharpened her understanding of prejudice and injustice against other groups and pushed her to embrace interracial activism. As Molly later described it, the turning point was her house. In a poignant moment in her *Common Ground* article "After Pearl Harbor," Molly had confided her worries that, unless her husband could find work, they might lose their beloved house: "I had thought it was only in old-fashioned melodramas that people lost their homes." Once ordered to leave the West Coast, the Mittwers were obliged to rent out their home in order to sustain it. After they had interviewed several prospective tenants, a friend who worked with an interracial fellowship asked whether they would be willing to rent to an African American couple. Molly later recounted her shock at the request. While she had never felt any racial prejudices, she noted, she also had next to no experience of blacks in her world. "We were so astonished by the novelty of the idea that we did a split-second mental flip-flop. But in that 'end of a minute' we did some fast thinking. 'Negroes—er, ah. Okay gal you've always believed in democracy. Now's your chance to do your stuff.' So partly to our surprise we could hear ourselves saying casually, 'Why, yes—send them up.'"

The couple was the writer Chester Himes and his wife. Not only did the Mittwers agree to rent their house to Himes, a warm friendship immediately blossomed. The result, Molly said, was that she "began to take an intense personal interest in the welfare of all Negro Americans." Himes was equally affected by his close friendship with Mary Oyama Mittwer and grew sensitive to the plight of Japanese Americans. In his novel *If He Hollers Let Him Go*, Himes spoke of the affecting spectacle of "little Riki Oyana" singing "God Bless America" before his family was taken away. He also wrote an article about Japanese Americans for Los Angeles–based interracial magazine the *War Worker* (for which Larry Tajiri would subsequently serve as a columnist).

In 1945, after the lifting of exclusion, the Mittwer family returned to Los Angeles and reclaimed their home in Boyle Heights, where Molly restarted her salon. Her biggest coup was receiving Marlon Brando as a guest when he first came to Hollywood. (For a time, Molly housed a Nisei teenager, Chizuko Omori, who returned from camp without her family. The future author of "Rabbit Ramblings" remarked that she met Carey McWilliams and all sorts of other fascinating people at Molly's house). Molly also threw herself into promoting progressive causes and fighting racism. In 1946 she was selected for the board of directors of the International Film and Radio Guild, an educational association designed to defend minorities from racial stereotyping, and she served alongside such luminaries as Eddie "Rochester" Anderson and Lena Horne. She also led a letter-writing campaign to persuade Hollywood studios to make films about Japanese Americans.

In 1946 Molly undertook a daily column for the revived *Rafu Shimpo*, a column alternately titled "Reveille" and—in homage to the title of African American author Roi Ottley's book on Harlem—"New World Coming!"

In the column and various pieces in the *Pacific Citizen*, Molly campaigned on behalf of collective action to promote racial equality and urged Nisei to broaden their horizons and become politically active. Molly withdrew from *Rafu Shimpo* around 1950 and began writing for the local Nisei newspaper *Crossroads* and for the *Pacific Citizen*. Her column, entitled "Smoglites," centered on life in Los Angeles. She continued writing it, with decreasing frequency, over the following decade.

Molly also resumed her role as a promoter and encourager of literature and social reform. In May 1948 she joined Sakei Ishihara, Mary Kitano, and Tom Kumuro on the steering committee of LA Nisei for Wallace, to support Henry Wallace's Progressive Party campaign for the presidency, and helped found the progressive Nisei weekly *Crossroads*. In 1950 she helped form a playwright's circle, the Nisei Experimental Group, in coordination with Los Angeles City College (LACC). It featured the budding Nisei writers Albert and Gompers Saijo, plus an LACC student named Hiroshi Kashiwagi. Their first performance was of Kashiwagi's one-act play *The Plums Can Wait*, about conflict between two brothers on a Northern California farm.

After 1950 Molly gradually withdrew from her public role. In later years she kept up close relations with her scattered siblings (as well as her brother-in-law Henry Mittwer). Fred Mittwer died in 1981. While Molly participated in a Nisei writers' conference at UCLA in 1985, she remained virtually forgotten until the historian Valerie Matsumoto produced her groundbreaking article "Desperately Seeking Deirdre" in 1991, three years before Molly died. Her work, especially her powerful columns in the postwar *Rafu Shimpo*, awaits further rediscovery and analysis.[1]

Mary Oyama's brother-in-law Henry Mittwer carved out a long career of his own, successively as an artist, engineer, and designer, and later as a Buddhist monk. Henry Mittwer was born in Yokohama in 1918. He later recounted the story that his American-born father R. J. H. Mittwer, first visited Japan in 1898 as a sailor in the US Navy while en route to the Philippines for combat in the Spanish-American War. While this story is not verified, it is certain that R. J. H. Mittwer ended up living in Japan and traveling widely in Asia, where he worked as a distributor of American films, and marrying a geisha from Tokyo. The couple had three sons, of whom Henry was the youngest. After the great 1923 Kanto earthquake, during which the Mittwers were forced to abandon their house for several days and camp out in their yard, the family moved to Shanghai. There they lived for nearly three years before returning to Japan. Soon after, R. J. H. Mittwer left for the United States with his middle son, Fred, who was nine years Henry's senior. Henry and his eldest brother, John, remained with their mother in Yokohama, where Henry attended St. Joseph's Academy, a cosmopolitan, English-speaking Catholic school. Initially the plan was to ultimately bring the entire family to America. However, in the Great Depression Mr. Mittwer lost his business and savings and ceased sending money back to Japan, and the Mittwers there were reduced to poverty. Henry was forced to quit school at age sixteen and seek employment.

In 1940, as war dawned between Japan and the United States, Henry Mittwer managed to buy a steamship ticket to the United States in order to seek out his father. Henry was a US citizen by birth, but it was his first trip to America. Though he did not look Japanese, he spoke Japanese better than English and was not accustomed to American life. He first reconnected with his brother Fred, who took him to the New York Hotel in Los Angeles's Little Tokyo to meet his father. The elder Mittwer, whom Henry would later describe as "frail and defeated," did not recognize him when they first met, after their twelve-year separation. While Henry intended to return to Japan, the approach of war made such a return impossible. He settled in Los Angeles and remained close with brother Fred and his wife, Mary Oyama Mittwer. He found work at a Japanese store and met a local Nisei named Sachiko.

Following the Japanese attack on Pearl Harbor, Henry was thrown out of work. Although Henry was a skilled electrician, he had trouble finding employment because of his ancestry and the language barrier. In 1942, following Executive Order 9066, Henry Mittwer was rounded up and confined. As he later related, "My father took me to see a district attorney he knew, who advised me to go to a detention camp." (At the same time, his brother John was detained in Japan for being a US citizen and confined at a farm in Hakone.)

Sent to the Manzanar camp in Owens Valley, California, Henry passed the time by working at the camp hospital. During the so-called "Manzanar riot" in December 1942, Mittwer joined the crowd of protesters and threw stones at military police and gained a reputation as a troublemaker. Despite this, because of his mixed ancestry he faced accusations by other dissidents that he was an administration spy. Unwilling to live amid such pressures, he applied for and received a transfer to the Gila River camp in Arizona, so that he could join Sachiko, who had been confined there. The two were married in Arizona on December 29, 1942. While in camp, they had two children. However, in 1943, when faced with the loyalty questionnaire imposed on camp inmates, Mittwer gave a "wrong" answer. In response to question 27, which asked whether he was willing to serve in the US military, he responded, "I cannot point the barrel of a gun at the country where my mother awaits me." Mittwer was sent to the segregation center at Tule Lake, in Northern California, where he renounced his US citizenship. (Since Henry never had Japanese citizenship—at that time birthright citizenship in Japan passed solely through the father—his action left him stateless.)

Following the end of the war, Mittwer's wife and children were allowed to leave camp and migrate to Chicago. However, Henry was threatened with deportation and held in a detention center in San Francisco for three months. With the aid of attorney Wayne Collins, he brought a habeas corpus suit in federal court, arguing that he had been illegally detained and had been coerced into renouncing his citizenship at Tule Lake by threats of physical violence. He was released from custody in 1947, and his citizenship was finally restored in 1951.

Following his release, Henry Mittwer lived briefly at Seabrook Farms, in New Jersey, a frozen food production center that was home to many resettlers. Soon after, however, he and his family migrated back to the Los Angeles area. There Mittwer attended John Muir College, an adult night school where he studied ceramics, and pursued his dream of becoming a furniture designer. In the early 1950s Henry opened a furniture design business in Pasadena. His Japanese-influenced tables were selected for the Museum of Modern Art's *Good Design* exhibition in 1952. A coffee-cocktail table he designed was featured in *Interior* magazine and in *Retailing Daily*. Other designs were featured in the magazine *Art and Architecture*, and in Esempi, the Italian design book series.

Mittwer engaged in public activities that supported his furniture business. In 1953 he lectured on Asian style at a local JACL branch. Referring to the attraction of simple lines of architecture, he asserted prophetically that Asian design in furniture and pottery would become popular in Southern California. In 1955 he proposed a three-week "cherry blossom" tour of Japan, where he would guide guests around various spring festivals, but the trip seems not to have occurred.

A series of catastrophic life events then altered Mittwer's life path. First, in 1955 his mother died before he could see her again. His furniture business proved insufficient to support a wife and two children (plus a third child, born in 1956). He thus gave it up and found a job working for the Endevco Corporation, designing and making precision instruments for use in airplanes and rockets. Meanwhile he had become attracted to the ideas of Zen Buddhism. Henry made regular visits to the meditation hall run by the Zen monk Nyogen Senzaki and started regular meditation sessions—as he put it, "to clear the cobwebs from my brain." Around this time, Mittwer was struck by a serious lung disease, which nearly killed him, and he had half of one lung removed.

In 1961 Henry Mittwer returned alone to Japan, where the air was fresher than in Los Angeles, and visited Kyoto's Myoshinji Temple, the home temple of his teacher Senzaki. There he found peace and sanctuary. Mittwer became a disciple of the chief abbot, Daiko Furukawa, and was engaged to assist with visiting American priests. As Mittwer later related, "One day I was asked, 'Why don't you become a priest?' So I was tonsured." After a long separation, Mittwer's wife and daughters finally came to Japan in 1965 and lived together with him on the temple grounds.

After Furukawa's early death, Mittwer met Hirata Seiko, the abbot of Tenryuji Temple, a complex of wooden buildings and gardens in Kyoto. Seiko invited him to become his student, and Mittwer shifted his base to Tenryuji, where he remained active into his nineties. Beyond his religious duties, he made pottery, holding exhibitions annually in Tokyo, and threw himself into ikebana (flower arranging). He served four terms as president of the Kyoto chapter of Ikebana International and lectured widely. He wrote a book in English, *The Art of Chabana: Flowers for the Tea Ceremony* (Charles E. Tuttle, 1974), and several other books in Japanese, including his 1983 memoirs, *Sokoku to bokoku no hazama de* ("Between My Fatherland and My Motherland"); *Arashiyama no fumoto kara* ("From the Foot of Arashiyama"), a 1992 book of essays about temple life; and *Jisei no Kotoba* ("Poems for Leaving the World"), a 2003 dialogue with the noted author and Buddhist priest Tsutomu Mizukami about life, death and Zen. He also helped translate a Japanese treatise on classical Chinese science.

In his last years, Mittwer wrote an original screenplay, "Akai Kutsu" ("Red Shoes") based on Ujo Noguchi's children's song of the same name, about a Japanese orphan adopted by an American missionary couple. He worked to interest filmmakers and government officials in the project but was unable to find a producer before his death in June 2012. A set of screenwriters and filmmakers then decided to "take over Mr. Mittwer's passion," as one of them termed it, and selected Takayuki Nakamura to direct. The five-minute animated short, "Henry's Red Shoes," premiered in December 2014.

Ambrose Amadeus Uchiyamada

One remarkable hapa poet and journalist had the magnificent name Ambrose Amadeus Uchiyamada. He grew up under unusual circumstances. His father, Thomas Morkiyo Uchiyamada, a university-trained engineer from Japan, came to the United States for further schooling in the first years of the twentieth century. Family lore has it that he met his Irish-born wife Mary in California, where she was working as a "Harvey Girl" at a railway station eatery. After she fell ill, Thomas helped nurse her back to health, whereupon the two fell in love. (White-Asian marriage was at that time illegal in California, so they traveled to New Mexico to wed.).

Ambrose, known to his family and friends as Ambie, was born in Southern California on March 21, 1913, the second of four surviving children of the couple. Soon after, Thomas suffered an attack of polio that left him

Ambrose Amadeus Uchi-yamada, Menomonee Falls, Wisconsin, 1934. Photographer and source unknown, author's personal collection.

temporarily disabled, and he took the family back to Japan so he could recuperate. He did not prepare his Japanese relatives for the news that he was bringing a white wife and mixed-race children, however, and his appearance caused a stir. The young mixed-race family experienced such prejudice from Thomas's family that after two years they returned to the United States.

Once returned, they faced racial discrimination in America. Despite his qualifications, Thomas was able to get only short-term replacement jobs as an engineer. Instead, both spouses took menial jobs. Money was so tight that, rather than pay for lodging, the family lived for two years in a large tent in the Arroyo Seco region. For a time, Ambrose and his father worked as sugar beet laborers in Utah. Following a work accident, Mary

Uchiyamada developed cancer and died young. Her husband, worn out by sorrow and illness, thereafter was confined in a state farm for alcoholics, and he eventually died there.

Even before their mother's death, the children were sent to live at the Los Angeles–based Maryknoll Home for Japanese Children, where they also received schooling. During his school years, Ambie distinguished himself as a writer and actor. According to his sister Margaret Uchiyamada Takahashi, Ambie was an avid performer from a young age. In an unpublished memoir, she later recalled living in Long Beach and going to the local amusement park, the Pike, where Ambie would volunteer for the sideshows and go up on the stage. "Once he entered a buck and wing contest. He couldn't even jig—but he got up and jigged away." Ultimately writing and performing became for him a form of escape from school. "He felt like a pauper and didn't want to be there, but he studied hard and made good grades except in math. His compositions were far above his grade level. When the downtown public library was built, all the schools submitted their best composition. The winner would lead the parade. Ambrose won and led all the children dressed as storybook characters."

Ambie was let out of the orphanage as a teenager and worked as a houseboy and domestic for white families to support himself. With help from sympathetic Maryknoll brothers, he received a scholarship to Marquette University in Milwaukee, Wisconsin, where he majored in journalism. In 1933 he won the freshman oratorical contest with "Defense of the Vagabond" and finished second in interpretation with "Richard III." The following year he won another award, from the *Marquette Journal*, the student literary magazine, for his poems "Lines Inscribed" and "Thou and I." In his senior year he performed a dramatic reading of excerpts of Edmond Rostand's *Cyrano de Bergerac* for the International Club.

After leaving Marquette in 1935, Ambie returned to California, where he joined Japanese American literary circles. In the following years he published numerous works in West Coast Nisei journals and literary magazines. His selection in the 1935 journal *Leaves* was a greenroom dialogue between two musicians on the relative importance of talent and fearless initiative. His contribution to the 1936 journal *Gyo-Sho* was a wistful poem, "Ah, Love—Do You Remember?" It concluded:

Ah love, I have found...
That the world is only a bubble
And the night's cloak merely a shadow
And the stars—(ah, fool!)—the stars were never diamonds...
Ah, if you can, forgive your long-ago lover
For those blind eyes that could not see...
For the rash promises he could not keep.

Ambie made a strong impression on his colleagues. Larry Tajiri, English editor of *Kashu Mainichi* and *Nichi Bei Shimizu* and an arbiter of taste, referred to Ambrose's poetry as a highlight of Nisei writing. Mary Oyama Mittwer later published a warm reminiscence in which she recalled him as a "dashing Irish-Japanese poet-thespian-vagabond" who hitchhiked and rode the rails from Milwaukee to Los Angeles in the mid-1930s. Fellow journalist Buddy Uno drove a group of them to the beach, where they paraded around and ate popcorn. Ambie found a children's playground and raced around, singing "Ah, Sweet Mystery of Life" at the top of his lungs. Then they delivered him to the Maryknoll Home where he was staying (and where his younger brother Raymond ecstatically greeted him). Mittwer concluded her reminiscence by describing how Ambie had gallantly kissed her hand in farewell.

Ambie's later life is somewhat more hazy. Sometime before World War II he moved to New York, where he worked as an editorial assistant at *Time* magazine. Following the outbreak of World War II, his younger sister Margaret and her family and their brother Raymond were confined by the US government. Ambie was conscripted into the US Army but protested being drafted because of his family's treatment. To avoid prison, he ultimately agreed to join the US Army Medical Corps. During this time, he met and married Hilda Castle (Kastelowitz), a Jewish-American woman doing graduate work in physics at Columbia University. (Like Thomas Uchiyamada, she had been stricken with polio and walked with a limp.) After training on Long Island at Camp Upton, Ambie was stationed in Chicago. Hilda followed him and was hired for work at the University of Chicago, working on neutron cross-sections for the Manhattan Project. Her team performed computations on plutonium piles (nuclear reactors) and helped design the famous pile at Hanford, Washington. Ambie was ultimately sent for service in England and Germany before being discharged in mid-1945.

In the postwar years, Ambie and Hilda returned to New York. Ambie enrolled at the New School, where he received a bachelor's degree in literature and worked as an assistant editor at *Architectural Forum*. He later pursued graduate work in literature at Boston University and New York University. In addition to working together with his wife at the General Dynamics Corporation on submarine control systems, he spent several years teaching English, first at the New York State Agricultural and Technical College (today's Alfred State College) and then at Penn State Altoona, where Hilda taught physics. He does not appear to have published much, neither scholarly articles nor creative literature. The couple lived their retirement years in Bangor, Maine. In 1991 he wrote an essay, "Beach Walking," for the magazine *Down East*. Ambie passed away on October 24, 2002, at age eighty-nine. Hilda followed seven years later.

K. K. and Clarke Kawakami, Journalists

WITH CHRIS SUH

One intriguing aspect of Japanese immigrant experience before World War II was the diverse intellectual life of community members. Although most early Issei were farmers or laborers, a significant group of writers and thinkers emerged among them. These people found work as Buddhist priests, schoolteachers, or newspaper editors in Japanese communities. As Eiichiro Azuma shows, they wrote primarily in Japanese, identified with the old country, and were heavily invested in building a *shin nippon*, a new Japan in the New World. Yet overlapping with them was a selection of students, artists, and professionals who might be termed cosmopolitan Issei. They generally lived outside ethnic communities, developed primary

K. K. Kawakami in the early 1920s.
From *Japan: Overseas Monthly*, 1922.

contacts with whites, and willingly absorbed themselves in Western culture. Unlike the majority of Issei, they wrote in English, producing novels, poems, and plays as well as nonfiction. This audacious move symbolized their quest for a diverse readership and their demand for recognition as equal players in conversations about America. Perhaps the most notable representative of the cosmopolitans is K. K. (Kiyoshi Karl) Kawakami. During the prewar decades Kawakami produced numerous books and articles in English, plus a pair of books in French. These works reflected the odd evolution of Kawakami's career. At first critical of Japan and its "feudal" society, he later became an influential apologist for Japanese imperialism, then still later turned against Tokyo and supported the United States during World War II.

Kawakami was born in Japan in 1873 (according to one source his birth name was Miyashita Yūshichi). Orphaned at an early age, he nonetheless was able to attend school and learn English. After moving to Tokyo at age seventeen, he enrolled in legal studies and then attended Aoyama Gakuin, a Methodist school where he presumably learned English. According to one source, he also graduated from the law school Tokyo Hogakuin (the future Chuo University). Kawakami converted to Christian socialism, and he became one of founding members of the *Shakai Shugi Kenkyūkai* (the Society for the Study of Socialism) and the *Shakai Minshūtō* (the Socialist Democratic Party) alongside the better-known socialists Abe Isoo, Katayama Sen, and Kōtoku Shūsui. Inspired by Karl Marx, Kawakami took the English name "Karl" and thereafter referred to himself as Kiyoshi Karl (or K. K.) Kawakami. He wrote editorials for *Yoruzo Chōhō*, then under the editorship of the American-educated Christian author and intellectual Kanzo Uchimura.

Following the collapse of Japan's first socialist party in 1901, Kawakami left for the United States, where he received a fellowship in political science at the State University of Iowa. His master's thesis was published as *The Political Ideas of Modern Japan* by the University Press (Iowa) and the Japanese firm Shōkwabō, both in 1903. After graduating from Iowa, Kawakami continued his studies at the University of Wisconsin but did not finish his doctoral work. Instead he helped found the Seattle Japanese Socialist Party with Katayama, and worked for the Japanese Commission at the 1904 Louisiana Purchase Exposition in St. Louis. During this time he also worked as a foreign correspondent for the Japanese newspaper *Yorozu Chōhō*, which had begun to publish his writings during his Tokyo days. In 1905 Kawakami traveled to New Hampshire to cover the Treaty of Portsmouth, which ended the Russo-Japanese War. In 1907 he married Mildred Clarke, a white woman, and moved to her hometown of Momence, Illinois, where he spent the next several years. During this time the couple had two children, Clarke and Yuri.

By this time, Kawakami had become disillusioned with socialism. Attracted by the plight of his fellow Issei, he published numerous articles in English defending Japanese immigrants in California as well as Japanese imperialists in Asia. Many of these articles were published in his 1912 book *American-Japanese Relations*, which was highly praised by the *New York Times* for its "everlasting righteousness and common sense." The *Times* reviewer approved of Kawakami's conclusion that the Gentlemen's Agreement would solve the immigration problem, reflecting what "scientific inquirers, the best businessmen and the statesmen, whose eyes are not on votes, have long held."

In 1913 Kawakami moved to San Francisco (where his youngest child, Marcia, was born) As general secretary of the Japanese Association of America, he took an active role in the struggle to defend Japanese immigrants against nativist pressures for exclusion. In 1914 he became the head of the Pacific Press Bureau, established by the Japanese consulate in San Francisco to create a positive image of the Issei. In 1919 Kawakami joined forces with missionary and publicist Sidney Gulick to press for liberalized immigration policies, for which the two were publicly accused by California's US senator James Phelan of being Japanese government agents.) Kawakami produced a series of books that argued for Japanese inclusion into American society.

What is particularly striking about these works was Kawakami's self-presentation. In his 1914 book *Asia at the Door*, published shortly after passage of the 1913 Alien Land Act in California, Kawakami spoke as an American, not as Japanese or Japanese American. "Fate decreed that I should make my home in America and have American relatives and friends, who do not hesitate to take me into confidence and reveal to me both the lighter and darker phase of American life."[2] As a self-appointed insider, he undertook a frankly elitist defense of Japanese immigration. "The restriction of immigration is no doubt one of our sovereign rights, but in exercising such rights we must not single out . . . a civilized and progressive nation [as] the object of discrimination. . . . It was this sense of justice which inspired our forefathers and which made our country unique and spiritually great in the concourse of nations." A just policy toward Japanese immigrants, whom the United States had the responsibility to protect and uplift, was part of America's long mission to free Japan from the legacy of its "oppressive past" and instill in its people "the idea of personal rights and freedom essential to a constitutional government." Meanwhile, the treatment of Japanese immigrants in America encapsulated a choice for the West: equal friendship or conflict with a rising Asian continent.

Kawakami's position was fundamentally contradictory. He maintained that immigration ought to be restricted to only the "better" classes, and he was ready to concur with nativism and white supremacy as long as Japanese were recognized as among the superiors. Indeed, he asserted that it was natural for Californians to consider themselves a superior race. In his book he speaks condescendingly of immigrants from southern and eastern Europe and continually contrasts Japanese immigrants with the Chinese, whom he calls variously a race of effeminate "ideal servants," a criminal gang of "hatchet men," and gamblers. (He reported that Sun Yat-Sen's revolution was financed by the Chinese gambling parlors in California that profited from the Japanese trade.) In fact, the only group that came in for more scathing criticism than the Chinese in the book were the native Hawaiians, whom he called "the offspring of animal rather than of the intellectual faculties, governed by traditional customs of a very low order."

Yet Kawakami's standard of "desirability" in judging classes of immigrants was not simply racial. He insisted, "No man is worthwhile who does not respect himself and the race of which he is a member. Neither is he a desirable member of the democracy who cherishes prejudice against other races." Nor was it entirely social. He decried the dishonesty and deceit of both Japanese and Americans of "a certain class." But at the same time he deplored the influence of the Japanese consul in Hawai'i and that of Buddhist priests and missionaries there in chiefly economic terms, the former for collaborating with white planters in enforcing exploitative contracts and preventing workers from migrating to the mainland, and the Buddhists for spreading narrow pro-Japanese propaganda and extorting contributions from poor parishioners. Nor was Kawakami entirely an advocate of assimilation. To be sure, he believed that the principal point in favor of Japanese immigrants was their capacity to be quickly "Americanized" and pointed with pride to the offspring of white-Japanese intermarriages as appearing "completely American" (i.e., white). Nevertheless, he praised Japanese schools on the West Coast and in Hawai'i for instilling cosmopolitan ideas in children and promoting cultural interchange. Kawakami asserted that Japanese Americans stood at the border between West and East and that their treatment by white Americans, albeit minor in itself, symbolized the relations between the two worlds.

Kawakami's cosmopolitan optimism was soon strained by the success of anti-Japanese legislation, including California's Alien Land Act, which he termed part of a policy of "extermination." In his next book, *The Real*

Japanese Question (1920), he bitterly denounced the politicians who were in his mind chiefly responsible not only for the exclusionary legislation but also for stirring up racial prejudice. The book generally rehashed the arguments Kawakami had already presented in *Asia at the Door*. Though he expressed even more condescension toward the Chinese, he criticized US immigration law as absurd for excluding qualified Chinese and Japanese immigrants yet allowing citizenship to undesirable "non-Caucasians" such as Mexicans, Hungarians, "Hottentots," Finns, Persians, and Syrians. The most striking change, however, is in Kawakami's rhetorical strategy. No longer would the author describe himself as an American or assume that right-thinking people opposed immigration restriction. Instead of speaking about the innate assimilability of the Japanese, he asked only for tolerance.

Following the passage of the 1920 Alien Land Act in California, the Pacific Press Bureau was disbanded. Kawakami and his family moved to Washington, DC in 1922. In the following years, he served as the Washington correspondent for the *Osaka Mainichi Shimbun* and the *Tokyo Nichi Nichi Shimbun* and also wrote regularly for the *Washington Post* and such magazines as *Japan: Overseas Travel Magazine* and *Japanese Student*. He also wrote books, such as a biography of chemist Jokichi Takamine, and articles on the United States for Japanese newspapers. In 1937 he traveled to Italy as a representative of Japanese newspapers and interviewed Italian dictator Benito Mussolini.

During these years Kawakami became known for championing Japan's foreign policy, including the Japanese occupation of Manchuria. Although Kawakami criticized the decision of Japanese policy makers to sign the Anti-Comintern Pact with Nazi Germany in 1936, he continued to defend Japan's actions in Asia. After Japan invaded China in 1937, Kawakami attempted to convince his American readers that Japan was fighting a war to secure American, British, and Japanese commercial interests in China against the Soviet-led communists. As late as the summer of 1940, he published an article in *Foreign Affairs* portraying Japan's actions in China as an effort to enforce the Open Door policy. He stopped defending the Japanese government after it signed the Tripartite Pact with Germany and Italy in September 1940, arguing that Japan was "devoid of a forceful leadership."

Despite the change of position, Kawakami was apprehended as a potentially dangerous alien on December 8, 1941, the day after Japan bombed Pearl Harbor, because he was known as the leading prewar defender of Japanese foreign policy. He remained in detention for several weeks at the US Immigration Station at Gloucester City, New Jersey, waiting to appear before the Alien Enemy Hearing Board at Fort Howard, Maryland. During this time he received important support from several prominent Americans, including Felix Morley, the president of Haverford College and former editor of the *Washington Post*. On February 11, 1942, Kawakami was paroled by order of Attorney General Francis Biddle. He spent most of the war years in Washington. Toward the end of the war he began publishing occasional articles on Japan for the *Evening Star* newspaper and reemerged in public, continuing his argument from the 1930s that the United States and Japan needed to cooperate to fight the Communist threat. Many of these writings were published in *Human Events*, a conservative, anticommunist magazine. Kawakami passed away on October 12, 1949, in Washington, DC.

K. K. Kawakami's son, Clarke Hiroshi Kawakami, a man who made his mark in many different fields, was born in Momence, Illinois in 1909. The young Clarke spent his early years in San Francisco, then in 1922 moved to Washington, DC, where he attended Central High School. Clarke went on to attend Harvard University, where he studied government and international relations. Hoping to make a career as a diplomat, he applied to the State Department upon graduation in 1930, but despite his stellar record he was turned down. It is not clear how much the refusal was based on racism and how much US officials feared his father's pro-Japan influence.

Rebuffed by the State Department, Clarke Kawakami accepted a fellowship from the École Libre des Sciences Politiques in France and spent a year there doing graduate studies. The next year he moved to Geneva. With help from his father's connections, he was hired as an interpreter by the Japanese delegation at the World Disarmament Conference at the League of Nations, but soon after his arrival Japan withdrew from the League of Nations, and Clarke lost his job. While in Europe, Clarke met and married Helen Machilda, a German woman who worked as a secretary at the Japanese legation. He and Helen moved to Washington, DC, where Clarke served as a press attaché for diplomat Yōsuke Matsuoka (according to one source, despite Kawakami's poor Japanese, Matsuoka preferred Clarke because of his striking good looks). In the summer of 1933 Clarke and Helen moved to Japan. With Matsuoka's patronage, Clarke was hired as a reporter for the Japanese Associated Press Shimbun Rengo (later known as Dōmei); since he could not write in Japanese, he wrote all his articles in English. Helen worked as a secretary for Kokusai Steamship Company. Meanwhile Clarke joined a Harvard classmate in touring occupied Manchuria, then collaborated on production of a bilingual propaganda volume about the Japanese puppet state of Manchukuo.

In late 1935 Clarke met Chieko (Susuga) Takehisa, a famous stage and screen actress, at a Christmas party. The two soon fell in love, and Clarke asked Helen for a divorce. Helen was not pleased but finally agreed in exchange for Clarke assisting her in getting US citizenship as his spouse. As a result, the divorce took several years. In 1939 Clarke moved to London as Dōmei's European correspondent, and then in June 1940 he returned to Washington. While there he lived at his parents' house and filed a series of English-language articles on US foreign policy for Dōmei. He had great difficulty securing a visa for his betrothed because of the Japanese exclusion laws. Finally he persuaded Secretary of State Cordell Hull to order the State Department to issue her a one-year student visa. One year later, in April 1941, Chieko came to Washington, and the two were wed in August.

Pearl Harbor led to drastic changes in Clarke Kawakami's life. As noted, his father K. K. Kawakami was briefly interned as a potentially dangerous alien. Once the war began, Chieko decided to go back to Japan, and in the spring of 1942 she left on the *Gripsholm* "exchange ship," despite Clarke's opposition. Clarke's job with Dōmei was suspended by the outbreak of war. He formally resigned from his post and publicly condemned Japan's attack as shameful and double-dealing. In a letter he wrote to his Washington newspaper colleagues explaining his position—which was then publicly released by the U.S. State Department—Kawakami described the attack as "the blackest and most shameful page in Japanese History" and expressed his intention to enlist in the US Army so that he could help "crush forever the type of militarist rule which drugs and drags peaceful people in to war, wherever it exists." He tried to enlist in the army (from which he had obtained a deferment before the war) but was declined on grounds of his Japanese ancestry—according to one source he wrote "Eurasian" in response to the question of "race," but the army corrected it to "Japanese." Clarke wrote many articles on Japan and sent them to journals such as the *Saturday Evening Post* and newspapers such as the *New York Times* and *Washington Star*, without success. After several months he was able to secure a position as correspondent with the *Washington Post*. The series of articles he produced on Japan during mid-1942 reveal a clear understanding of Japanese society.

In the spring of 1943 Kawakami succeeded in enlisting in the US Army Military Intelligence Service (MIS) program and was sent to Camp Savage in Minnesota for training as Japanese specialist. Raised to the rank of lieutenant, in spring 1944 he was attached to the Office of War Information's Psychological Warfare Section and sent to the India-Burma front. Two prominent leftist Nisei, Koji Ariyoshi and Karl Yoneda, were also in his group. Clarke drafted propaganda flyers that were translated into Japanese by Yoneda and sent into Japanese-occupied Burma. He worked with State Department diplomat John Emmerson on reports of interrogations of Japanese POWs. In early 1945 he was sent to Kunming, China, to work with a psychological warfare unit. He prepared leaflets targeted to the Japanese, underlining terms and conditions of surrender. Once the war ended he joined American and Chinese soldiers in processing the surrender of occupying Japanese troops and working with Allied rescue units. For his efforts, he was awarded the Bronze Star.

While in Shanghai at war's end, Clarke learned that his wife Chieko had survived and was active in the Japanese film industry. Hoping to find her, in November 1945 he returned to Japan, where he was attached to General MacArthur's staff at GHQ and helped organize the US occupation. He did find Chieko, and she was astonished to see him. Having heard of Nisei combat units, she had assumed he was in Europe. The couple reunited and had three children in in the following years. After a short visit to the United States, during which Kawakami was officially discharged, he returned to Japan to serve in the Allied Translators and Interpreters Service (ATIS) as a civilian War Department employee. At first he was employed with ATIS's Periodicals Section, directing the translation of articles from the Japanese press. He later worked with the G-2 Historical section to produce a history of MacArthur's wartime campaigns. While he did not keep close contact with Japanese communities in the United States, he furnished an introduction for a copy of the new Japanese postwar constitution that appeared in the San Francisco *Progressive News* in 1946.

Kawakami and his family returned to the United States in 1950. Once back in Washington, Kawakami served as research assistant to Commodore Richard Bates of the Naval War College on a history of the Battle of Leyte Gulf. Kawakami wrote articles for biweekly newsmagazine *The Reporter*, notably one on anti-Americanism in Japan. He also helped translate and edit a book by two Imperial Navy officers, *Midway: The Battle That Doomed Japan* (1955). The book was widely reviewed and went through several editions in multiple languages. In 1955 Kawakami was hired as a staffer by the new US Information Agency (USIA) and was named associate editor of its journal *Problems of Communism*. He remained with the USIA until his retirement in 1976. He died in 1985.

CHAPTER THREE

Wartime Confinement and Japanese Americans

NIKKEI STORIES

Japanese Americans and Pearl Harbor: Another Sort of Infamy

The Japanese attack on Pearl Harbor and the outbreak of World War II in the Pacific triggered the mass removal of 120,000 American citizens and long-time residents of Japanese ancestry from the US Pacific Coast during mid-1942 and eventually their confinement in government camps. As a historian of the wartime events, I was asked some years ago by the editors of a historical forum on Pearl Harbor to contribute a reflection on its meaning for Japanese Americans. My first response was to inform them somewhat stiffly that I really had nothing to say about Tokyo's bombing raid, since Japanese Americans were in no way responsible for it. I was quickly reassured by the editors that the assignment was not about causal links or historical revisionism but about the event itself and its legacy in terms of commemoration and collective memory within the community. Again I hesitated: it is tricky and complex business

One view of the Japanese attack on Pearl Harbor. Official US Navy photograph.

to generalize about the collective psyche of any group. Yet I recalled that in speaking to countless individual Nisei I had been struck forcefully by how deeply December 7 remained for them a day of infamy and trauma. For Japanese Americans, the words "Pearl Harbor" are an accusation, a standing charge against them of a crime they did not commit, and one that has generated its own reactions throughout history. After some further thought, I agreed to touch on some issues that seemed to me particularly relevant.

In discussing Japanese Americans and Pearl Harbor, it is worth noting that Japanese Americans do indeed have an important connection to the attack. Before readers panic, however, let me make clear that the connection is nothing resembling the racist mythology about Japanese spies and fifth columnists that still persists in the imaginations of right-wing columnist Michelle Malkin and her supporters. On the contrary, the connection is precisely in the government's preexisting, exaggerated fears of Japanese American spies, which played a central role in amplifying the disaster at Pearl Harbor and its aftermath. In the fall of 1941, commanding army general Walter Short ordered the airplanes based at Hickam Field bunched close together on the ground, in order to protect them more easily against the danger of sabotage by ethnic Japanese in Hawai'i. Japanese bombs caught the American planes thus immobilized during the first wave of attacks and swiftly put over 250 of them out of commission, thereby crippling any defense of the naval base.[1] Furthermore, in the first hours after the attack, government agents in Hawai'i and on the mainland began mass arrests of Japanese community leaders—teachers, ministers, and businessmen—whom they held incommunicado for months without charge. Those rounded up had been previously marked for internment, not because of any action on their part but because their position in the community made them suspect.

Nonetheless, the attack gave rise to a central divergence in status between the "local Japanese" in Hawai'i and their mainland counterparts. The attack had an immediate and direct impact on local Japanese communities in the territory. First, dozens of ethnic Japanese civilians in Hawai'i were killed or wounded by stray bombs. While official lists of the fifty-seven recorded civilian casualties did not distinguish victims by national origin, a check reveals numerous Japanese names (which would be logical, given the significant percentage of local Japanese in Oahu).[2] Nisei soldiers rushed to their posts during the attack to fire at the enemy, while Nisei Red Cross workers helped care for the wounded. A telephone summons to male Nisei graduates of the University of Hawai'i, who had gone through required ROTC courses, led to the immediate organization of a militia unit, the Hawai'i Territorial Guard. The local Japanese, indispensable to the territory's plantation workforce and with representatives close to the power structure, were spared mass confinement. At the same time, General Short, brandishing the text of a proclamation of martial law secretly drafted by Colonel Thomas Green of the Provost Marshal General's office, stormed into the office of territorial governor Thomas Poindexter. Warning of potential disloyalty by local Japanese and invoking the menace of a military takeover, Short forced the governor to sign the proclamation sight unseen, then declared himself military governor and suspended the US Constitution. Full civilian rule would not be restored in Hawai'i until October 1944.

On the mainland, reactions among Japanese Americans, like others, were variable. Mainland Nisei organizations and individuals nationwide publicly expressed outrage over the attack and offered the government their full support. Young men rushed to join the US Army, but the War Department immediately froze Nisei enlistments, and almost all Nisei were refused. In the first days after the attack, there was no perceptible public outcry against Japanese Americans. However, in early 1942, the conjunction of Japan's victories in the Pacific, the presence in the Western Defense Command of craven and ambitious military officers fearful of invasion and impatient with civilian control, and the instigation of powerful nativist and commercial lobbying groups with a self-interest in removing their non-white competitors all created the conditions for mass removal of the entire ethnic Japanese population from the Pacific Coast.

It would be an exaggeration to say that the Pearl Harbor attack in itself settled the respective fates of the Japanese Americans in Hawai'i and the mainland—economic and political factors played a decisive role as well. Still, the visible support and heroism that the local Japanese in the former region had the opportunity to display helped reassure officials, civilian and military alike, that Nisei could be trusted. In the same way, through their exemplary patriotism and contribution to the war effort, these Nisei were able to emerge from the shadow of mainstream suspicion and play a dominant role in Hawaiian society in the postwar years. Japanese Americans on the mainland, already a small and relatively isolated group, were further excluded after the outbreak of war and stripped of the largest part of their community leadership. They thus made easy and tempting targets to pick off.

Furthermore, the onus of the Pearl Harbor attack, however unjust, proved durable and largely unshakable for Japanese Americans. It manifested itself in numerous ways. On one level, individuals were targeted for abuse or mockery on the anniversary. For example, Asian American studies pioneer Don Nakanishi later recalled that when he left his native California to enroll at Yale University in 1967, it was an almost entirely white institution. On December 7, while he was sitting in his dorm, white students entered the room and pelted him with water balloons, yelling "Attack Pearl Harbor!" He was humiliated, he later said. "I'd never faced anything like that before."[3] A year later, when student strikes rocked San Francisco State University's campus, the Canada-born Nisei S. I. Hayakawa agreed to serve as acting president of the university. California governor Ronald Reagan (who had gained a reputation during the early postwar era as a friend of Japanese Americans) reportedly joked that if Hayakawa would take the job he would be "forgiven for Pearl Harbor."[4] There were also less prankish sides to the conflation of Japanese Americans with Japan's military. In 1981 John J. McCloy, who as assistant secretary of war had been one of the prime movers in bringing about Executive Order 9066, testified before the US Commission on Wartime Relocation and Internment of Civilians. McCloy caused widespread shock in the hearing room when he declared that the mass removal of Japanese Americans was a case of just retribution for the Pearl Harbor attack.

I discovered a poignant echo of this misguided association when I first began doing research for my book *By Order of the President*. I found that a number of Nisei, on hearing that I was studying the question of Franklin Roosevelt and Japanese Americans, would ask me whether Roosevelt had had foreknowledge of an attack on Pearl Harbor and had permitted it to occur in order to bring the United States into the war (or, more precisely, they would ask me to confirm their belief that he had done so). At first I would answer as best as I could that there was no conclusive evidence to support such ideas. After a while, it dawned on me why so many Nisei were asking the question: they still felt stigmatized by Japan's surprise attack, and they believed—whether consciously or not—that if it could be shown that Roosevelt had deliberately allowed the attack to proceed, that would mean somehow that Japan's military was innocent and that they in turn were blameless. Realizing this, I felt enormous compassion for the Japanese Americans who had been so brutalized for their connection with Japan that they needed to believe that FDR was the manipulator. They still could not quite grasp that they themselves were innocent, irrespective of the nature of the attack. The culminating irony is that the comfort they seek is largely illusory. Whatever FDR did or did not know beforehand, the fact remains that Japan deliberately planned and executed a surprise attack, and it was this attack that plunged the two nations into open war.

The attack was a tactical masterpiece but a strategic blunder of amazing proportions in uniting the formerly divided people of the United States behind war against Japan.

Tsuyoshi Matsumoto: Teacher and Artist

The Japanese raid on Pearl Harbor in December 1941 had immediate repercussions for Japanese Americans living throughout the United States and its territories—not least the Issei and Nisei civilians in Hawai'i living near the naval base who were wounded by falling bombs. Amid the nationwide confusion and anger that resulted from the attack, people with Japanese faces were targeted for hostility, harassment, and insults as well as official discrimination.

Particularly vulnerable were Japanese immigrants. Barred by law from naturalization, however long they had resided in the United States, the Issei had none of the legal protections of citizenship. Even before Congress voted a declaration of war on December 8, President Franklin D. Roosevelt signed Presidential Proclamations 2525, 2526, and 2527, which transformed the entire Issei population at a stroke into enemy aliens who were subjected to a curfew, limitations on travel, and freezing of bank deposits.

In the days that followed, hundreds of immigrant community leaders were arrested and held by the Justice Department. Other individuals were detained or held for questioning by the FBI. Local authorities, especially in areas with long-established Japanese populations, were generally supportive or neutral. However, there were cases of malicious treatment. Perhaps the most curious were those of the brothers Tsuyoshi "Mat" Matsumoto and Toru Matsumoto.

Tsuyoshi Matsumoto's wartime experience lay at the center of his many-sided life. He was born in 1908 in Hokkaido, Japan, the son of a doctor. His Christian mother sent the Matsumoto children to church. After attending Meiji Gakuin University, a missionary college in Tokyo, he arrived in the United States in 1930. There he studied at the San Francisco Theological Seminary. In 1933 he received a bachelor of divinity degree and was licensed as a Presbyterian minister. He then moved to New York and enrolled at Union Theological Seminary as a theology and music major. In May 1935 he received a master's degree in sacred music (with a thesis on Japanese hymnology), after which he returned to Japan. Once in Japan, he distinguished himself as an antimilitarist through his public speeches on pacifism and pro-American magazine articles. Although he had previously expressed an intention to serve as a missionary, he forsake the pulpit for music and took work as a guest organist at Nippon Gekijo, the first theater in Tokyo with a pipe organ. While serving as organist, he met Emiko Nakamura, a half-Japanese ballerina and film actress ten years his junior. Emi's Russian father Alexander Lebedeff had moved to Japan (fleeing the Bolshevik Revolution, according to one source), and she had grown up there.

Even as the two courted, the upsurge of militarism in Japan made life precarious for Matsumoto because of his pacifist principles. In mid-1937, at the time of the Japanese invasion of China, Matsumoto received an urgent telegram inviting him to take a job in the United States and sending money for his passage. When he arrived in the United States that September, however, Matsumoto discovered that there was no job waiting: the telegram had been sent by friends who feared he would be arrested or conscripted by the militarists. After chipping in to pay his fare and provide a scholarship fund, they had sent the telegram as a part of a scheme to persuade him to leave Japan. Matsumoto subsequently enrolled at Columbia University's Teachers College, where he remained for a year. Emiko joined him in New York. In mid-1938 he moved to California—a *New World Sun* article lists him in August 1938 as playing organ at a church service in Little Tokyo. For a time he lived in Watsonville, where he and Emi were married and where he preached and taught music in the Japanese community. During the next years, the Matsumotos lived in Los Angeles, where Tsuyoshi studied for a master's degree in Asiatic Studies at University of Southern California. At first they lived in a small bungalow near Hollenbeck Park. A 1940 census form lists them as boarders in a rooming house run by an elderly Swedish couple. Soon after, Emi's passport expired, and she was forced to return to Japan. While her absence was meant to be temporary, the war intervened and the Matsumotos were separated for eight years.

During his years in Los Angeles, Matsumoto—a rare young and bilingual Issei—bonded strongly with community elders. They commissioned him to translate *Zaibei Nihonjinshi*, a Japanese-language community history. (Actually, two manuscripts are attributed to him: "History of the Resident Japanese in Southern California" and "The Japanese in California: An Account of their Contributions to the Development of the State and Their Part in Community Life.") Matsumoto also worked closely with Nisei, to whom he was closer in age. For instance, in May 1940 he was the guest speaker at a Young People's Christian Conference retreat. A year later he directed a concert of sacred music at a Los Angeles church, with a choir of with 125 local Nisei and with soprano Tomi Kanazawa as soloist.

During this period Matsumoto served as a columnist for the English section of *Rafu Shimpo*. He distinguished himself with his Christian approach to social issues and his encouragement of Japanese American fraternization with blacks, Chinese Americans, and Mexican Americans. He reminded his Nisei readers that as a group exposed to discrimination and exclusion they shared a great deal with African Americans. "The more I learn about colored people, the more I realize the need of closer cooperation and better understanding between them and ourselves. We have many things in common." In another column he deplored Japanese community anti-Semitism: "Some of my most respected American friends shamelessly admit their violent anti-Jewish sentiments," he stated. Matsumoto added that many Nisei expressed dislike for Jews and asserted that their unjust words made for further difficulties for Jews and other "much abused minority groups."

In the fall of 1941, Matsumoto was engaged as a music teacher at the Trinity School, an African American school in Athens, Alabama, run by the American Missionary Association (AMA). The job came at the invitation of the school's director, Jay T. Wright, a former Union Theological Seminary classmate of Matsumoto's. Shortly afterward, the Japanese raid on Pearl Harbor occurred, plunging the country into war. The following day, Matsumoto was summarily arrested, taken to the Limestone County, Alabama, courthouse, and placed into a cage by local officials, allegedly so that people could see "what a real 'Jap' looked like." He was then taken into custody at Alabama's Fort McClellan, where he remained for two months. During his time in custody, he pursued his hobby of drawing and became friendly with soldiers who would come to his cell at night to have their portraits done.

Matsumoto's arrest led to all sorts of pressure on Wright. Ruth Morton, the AMA's director of community schools, wrote to Wright stating that Matsumoto's continued presence represented "a delicate situation" for the school and requesting an immediate report on his immigration status. Another teacher wired Morton that the arrest and the wild rumors spreading from it could "imperil" Trinity's existence and recommended an investigation to protect the school. Wright traveled to Memphis to consult with the head of the AMA, General Secretary Fred E. Brownlee, then serving as acting president of LeMoyne College (today's LeMoyne-Owen College). Brownlee, in turn, wrote to Matsumoto to express concern over his care and to ask if he needed reading material. This sparked a friendly correspondence between the two men. Matsumoto wrote to Brownlee about the curious feeling he had being taken out by soldiers for daily walks, like a pampered dog in New York City.

After undergoing a loyalty hearing by the Alien Enemy Control Board, in February 1942 Matsumoto was released from confinement and returned to Athens. Wright later insisted that the agents left Matsumoto in Wright's custody and warned that he was not to leave. However, Justice Department authorities informed Wright that Matsumoto's release was unconditional. Nevertheless, influential locals continued to express hostility toward his presence. Following a sensational editorial in the weekly *Alabama Courier* newspaper, Athens mayor J. C. Richardson protested to Brownlee: "I understand that you have been informed about the Jap that is out at Trinity. That should never be, in times of war or peace. The people here resent it, both white and colored, very much. We are at a lost [*sic*] to understand why he ever came here and at a greater lost to understand, why he still remains." Richardson called for Wright's resignation. While Brownlee resisted the pressure to dismiss his employee, Matsumoto did not remain long in Alabama.

During the war years, Matsumoto worked as an instructor in Japanese language for military intelligence, first at the University of Michigan and later at the University of Chicago. In a pair of postwar articles, "No Sur-render at All," in *The Nation* and "We Fight the Emperor," in *Asia and the Americas*, Matsumoto argued that the Japanese had abandoned neither their will to conquer nor their hatred of foreigners and should still be treated as a hostile military power. In February 1946, once the army began accepting Japanese aliens, he enlisted and was posted as a Japanese instruc-tor at the Presidio Army Language School in Monterey.

In June 1947 Matsumoto was discharged from the army with the rank of technical sergeant, following which he was engaged as a professor of Japanese language at University of Hawai'i (he was thus in the interesting position of continuing to instruct members of the returning 442nd Infantry Regiment and Military Intelligence Service veterans he had helped during the war). A year later he was finally reunited with Emi. Despite his wartime service to the US government, Matsumoto was faced with deportation, as his student visa had expired. Thanks to a private bill sponsored by Penn-sylvania representative Francis Walter (later known for his cosponsorship of the 1952 McCarran-Walter immigration bill) and enacted in April 1948, he was able to remain in the country and become a US citizen.

In 1950 Matsumoto and Emi returned to Japan. There they spent what he referred to as "two decades of stability" and raised two children. Matsu-moto worked as civil relations director at Commander Fleet Activities Yokusuka (a US naval base), and studied for a doctorate at Tokyo Univer-sity. During these years he wrote a weekly column, "People to People and How," in the US Navy newspaper the *Seahawk*. It featured light-hearted, humorous articles about Japanese customs and cultural misunderstand-ings. In 1964 Matsumoto published a book, *How to Earn Tourist Dollars*, as a guide for Japanese entrepreneurs hoping to profit from the 1964 Tokyo Olympics.

During these years Matsumoto returned to sketching, and he began exhibiting at galleries around Tokyo. In 1958 a show of his abstract and expressionist art was held at the American Cultural Center in Yokohama. Matsumoto began intensive study of pines, the Japanese symbol of good luck and longevity. (There was also a personal element in that "Matsumoto" means "root of the pine.") In 1968, at the age of sixty, Matsumoto retired to pursue his art and moved to New York, where he worked and exhibited.

In 1971, while looking for a retirement location, Matsumoto visited the Torrey Pines state natural reserve in La Jolla, California, famous for its pine trees. According to one article, he spent hours wandering the trails at Torrey Pines and admiring the trees. In the process, he lost his wallet and keys and had to borrow money for a taxi home. In 1973 the family moved to San Diego and opened an art gallery in nearby La Jolla. Matsumoto devoted the last decade of his life to drawing his beloved pines, spending many days at the reserve. He filled forty-five large sketchbooks with about eight hundred "studies of the pine," as he called them, and he redrew many of these studies into finalized pencil drawings. He died in 1982, bequeathing his artworks to the Torrey Pines State Reserve. In 2017, with assistance from Matsumoto's daughter Helen Kagan, an exhibition of his art was held at the Geisel Library at UC San Diego. His art remains a living legacy of the man and his spirituality.

Toru Matsumoto: Brother and Stranger

My *Discover Nikkei* article on Tsuyoshi Matsumoto (see preceding piece) prompted interest from readers in other members of the Matsumoto family, such as Tsuyoshi's sister Takako Shibusawa, a leader in social welfare work in postwar Japan, and especially Tsuyoshi's younger brother Toru. Toru Matsumoto (1913–79) was actually the more-renowned brother during his lifetime: in the United States during the 1940s he was known as the author of multiple books, including the notable 1946 memoir *A Brother Is a Stranger*. Following his return to Japan, he became celebrated as a radio personality and teacher of English. Oddly, while Toru lived in the United States during roughly the same years as Tsuyoshi and had somewhat parallel experiences, his memoir almost totally excludes his elder brother.

Toru Matsumoto, like his brother, was born in Hokkaido, the son of a doctor father and a Christian mother. His great-grandfather Shohachi Matsumoto, who attended University of Michigan in 1885, was reputedly

Toru Matsumoto speaking in New York, 1945. War Relocation Authority portrait. Bancroft Library, University of California, Berkeley.

one of the first Japanese students to be educated in the United States. In his memoir Matsumoto tells the story of how his father, impatient at the restrictions imposed by his devout wife, abandoned the family when Toru was five years old, plunging the family into financial difficulties. Over the next years Matsumoto's mother moved with the children to Takasaki, near Tokyo. There she raised the children as a single parent, doing sewing and tailoring to support the family. In the absence of their father, Toru's eldest brother Yuji assumed responsibility. Ultimately Matsumoto's father returned, but he died soon after, and the family remained poverty-stricken. Toru became part of a close-knit group of friends who dubbed themselves "the Seven Stars."

Through Tsuyoshi's connections, young Toru was able to attend his brother's alma mater, Meiji Gakuin, where he became close to Daikichiro Tagawa, Meiji's president, and developed his distaste for Japanese authoritarianism. After graduating in 1935, Matsumoto left Japan. He later termed it an act in protest of Japanese military policies. Upon arriving in New York, Toru joined Tsuyoshi at Union Theological Seminary, where the brothers roomed together for one semester. Once Tsuyoshi graduated, Toru roomed with James H. Robinson, an African American ministerial student who was later a prominent clergyman and humanitarian. Matsumoto graduated with a bachelor of divinity in 1938. During his time at Union, Matsumoto met Emma Nishimura, a westernized Japanese woman studying in New York. The marriage led to lasting conflict with Toru's brother Yuji, who disapproved of the match. Their first son, Ted, was born in 1939.

Throughout his time in New York, Matsumoto served as general secretary of the Japanese Student Christian Association (JSCA) and worked with the World Student Service Fund to raise money to aid students in war-torn countries, mostly Chinese students. His status as a representative of Japanese students placed him in a permanent dilemma when he was asked in public forums to defend Japanese foreign policy that he privately deplored. He later recounted that he staged a public debate with a Chinese colleague in which each took the other's position: Matsumoto criticized Japanese policy in China, while his Chinese counterpart deplored Western interference in Asia that hindered accord between Japan and China. Forced to return to Japan in 1940 due to visa problems, Matsumoto stopped on the West Coast while en route and addressed a meeting of the JACL. Curiously, Matsumoto interviewed Nisei college and university graduates seeking positions in East Asia to help them file their applications and records. In his memoir Matsumoto recounts how during his time in Japan, he was placed under surveillance by the government and suffered from his brother Yuji's schemes to break up his marriage. He was ultimately forced to flee to New York, leaving his wife and son behind, but they were able soon afterward to rejoin him.

Following the Japanese attack on Pearl Harbor, Matsumoto was interned by the Department of Justice, first at Ellis Island and Camp Upton, New York, and later at Fort Meade, Maryland. His account in his memoirs of his internment experience is horrific. Matsumoto faced hostile and punitive military authorities, harsh living conditions (including residence in a leaky tent in pouring rain), and friction with pro-Japanese internees suspicious of him because of his Christian pacifist views, fluent English, and lack of interest in repatriation.

After eleven months of internment, Matsumoto was finally paroled in late 1942. Upon his release he was named executive assistant to George E. Rundquist, secretary of the Committee on Resettlement of Japanese-Americans for the Federal Council of Churches and Home Missions Council of North America. He also worked with the International Committee of the YMCA. The Matsumotos settled in the suburb of Larchmont. There the Matsumotos made national headlines in 1943 after the Victory Garden that Emma and son Teddy had planted was trampled and slashed by vandals. Local officials and club women responded by transplanting their own seedlings and tending the garden, while liberal newspapers expressed regret for the action. Matsumoto made further headlines in 1944 when he was ordained as a minister of the Dutch Reformed Church. While New York City officials sent police to guard his ordination ceremony, fearing attacks on the new pastor as a Japanese alien, there was no negative demonstration. During 1945 Matsumoto visited the WRA camps at Heart Mountain and Minidoka and propagandized for resettlement.

Following the end of World War II, Matsumoto pursued a doctorate in education at Columbia University. During this period, he and Emma had two more children. He meanwhile distinguished himself as a public intellectual. He wrote a pair of articles on the Japanese people for *Asia* magazine (again following brother Tsuyoshi) and threw himself into writing books. His study *Beyond Prejudice: A Story of the Church and Japanese Americans* was published by Friendship Press in 1946. It told the story of Protestant groups and their wartime support for Japanese Americans. Meanwhile Matsumoto turned to work on a memoir that he had started writing while interned at Fort Meade. Coauthored by a Larchmont neighbor, the sex therapist and educator Marion O. Lerrigo, the work was completed and published in mid-1946 under the title *A Brother Is a Stranger* and featured an introduction by the Nobel laureate novelist Pearl S. Buck. It was one of the first books to discuss the wartime confinement of Japanese Americans, as well as describing Matsumoto's own experience in East Coast internment. The book received a fair amount of media coverage and respectable reviews. In 1949 Matsumoto published two further volumes. His novel *The Seven Stars*, also published by Friendship Press, was a fictionalized account of the life experiences of his circle of high school friends in Japan, amid the background of Japan's descent into militarism and war. The book was also notable for a set of drawings by Nisei artist Miné Okubo, which helped launch her postwar career as a book illustrator. Matsumoto's other book, *I Attacked Pearl Harbor*, was a translation of a Japanese-language memoir by Kazuo Sakamaki, commander of one of the Japanese midget submarines that took part in the Japanese raid on Pearl Harbor. During these years, Matsumoto also devoted himself to lecture tours and speaking engagements. For instance, in the fall of 1945 he spoke at Springfield, Massachusetts, a talk titled "Chances of Japanese for Rehabilitation." In 1947 he addressed a Hudson Valley youth rally.

In 1949 Matsumoto received his EdD degree, with a dissertation on "a proposed program of voluntary religious education at Meiji Gakuin, Tokyo, Japan." He then returned to Japan with the goal of easing the teacher shortage there. He announced that he would assume the duties of president of Meiji Gakuin (the institution had just begun admitting women the previous year—the first Japanese university to go coed). But either he did not assume the presidency or it did not last, because he was thereafter identified as "professor of English." His wife and three children remained in Larchmont. Matsumoto returned to New York from July to October 1950 and helped publicize *Toru's People*, a thirty-minute film on Japan made by the Protestant Film Commission for which he served as narrator. The film asked, "What are the Japanese people like today and how do they live?" and responded by focusing on a representative family.

In October 1950 Matsumoto moved permanently to Japan. The following year he started radio broadcasting. As the host of an NHK program he provided fifteen-minute lessons in conversational English. He soon became well known for his theory of thinking in English as a basis of language learning (and also for his parting phrase—he was notable for saying "so long" rather than "good-bye"). He continued teaching English on NHK for twenty-two years and also wrote several books on the English language, including *Eigo de kangaeru hon* (Think in English) and *Eigo gakushūsha no tame no Kirisutokyō nyūmon* (Introduction to Christianity for English Learners). In 1961 he began what would become a long-running program, *Let's Speak Japanese*, which offered twice-weekly lessons in spoken Japanese for English-speaking listeners in the South Pacific. Matsumoto compiled *The Random Dictionary: A Glossary of Foreign Words in Today's Spoken Japanese* (1974) and also published a book of children's stories, *Inaba no Shirousagi* (The White Rabbit of Inaba) (1968) and a novel, *Tobosha* (Hunted) (1978).

By the time Toru Matsumoto died in 1979, his pro-democratic activism had been largely forgotten. However, as current-day scholars such as David Hollinger, Stephanie Hinnershitz, Anne Blankenship, and Beth Hessel have begun unearthing the complicated tale of connections between white

Christians and Japanese Americans, especially those in the camps, Matsu-moto's works stand as early and useful resources.

Parallel Wars: Japanese American and Japanese Canadian Internment Films

Films that portray the removal and confinement of ethnic Japanese in North America during World War II, especially those that tell their stories through the interactions between Japanese families and white characters, allow us to reflect on the ways these films were shaped by dominant narratives about race relations. One eternal dilemma surrounding so-called "message films"—films that deal with social problems, particularly with minorities—is how to get white audiences, who may share endemic prejudices, to identify with characters facing injustice because of their racial or ethnic difference. During the classic Hollywood studio era, this most often involved variations on the "passing" narrative, in which a black person passed for white. In films from *Imitation of Life* (1934, 1957) to *Pinky* (1949) to the different remakes of *Show Boat* (1936, 1951), scripts dramatized the difference in treatment that the white-appearing person (female in all the above cases) received when crossing the "color line."[5] Variations on this narrative emerged. Sometimes, as in *Gentleman's Agreement* (1947) or *Black Like Me* (1964) the main character himself, a white man, passes in reverse, posing as the ethnic or racial other; in *Lost Boundaries* (1949), members of a family learn of their racial difference after being unaware of it. Although "passing" narratives had historic roots in African American literature, they became discredited and largely vanished by the 1970s.[6] In the wake of the Black Power movement, scholars such as Thomas Cripps and Donald Bogle complained that these representations perpetuated images of minorities as "other" rather than valorizing their actual subjectivity—in essence, the audience is made to feel bad not about the treatment of blacks but that white people should be subjected to such treatment.[7]

Japanese Canadian fishing boats impounded by the Canadian government, 1942. Special Collections, Vancouver Public Library.

The elimination of this trope did not necessarily signal a focus on minority protagonists but rather the expansion of an existing trope: the white hero. His presence—it is most frequently an individual man—is designed to give the white audience an accessible character with whom they can identify and through whose eyes they can grasp the nature of the injustice to the "other." This character can take different forms. One, which undergirds such diverse works as *The Defiant Ones* (1958) and the Japanese American war film *Go for Broke* (1951), is the white man who begins by sharing widespread prejudices and learns through his contact with the other to overcome them. Another form is the white man who is already antiracist but must befriend and help the other despite threats to himself—the classic model being Gregory Peck's Atticus Finch in *To Kill a Mockingbird* (1962), a lawyer who defends a black man charged with rape in 1930s Alabama despite community opposition. In both cases the focus is on the white man and his actions rather than on the victims of racism.

This trope became especially popular during the 1980s. In Richard Attenborough's *Cry Freedom*, set in 1970s South Africa, Kevin Kline's Donald Woods displaced Denzel Washington's Stephen Biko, the film's

Tsuru Aoki, publicity still, *Hell to Eternity* (1960). Atlantic Pictures / Allied Artists.

ostensible subject, as its moral center. In Kevin Costner's *Dances with Wolves*, a white man (played by Costner) is accepted into the Sioux nation and is distressed by the savagery of whites in the West. The most controversial white hero film was Alan Parker's *Mississippi Burning*, which dramatized in semi-fictionalized form the 1964 Freedom Summer and the killings of the civil rights activists Cheney, Schwerner, and Goodman. Parker fixes on a white Southern FBI agent, played by Gene Hackman, who uses his skills to identify the murderers. Parker was the target of widespread criticism by scholars and movement survivors for portraying the FBI, an agency largely hostile to civil rights (and engaged in wiretapping Martin Luther King Jr), as heroic. Despite concerns about historical license and distortion, these films were successful at the box office and spawned copies. Denzel Washington even did a role reversal. In *Philadelphia* (1993) he plays a version of the white hero in the form of a black lawyer who overcomes his own homophobia to take the case of a man suing the firm that fired him for being gay.[8]

All this being so, it was perhaps inevitable that the two mainstream Hollywood narratives about Japanese American removal would bear this trope. The first was *Come See the Paradise* (1990), directed by Alan Parker, creator of *Mississippi Burning*. Here again the film revolves around a white man (played by Dennis Quaid), in this case one whose Nisei wife and half-Japanese children are taken away from him under Executive Order 9066, after which he attempts to save them. Compared to the story of this mythical white man—and, to a much lesser extent, his Nisei wife—the film's Japanese American characters remain undeveloped. To this injury is added the insult of historical inaccuracy—in reality, ethnic Japanese wives of white men and their mixed-race children were officially exempted from removal, whereas Nikkei husbands of white wives (including Communist activist Karl Yoneda, the real-life prototype of Parker's protagonist) were confined. The other film, Scott Hicks's 1999 *Snow Falling on Cedars*, dramatizes the trial of a small-town Nisei man unjustly accused of murder. He is allowed to demonstrate some rage and complexity of character. However, he is saved by the timely intervention of a white man (played by Ethan Hawke), who is revealed as the onetime sweetheart of his wife. Hawke's character is the only fully realized one—he sees the injustice but must grow past his own bitterness to offer assistance (which likewise means renouncing all hope of reconnection with his ex-lover). In a scene directly inspired by *To Kill a Mockingbird*, the town's Japanese community, seated in the balcony of the courtroom, pays homage by bowing to their white champion.

The question today is how much the white hero trope also marks alternative cinema. Two films I wish to focus on are *Hell to Eternity* and *The War between Us*. Each contains such elements, but each also subverts them. *Hell to Eternity*, directed by Phil Karlson and released in 1960, is on the surface a quintessential white hero film. It portrays the valor of a white man, Guy Gabaldon (played by Jeffrey Hunter), who singlehandedly persuaded some two thousand Japanese soldiers on the island of Saipan to surrender. At the start of the film, Guy, a child from a broken home, is adopted by the Unes, a Japanese American family, and learns to speak Japanese in order to communicate with his Issei foster mother (luminously played by former silent film star Tsuru Aoki, in her only sound film role), whom he also begins to teach English. Once war comes, he is alienated by the discrimination he sees. He gets harassed by racist toughs when he goes out with a Nisei girl, Esther (Miiko Taka), on the morning of Pearl Harbor. (Guy's date with Esther is portrayed as platonic—an interracial romance in 1960 would presumably have been too daring.) Meanwhile his Nisei brothers George and Kaz attempt to enlist and are refused.[9] Finally his family and their neighbors are moved out by the army. Guy is rejected for service in the army and is rootless. Sometime later he receives a letter from his brother George (George Takei), who has been accepted for service in the army. He suggests that Guy visit their foster parents in "Camp Manzanar," where, we are told, the authorities have transferred them (implicitly away from the "real" camps) because of their father's delicate health.

As a result, Guy travels to Manzanar and sees his Issei mother. This is the first representation of the camps in Hollywood cinema. Perhaps because the producers needed army assistance, the image of the camp is greatly sanitized. After a quick establishing shot of barracks in a verdant valley, the Unes are shown in a small but comfortable room. There is no suggestion that the entire family is housed in one twenty-by-twenty-five-foot shack; instead there is an door that suggests other rooms or at least a closet. There is a window with curtains, a table and chairs, a bureau with knickknacks, and a side table with photos. Outside is a trellis with vines. When Guy sees Mrs. Une, she tells him that his Nisei brothers have volunteered for military service from camp, in order to make a better world, and are serving in Europe. She tells him that he too should find some way to join. Once this is done, Guy enlists in the army as a translator, and the camps are never brought up again. Instead the film turns into what one critic called a "war and sex" movie.[10]

Not only is Guy the focus of the plot, he is the only antiracist. When Guy, Esther, and George watch Japanese Americans quietly leaving their houses and being loaded on trucks for Santa Anita, Guy is the only one to express outrage. George mentions that they are headed for "relocation camps," and Guy says "more like concentration camps." Esther pleads with him not to blame the Japanese Americans for following orders and says that at least in the camps everyone will be "the same" and will not face hostility for being Japanese. Guy snaps, "But you're not Japanese, you're Americans." He then asks his older Nisei brother how the government could treat Japanese Americans this way but not Italians or Germans. His brother responds, "I can't answer that. Right or wrong, our government's doing what they think is right. No one bats one thousand."

However, the film also diverges in part from the pattern. First, the real Guy Gabaldon was Mexican American. While the film makes only the barest mention of this, and all reference to his Hispanic culture and family is erased, we understand that he is a tough kid. We see that he has tattooed arms, even as a twelve-year-old, and frequently fights (although his foster mother's tenderness succeeds in winning his avowal of love for her). Also, the film pulls a daring, if momentary, reversal. When Guy visits his mother in Manzanar, she laments that everything she and her husband had is gone but expresses faith that her sons will save the world from its mess and make everyone happy: "Mother, father of Une family work hard all lives build good . . . foundation for future. Not any years left for old people to build again. Sons must build, Kaz, George, Guy must build home again. Must build world again. All papa sans, all mama sans all over the world is same. This you believe?" Guy asks, "What difference does it make what one man believes?" She answers, "One man must believe. Else why Kaz, why George go far away across ocean to kill men look like brother they love?" Instead of developing the familiar theme of Japanese Americans looking like the enemy, the film refers to white people in that role.

The War between Us, a Canadian television film directed by Anne Wheeler and released in 1995, is a considerably more sophisticated and critical film (from a different generation, in fairness). It dramatizes the wartime confinement of twenty-two thousand West Coast Japanese Canadians by the Canadian government. In February 1942, one week after US president Franklin Roosevelt issued Executive Order 9066, Canadian prime minister W. L. Mackenzie King ordered all people of Japanese ancestry, regardless of citizenship, removed from the Pacific Coast of Canada. After being taken from their homes by a newly established agency, the British Columbia Security Commission (BCSC), the bulk of those removed were forced into settlements in abandoned mining towns in southeastern British Columbia. Unlike in the United States, the Japanese Canadians were given no financial assistance other than housing and a bare minimum of elementary schooling for children and medical care.

Instead the Canadian government forced the families to pay the expenses of their confinement. In order to extract money from community members and also to assure that they would not return to the West Coast, starting in 1943 an official custodian of "enemy property" sold off all real estate and personal properties of the Japanese Canadians, generally at bargain prices. As the war drew to a close, the government perpetrated a further injustice by forcing Japanese Canadians to move, immediately and permanently, even farther away from the West Coast. If they preferred to stay in the confinement sites where they were, they would be deemed to have agreed to postwar deportation to Japan. While Japanese Canadians and their allies eventually were able to have this unjust policy reversed, thousands of inmates were bullied into surrendering their citizenship and their country.

The principal action of *The War between Us* takes place in New Denver, the Slocan Valley town where thousands of Japanese Canadians from the Pacific Coast were forcibly resettled in mid-1942 by the BCSC. Ed Parnham (Robert Wisden) and his neighbors are initially reluctant to accept the "Japs," but they quickly recognize that the inmates will improve the devastated economy of their abandoned mining towns. Ed's wife Peg Parnham (Shannon Lawson) and a friend open a general store to sell clothes to the inmates. Then the action moves to Vancouver, where we see Mr. Kawashima (Robert Ito), a prosperous businessman, and his daughter Aya (Mieko Ouchi), who works in his office. After war is declared, they are forced to surrender their brand-new car to the authorities. Soon they are removed by official order. Mrs. Kawashima (Ruby Truly) must quickly pack the family's belongings.

The Kawashimas, along with other families, arrive in New Denver and proceed to settle in the freezing and dilapidated shack they have been assigned. In order to pay for supplies and support family members while they await income from the rental of their house and from Mr. Kawashima's business, Aya Kawashima must take work as a maid (and later shop assistant) for the Parnhams. Although the members of the Kawashima family initially try to make the best of their situation amid the hostile surroundings, they are horrified by the news that the federal government has confiscated their belongings. Mr. Kawashima, a World War I veteran, is so embittered by his treatment that he insists on taking the family and repatriating to Japan after the war.[11]

In this film, the main white characters, Ed and Peg Parnham, are humanized by their contact with the Japanese Canadians. From being wary and ignorant, they turn into friends and begin to criticize government policy. Ed eventually punches out Tom McIntyre (Kevin McNulty), the racist local representative of the BCSC, because of his anger at the deportation policy, and Japanese Canadians question their own complicity: "How did it happen? How did we end up on the wrong side?"[12] However, the narrative offers twists on standard narratives via the inclusion of discordant gender and class elements. First, whereas in both *Come See the Paradise* and *Snow Falling on Cedars*, like the old "passing" narratives, the romance is between a white man and a Nisei woman, what challenges and ultimately unites the Kawashimas and the Parnhams is the romance between Aya's brother Mas (Edmond Kato Wong) and the Parnhams' daughter Marg (Juno Riddell).

Furthermore, in *The War between Us*, it is not the whites who step in to assist Japanese. Rather, it is Japanese Canadians who come to the aid of the whites, whose town economy and their stores depend on their patronage. (The Kawashimas permit Aya to work as a domestic, in a job they agree is beneath her, only because they refuse to go on relief or accept charity for reasons of self-respect). Indeed, the Parnhams and their neighbors are portrayed as more rustic than their new neighbors. In one scene, a white family celebrates the arrival of electric lighting in their town, which the government has brought in exchange for their sheltering Japanese Canadians. The urbanized Japanese Canadians look on and laugh scornfully at the excitement of "the savages." When Mas expresses his ambition to go to Harvard, Yale, or Oxford, he is stunned that Marg has never heard of these places. When Aya begins helping Peg in her shop, and Mr. McIntyre patronizingly says that it will give her some useful experience, she loses her cool and reveals that she has a college degree and was accustomed to keeping the books at her father's shipbuilding business.

Finally, *The War between Us* violates the established narrative strategy in its complex portrait of the Japanese Canadians. There is generational conflict and family violence, and the question of loyalty is shown in complex fashion. For instance, there is a scene that takes place inside the women's bathhouse the Japanese community has built, during which a set of older women express their confidence that Japan will win the war, because they have heard it said on the radio. In a memorable line, Aya says that her parents feel shame over their situation, and that even her brother does, but she refuses to feel shame over what has been done to her by the country she loves. Nonetheless, she ultimately decides to accompany her parents to Japan, in order to help them resettle. When asked why she can't simply pick up the pieces after the war and start over, she responds, "There are no pieces." By refusing to turn its Japanese Canadian characters into paragons of virtue or patriotism, the makers of *The War between Us* keep them in the foreground and ultimately render their plight more moving.

The Unknown History of the Japanese American Committee for Democracy

The Japanese American Committee for Democracy (JACD), a New York–based social and political group of the 1940s, has been effectively ignored in the history of Japanese Americans. The JACD held rallies to support the American war effort in World War II, helped Japanese Americans in New York to find jobs and housing, and provided a forum for like-minded Issei and Nisei to meet and socialize. Its monthly *News Letter* offers historians a vital resource on what was going on in Nikkei circles in New York—especially during the early months of 1942, when the city was home to the largest free community of Japanese Americans on the mainland.

The JACD was founded in New York in 1941. During the prewar period, the local community, largely composed of Issei, remained dominated by consular officials, Japanese businessmen, and employees of Japanese firms solidly pro-Tokyo in sentiment. Japanese news predominated in the community's semiofficial organ, the *Nichibei Jiho*. The English-language *Japanese American Gazette*, which started out as the *Jiho*'s English page before

Japanese American Committee for Democracy directors Ernest and Chizu Iiyama (*left and center*) in later years, with historian Lynne Horiuchi (*right*). Photo by Greg Robinson. Author's personal collection.

spinning off into a separate journal in 1940, devoted much space to propaganda extolling the Japanese puppet state of Manchukuo.

Yet as Japan and the United States drew closer to open conflict, dissident community members mobilized. Hoping to counteract pro-Japanese forces within the community and protect members' rights in case of war, members of a circle of Issei artists and militants joined forces with activist Nisei such as journalists Larry Tajiri and Tooru Kanazawa to form the Committee for Democratic Treatment for Japanese Residents in Eastern States. The first director was Rev. Alfred Akamatsu, the young Japan-born pastor of New York's Japanese Methodist Church. The group remained largely dormant during its first months. However, in the wake of the Japanese attack on Pearl Harbor in December 1941 and the US entry into war, the situation changed drastically. New York's Japanese consulate closed, and over a thousand businessmen and community leaders were arrested as potentially disloyal and detained at Ellis Island by the Justice Department.

These events left a void in ethnic leadership. Progressive activists responded by calling a public meeting in the days that followed, and some 150 people attended. The meeting gave rise to a transformed organization, dubbed the Japanese American Committee for Democracy (JACD). The new organization elected a chairman, Thomas Komuro, established a structure of six subcommittees, and began a regular newsletter (Larry Tajiri edited the first issues, before he returned to the West Coast). An all-star collection of progressive celebrities, including Pearl S. Buck, Albert Einstein, and Franz Boas, signed on as advisory board members.

The committee's first priority was to organize social welfare work within the Japanese community. The Vocations and Welfare Committee provided information to those thrown out of work by the closure of Japanese businesses following Pearl Harbor and sought job aid from churches and government. Under the leadership of Reverend Akamatsu, the JACD organized a study of the New York Japanese community, to determine where aid was most needed. The JACD also engaged in protesting discrimination against Japanese Americans in New York. In mid-March 1942, the JACD sent a letter to Attorney General Biddle asking him to create a federal agency to create jobs for Japanese Americans unable to find jobs because of suspicion by potential employers.

To encourage Nisei participation and strengthen community morale, executive board member Toshi-Aline Ohta, a half-Japanese Nisei teenager active in artistic circles, organized various programs. In June 1942, for example, Ohta hosted a tea party for Nisei girls to encourage them to support the war effort. She also helped arrange dances and other entertainments, and ultimately she recruited musicians such as Leadbelly and Woody Guthrie to perform at JACD dances. After several months, she gradually withdrew from the group, and in 1943 she married the folksinger Pete Seeger.

Meanwhile, under the direction of a circle of seasoned Issei activists, notably the committee's executive secretary Yoshitaka Takagi, the JACD mobilized as a political action group with ties to the Communist Party. Although the number of actual party members in the JACD is a matter of dispute, and the group's militants were by no means simple-minded hacks, their platform and strategies were shaped in significant ways by the Communist Party and its wartime program of total victory over fascism. This was a double-edged sword as far as the committee was concerned. On the one hand, the emphasis on the larger anti-Axis struggle encouraged group members to look beyond their own group interests in support of democracy. On the other hand, the JACD's doctrine of full support for the war clashed with its recognition of the injustice done to West Coast Japanese Americans.

During the JACD's early weeks, there was no contradiction between its ethnic group status and support for the war effort. JACD leaders made patriotic statements endorsing America's war effort and organized a blood drive to aid soldiers. Group members provided government agencies such as the Office of War Information with translators, record albums, and other materials.

However, President Roosevelt's issuing of Executive Order 9066 on February 19, 1942, flung JACD leaders into a dilemma. Immediately after the order was issued, the JACD responded with a formal letter of support to the government. As the February 23, 1942, issue of the JACD *News Letter* reported, "In effect, our letter stated that while we realized that the majority of Japanese Americans are innocent, at the same time we recognized the possibility of fifth columnists working in their midst. As our committee is pledged to the full support of national defense, we offered to back whatever action the government deemed necessary to protect the strategic coastal zones and vital industrial areas." In May 1942 JACD members attending a conference of the pro-Communist action group American Committee for Protection of Foreign Born approved a resolution calling for the setting up of loyalty boards for "Germans, Italians, and Japanese" that could determine individual guilt, and the group opposed Senator Tom Stewart's bill to intern all persons of Japanese ancestry in the United States.

Still, the fundamental contradiction between the JACD's policies of opposing discrimination and giving full support to the government was laid bare in June when Socialist Party leader Norman Thomas—himself a leading rival of the Communists—organized a meeting through the Post War World Council to protest Executive Order 9066. At the meeting, Mike Masaoka of the Japanese American Citizens League (which had launched its own policy of collaboration with the government) stated that the treatment of Japanese Americans was "a test of democracy," and he warned, "If they can do that to one group they can do it to other groups." With Masaoka's support, Thomas introduced a resolution calling for the establishment of hearing boards to determine the loyalty of the "evacuees" and warning against the "military internment of unaccused persons in concentration camps." Although this resolution resembled the one the JACD had just approved in May, a JACD delegation offered a counter-resolution endorsing the government's claim that "military considerations made necessary the evacuation of all Americans of Japanese ancestry from certain areas on the West Coast" and supporting all measures to help ensure victory. While the JACD resolution was handily defeated, it reduced the momentum for Thomas's, which passed only narrowly. In a letter to the government shortly after, JACD secretary Yoshitaka Takagi formally disavowed any protest of EO 9066 as divisive.

Even as it sought to quell criticism of government discrimination against Japanese Americans, the JACD turned its attention to a large victory rally designed to promote "the end of all racial discrimination and the establishment of a mighty People's Front against fascism." According to the May 5, 1942, *News Letter*, the event was a great success. None of the speakers, apart from Pearl S. Buck, discussed the discrimination facing Japanese Americans, let alone denounced the injustice of the government's action. Rather, the keynote speakers, African American leader Adam Clayton Powell Jr. and Chinese musician Liu Liang Mo (a columnist for the African American *Pittsburgh Courier*), focused on equality for their respective groups and on friendship for the Soviet Union. The JACD continued the same policy in June 1942 when its invitation to join New York City's "victory parade" was rescinded by Mayor Fiorello LaGuardia on the absurd pretext that it might lead to violence against Japanese American marchers. Although the JACD called the mayor's act "ill-advised," its leaders urged acceptance of the decision in a spirit of unity.

By late fall 1942, the expulsion and incarceration of Japanese Americans was complete. The JACD was thus freed of its burden of defending the policy. While it did not call directly for the closing of the camps, which would constitute criticism of the government, it focused on encouraging resettlement. In its February 1943 *News Letter*, the JACD invited WRA director Dillon Myer to a forum on "Japanese Americans in the victory program." A positive program on Japanese Americans, the JACD claimed, was essential. In the following months, JACD members volunteered their services to the government as liaisons in resettlement and worked to find sponsors and housing so that inmates could leave the camps. In coalition with the National Maritime Union, JACD leaders lobbied the War Department and the WRA to speed up release of Japanese American merchant seamen from the camps.

Meanwhile, as young Nisei began leaving camps and migrating to New York, they turned to the JACD, whose offices became a gathering place for them. Numerous Nisei who had been active in journalism or political groups on the West Coast, including Eddie Shimano, Kenji Murase, Dyke Miyagawa, and Nori Ikeda Lafferty, resettled in the city and became active in the JACD. In order to let the new generation assume responsibility, the Issei leaders of the JACD formally resigned. Ernest Iiyama was named director of the organization, and his wife Chizu Iiyama took a leading role in producing the JACD *News Letter*. In addition to its support for resettlement, the JACD embraced interracial struggles for equality, reporting on efforts to fight lynching of African Americans in the South, and lobbying on behalf of the successful repeal in Congress of the Chinese Exclusion Act. The JACD also issued statements denouncing episodes of Japanese barbarity and opposing peace negotiations with Tokyo before victory over Japan. The JACD Arts Council, formed under the leadership of Yasuo Kuniyoshi and Isamu Noguchi, organized art shows and entertainments as well as issuing political statements. In the fall of 1944 the JACD joined with other ethnic groups in a rally supporting the reelection of President Franklin Roosevelt. In the last months of World War II, the JACD helped sponsor the Japanese People's Emancipation League, a Japanese resistance organization that operated in China in association with the Chinese Communist Party.

Once World War II ended, the JACD began to fade away. Its membership was consumed by the tasks of remaking their lives, and the JACD faced competition from the fledgling New York chapter of the JACL. In 1948 the remnants of the JACD reorganized as the Nisei for Wallace (also known as Nisei Progressives) to support Henry Wallace's third-party presidential candidacy. The Nisei Progressives continued into the early 1950s. However, like many other wartime political groups, it ultimately fell apart, a victim of postwar equality and McCarthy-era individual political withdrawal. A few JACD leaders, such as the Iiyamas and Toshi Ohta Seeger, continued their activism elsewhere. For others, such as Minn Matsuda and Kazu Iijima, their JACD experience helped guide them when in the late 1960s they formed a new political organization, Asian Americans for Action.

Interracial Marriage and Wartime Japanese American Confinement

The mass confinement of West Coast Japanese Americans during World War II represents a curious exception, though perhaps a less prominent one, in the history of official marriage discrimination against blacks and Asians in the United States.

During the spring of 1942, under authority of Executive Order 9066, issued by President Roosevelt, the army's Western Defense Command forcibly ejected from their homes the entire West Coast ethnic Japanese population. The extreme nature of the military's removal policy and the racist ideas that underlay it were starkly demonstrated by the order of the head of the Western Defense Command, General John DeWitt, that all people of Japanese ancestry be cleared from the West Coast, with no exceptions granted. Even the army language school at the Presidio of Monterey, with its ethnic Japanese instructors, was forced to move inland. DeWitt's deputy, Colonel Karl Bendetsen, carried out the "no exceptions" policy with horrifying literalness. Bendetsen and his aides stripped Japanese American children from their Caucasian foster families, and toured orphanages to make sure that any infant or child who appeared to have any Japanese ancestry would be removed. The Shonien orphanage, which housed Japanese American children, was forced to create a "children's village" at the Manzanar camp for the orphans in its charge. Apart from a few individuals who were incarcerated in prisons and those confined in hospitals and too ill to be moved, Japanese Americans of all ages were carried away. As DeWitt's final report on the evacuation stated, "Included among the evacuees were persons who were only part Japanese, some with as little as one-sixteenth Japanese blood; others who, prior to evacuation, were unaware of their Japanese ancestry; and many who had married Caucasians, Chinese, Filipinos, Negroes, Hawaiians, or Eskimos."[13] Not since the denial of citizenship rights in the Jim Crow South to those with tiny gradations of African ancestry had a single nonwhite ancestor been determined to have such an inherent corrupting force.

Strictly speaking, the army's policy did not touch the question of eugenics, either in its origins or its justification. Certainly none of the West

Coast politicians who fomented mass removal claimed that it was necessary to promote racial purity or to discourage reproduction by ethnic Japanese. In practice, however, the army designed a policy that gave preference to mixed marriages. According to this policy, which drew on a tortured mix of gender and sociological stereotypes, ethnic Japanese women who were married to white Americans or men from "friendly" countries (generally Filipinos), plus any underaged mixed-race children of these marriages, could apply to be exempted from removal on a case-by-case basis, depending on their overall level of "Americanization" (that is, assimilation to white American norms). However, if an ethnic Japanese woman divorced her husband or was widowed, she would then be immediately subject to removal.

Curiously, this policy reversed the decades-old trend in western states of discouraging intermarriage by legal means—white-Asian unions were banned in every state in the Western Defense Command except for Washington. (In theory, it even offered ethnic Japanese women an incentive to take white spouses, though there is no record of any ethnic Japanese marrying a non-Japanese to be saved from removal). More importantly, the preference did not work both ways. The army decreed that non-Japanese wives of Japanese American men (even wives of aliens who had lost their US citizenship through marriage and were deemed Japanese citizens) would be spared from removal—but their Japanese American husbands would not be spared. A number of white women, including artist Estelle Ishigo and activist Elaine Black Yoneda, accompanied their families to camp. As the policy evolved, the mixed-race children of these unions were allowed to leave camp and return to the West Coast, but only with the non-Japanese parent, on the theory that they would thereby be removed from the baneful influence of confined Japanese Americans and instead exposed to the allegedly positive influence white communities.

The strained logic and inconsistency of the army's policy was soon dramatized by a pair of Nisei. In March 1942 Mary Asaba Ventura, the Nisei wife of Filipino labor activist Mamerto Ventura, brought a habeas corpus petition in Seattle challenging the official curfew and restrictions imposed on American citizens of Japanese ancestry under Executive Order 9066. In April her petition was denied by a local judge, Lloyd D. Black. While officially Judge Black rejected the petition on the grounds that the restrictions on Mary Asaba Ventura did not amount to imprisonment, he also proclaimed that the order and the underlying laws were constitutional and rather gratuitously suggested that if she really was as loyal as she claimed, she ought to be glad to cooperate with the government. Fearing being separated from her family, Mary Asaba Ventura then petitioned the Western Defense Command to be spared removal, due to her marriage to a Filipino. However, her petition was denied, and she was sent on alone to confinement in Minidoka.

Another story was that of Theresa Takayoshi, a Nisei of mixed Irish and Japanese ancestry. As Paul Spickard relates, at the time of removal Takayoshi petitioned the Western Defense Command for exemption because she was of mixed ancestry. [14] While the army agreed to exempt her, military leaders ruled that her two young children would have to accompany their Nisei father into confinement. Rather than split up the family, Takayoshi agreed to accompany her family to Minidoka. In May 1943, after her husband joined the army, Takayoshi applied to the West Coast Defense Command to return to Seattle with her children and her mother. First Lady Eleanor Roosevelt wrote to the War Department to support her petition. However, even though Takayoshi had previously been granted exemption from confinement, and her mixed-race children should logically have been exempted, the army feared that permitting Japanese Americans back on the West Coast would dilute the justification for removal, and it denied her permission.

During the postwar years, numerous "war brides" were able to immigrate from Japan to the United States to join their predominantly non-Japanese husbands. In 1952 Congress passed the McCarran-Walter Act, which removed the remaining bars to immigration and naturalization rights for Asians. Meanwhile, the Supreme Court finally overturned existing state laws against interracial marriage in the *Loving v. Virginia* case in 1967. While it seems unlikely that the government's wartime policy favoring mixed-race couples strongly influenced the demise of laws targeting interracial couples, they did form a precedent for later federal government actions.

The Unknown History of Japanese Internment in Panama

WITH MAXIME MINNE

The historical narrative surrounding the wartime confinement of ethnic Japanese in the United States grows ever more complex. In the first two decades of the twenty-first century, historians and activists working with community organizations (in some cases with government funding) have made significant discoveries. The site of the Honouliuli Internment Camp in Hawai'i, long hidden from view, has been located and explored and was ultimately named a national monument. The Tuna Canyon Detention Station near Los Angeles, where Issei men arrested by the FBI after Pearl Harbor were held, has been rediscovered and its history documented. The War Relocation Authority's illicit "isolation center" at the former Indian boarding school at Leupp, Arizona, has been revealed in such works as filmmaker Claudia Katayanagi's documentary *A Bitter Legacy*. Scholar Anna Pegler-Gordon's research explores the wartime internment of Japanese aliens at Ellis Island in New York.

Yet amid all this new activity, the existence of one confinement site on US territory is still generally unacknowledged: that of the Panama Canal Zone, where Japanese aliens (along with Germans and Italians) were incarcerated throughout the war years. The Panama Canal, ceded by Panama to the United States via the Hay–Bunau-Varilla Treaty of 1903 and constructed between 1904 and 1914, was one of the major accomplishments of the early twentieth century in terms of technology and defense. Yet by its creation, this "path between the seas," about ten miles wide and fifty miles long, gave rise to repeated struggles and conflicts between Americans and Panamanians, and at a larger level between Washington and the entire region of Latin America. These struggles, shaped by race, culture, and politics, revolved around the question of sovereignty over the Canal Zone, the strip of territory surrounding the canal, which the United States controlled under the 1903 treaty and which cut the Republic of Panama in two. The bad feeling this separation created among Panamanians led to disturbances in the Canal Zone and in Panama. During this early period, the United States multiplied its military interventions inside Panama in order to maintain order in the country, in a total abuse of Panamanian sovereignty. Following requests by the Panamanians in 1921 and 1923, the United States agreed in 1926 to renegotiate the 1903 treaty. Nonetheless, this renegotiation failed to resolve Panamanian grievances concerning repeated violations of Panamanian sovereignty by Washington. During the 1930s, in connection with President Roosevelt's "Good Neighbor Policy" toward Latin America, a new agreement was reached between the two countries that postponed the question of sovereignty to the postwar period. (During the 1950s and 1960s, Panama would renew and extend its sovereignty claims amid rioting in the Canal Zone. The two nations signed a new treaty in 1977 providing for the handover of the canal, which would eventually take place in 1999).

As a result of the Roosevelt administration's diplomacy, the Panamanian government collaborated closely with the US War Department during World War II. During these years, the protection of the Canal Zone was of paramount interest to Washington, since the Panama Canal was central not just to the defense of the United States interests in the region but also to the security of all the nations in the Western Hemisphere that were engaged in the war. The canal was the only secure maritime line between the Atlantic and the Pacific Oceans. Moreover, the operations of German submarines in the Caribbean boldly dramatized the potential vulnerability of the canal and the need for reinforcement of the Canal Zone. In negotiations with the United States, Panama's government agreed to the potential formation of a new national army to support canal defense and promised to ensure coordination and cooperation between the Canal Zone Police and Panama's National Police. The area of most visible collaboration was in the wartime internment of Japanese aliens.

While the historical literature on Japanese Panamanians is scanty (there is no entry on Panama in *The Encyclopedia of Japanese Descendants in the Americas*), what seems clear is that throughout the prewar period there were Nikkei in the isthmus—by 1941 the community numbered an estimated four hundred. The *Chicago Tribune* stated in 1940 that Japanese made up a visible part of Colón's population. Some individuals resided inside the Canal Zone. For example, California-born Ralph Toshiki Kato was listed as living there in 1935.

As relations between the United States and Japan grew tense, authorities in Panama put pressure on Japanese citizens, viewed as a potential security threat, to depart. When the Japanese freighter *Sagami Maru* passed through the Panama Canal in fall 1940, the ship's crew reported that some twenty US Army officers boarded the ship for inspection. In July 1941, using the pretext of the need for repairs, American authorities closed the canal to Japanese ships. In the fall the government of Panama forbade Japanese citizens from doing business within its territory. In October 1941, according to historian C. Harvey Gardiner, the US ambassador to Panama, Edwin Wilson, began discussions with Panamanian foreign minister Octavio Fabrega. The Panamanians agreed that following any action by the United States to intern Japanese residents in the Canal Zone, Panama would arrest any Japanese on Panamanian territory and intern them on Taboga Island. All expenses and costs of internment and guarding would be paid by the United States government, which would hold Panama harmless against any claims that might arise as a result.

In November 1941, Attorney General Francis Biddle hinted that the government was planning mass confinement in Panama. Biddle announced that Justice Department experts had decided against wholesale arrests—it would be unwise to treat all Japanese living in the United States as enemies—but he added that the Canal Zone and Hawai'i were different and said that "temporary" mass arrests there were likely.

The various plans were translated swiftly into action following the Japanese bombing of Pearl Harbor in December 1941. According to Wilson's later testimony, within twenty minutes of the announcement of the Pearl Harbor attack, Panamanian authorities began rounding up Japanese and German aliens throughout the Republic. Once arrested, the Japanese were summarily turned over to US authorities and transported into the Canal Zone for internment in "concentration camps." The *New York Times* reported that 57 Japanese in Colón had been delivered to US authorities and that 114 more were expected from Panama City. The *Times* added that the Japanese were being held in a quarantine station in Balboa but that tent cities were being constructed to house the influx. Meanwhile, the Canal Zone Police, working in coordination with the Panamanians, took Japanese there into custody. *Newsday* stated that some three hundred

Japanese in the Canal Zone were being interned indefinitely as enemy aliens.

By January 1942, according to newspaperman Nat A. Barrows of the *Chicago Daily News*, 185 Japanese were held as civilian internees in a camp "somewhere in the Canal Zone," within a larger camp with separate facilities for Germans and Italians. Outside the camp, in a former private club, thirty-four women and forty-seven children were confined. Four hundred other enemy aliens had been arrested but then released after hearings, he claimed, while a Nisei from the Canal Zone had been transported to California. Barrows asserted that the Americans intended to hold the internees until the Republic of Panama built its own camp, which would take over all internees except for the fifteen who were arrested inside the Canal Zone. Barrows lauded the treatment of the Japanese: "Most of them never have had such good food and such good quarters before. In the daytime they lounge in the shade or do light work about the camp. In the evening they indulge in wrestling in an earthen ring or just sit expressionless studying their guards."

However, this idyllic picture is contradicted by Yoshitaro Amano, who described the Japanese aliens as being housed in makeshift tents in a concentration camp.[15] Amano also spoke of the demanding physical labor the Japanese, many middle-aged, were forced to perform. Amano's account is corroborated by the claims of the Japanese government. When in the spring of 1944 the United States lodged a formal protest against Japan for its treatment of American captives, Tokyo responded in a letter to the Swiss legation denying ill-treatment of prisoners and complaining of the treatment of Japanese nationals in U.S. custody: "The Japanese who were handed over to the United States army by the Authorities of Panama at the outbreak of the war were subjected to cruel treatment, being obliged to perform the work of transporting square timber, sharpening and repairing saws, digging holes in the ground for water closets, mixing gravel with cement and so forth." The letter continued, "The internment Authorities let the Japanese dig a hole and then fill it again immediately, or let them load a truck with mud with their bare hands using no tools. Neither drinking water nor any rest was allowed. The Japanese who were exhausted and worn were beaten or kicked and all this lasted over a month." The Japanese letter referred to the lack of medical care. "One Ouchi was gravely ill when he was handed over to the American Authorities in Panama, but the Authorities gave him neither medical treatment, nor liquid nourishment which was all he could take. His wife requested that he be taken into Panama hospital but the request was not heeded, and he was sent on to Fort Sill in April 1942 together with other Japanese internees. As no nurse was provided at the new camp, his fellow internees looked after him, but no medical treatment having been given, he finally died on May 1st."

In April 1942 the Japanese held in Panama were sent to the US mainland, where they were placed in internment camps. The Associated Press ran a photo of Japanese enemy aliens being evacuated from the Canal Zone in a railroad car with blackened windows. The caption (based on an undisclosed source) said that one of the men was a "Japanese naval officer," while two others were "Japanese Army reservists." The camps in the Canal Zone were subsequently mobilized by the US government to hold Japanese Peruvians and other Latin Americans who had been summarily taken into custody and shipped north to the Canal Zone. There the prisoners spent several days or months in confinement, forced to work without pay to clear jungle and construct living quarters amid the heat and the pouring rain. As Gardiner later reported, "Denied communication with their families, unaccustomed to hard labor, resenting the unsavory food and their inadequate shelter under intolerable weather conditions, the men understandably put forth no special effort. In return guards occasionally kicked, beat, or nicked with their bayonets some passive worker." Grace Shimizu, daughter of a Japanese Peruvian detained in the Canal Zone camp, later shared the testimony of another internee about being put to work clearing the jungle around the camp. "One humid day the internees, many of whom were elderly, were told to dig a pit. [One] thought he was digging his own grave. When they were told to fill the pit with buckets of human waste from the guards' latrines, then the older men were so tired that they could not run fast enough to please the guards, they were poked and shoved by guards with bayonets."[16]

The United States confined people in the Canal Zone without due process, even though they were supposed to be covered by the Constitution, while the Republic of Panama colluded with the United States to transfer citizens and legal residents for confinement. Why does this matter? First, because the fluid nature of sovereignty and control on US territory raises important questions of human rights. As we have seen in the matter of current-day confinement of "enemy combatants" at Guantánamo Bay in Cuba, constitutional rights of detainees are threatened where governments can create gray areas. Also, the confinement in Panama set a precedent. Indeed, Lisa C. Miyake proposes that the imprisonment of Japanese Panamanians in 1941 became a model for the subsequent internment of all suspicious Japanese Latin Americans.[17]

CHAPTER FOUR

Wartime Confinement and Japanese Americans

FRIENDS AND FOES

Japanese Americans, Dorothy Day, and the *Catholic Worker*

WITH MATTHIEU LANGLOIS

The release of Martin Scorsese's film *Silence,* on the persecution of Catholic missionaries in early modern Japan, has increased popular interest in the long and eventful encounter between Japanese Americans and Catholicism, a subject that has tended to pass unnoticed in chronicles of Nikkei life. This absence of discussion is peculiar, since in most places around the world where Japanese immigrant communities became established in the twentieth century—including Latin America, the Philippines, New Caledonia, and Quebec—Catholicism was the dominant religion. In these regions, the church played an important role in assisting the Nikkei, some of whom ended up intermarrying or converting to the majority religious culture or both. In contrast, the United States (like Australia and English

Dorothy Day, 1916. Courtesy of *Discover Nikkei.*

Canada) is an Anglo-Protestant society where Catholics have historically occupied a minority (and sometimes stigmatized) position.

In spite of their marginality, Catholic clergy and members of religious communities in different places have been important supporters of Issei and Nisei. Throughout the first half of the twentieth century, Catholic schools and colleges in the United States accepted numerous Nisei students. The medical school at Creighton University, a Catholic institution in Omaha, trained a generation of Nikkei physicians from Hawai'i and the mainland during the prewar years. Loyola University in New Orleans not only welcomed Nisei students but also eventually professors as well: by the mid-1950s there were four Nikkei on Loyola's faculty, including Father James Yamauchi, a biracial Nisei Jesuit who served as chairman of the Religious Studies Department. The Maryknoll missionaries operated an orphanage for Japanese American children in Los Angeles. Conversely, while only a small fraction of Japanese Americans embraced Catholicism, there were some notable converts, including early nineteenth-century migrant Joseph Heco; Nisei newspaper editors James Sakamoto and Harry Honda; Joseph Kurihara, World War I veteran and leading dissident in Manzanar; and Chicago-based attorney Franklin Chino, who even became an officer of the local branch of the Knights of Columbus.

Catholic support became especially noticeable in the wake of Executive Order 9066 and mass removal of West Coast Issei and Nisei. As Anne Blankenship reveals in her book *Christianity, Social Justice, and the Japanese American Incarceration during World War II*, after the attack on Pearl Harbor many members of the Catholic clergy stated their support of the Nikkei and decried the prejudices this community had to face. The Maryknoll missionaries worked, without success, to help Japanese Americans avert confinement. Maryknoll father Hugh Lavery and brother Theophane Walsh pushed the War Relocation Authority (WRA) to approve resettlement efforts. Walsh later moved to Chicago and aided Japanese American resettlers there. Maryknoll father Leo Tibesar, pastor of Our Lady Queen of Martyrs Church in Seattle, followed his Nikkei parishioners to Minidoka, where he lived and conducted services, and then on to Chicago at war's end. Father Edward J. Flanagan, the renowned founder of Boys Town, an Omaha-area home for abandoned youth, sponsored several Nisei for jobs at the institution to permit them and their families to resettle. Future Japanese American Citizens League president K. Patrick Okura was named staff psychologist.

One particularly intriguing story of Catholic engagement with Japanese Americans is that of the Catholic Worker movement. Founded in 1933 by Dorothy Day and directed by her until her death in 1980, the Catholic Worker is a progressive lay spiritual movement. It is known for its hospitality centers in poor areas of US cities where volunteers offer food and shelter. The organization's newspaper, the *Catholic Worker*, supports labor activism, peace, and human rights. In addition to these causes, Dorothy Day and her movement became distinguished for their outspoken opposition to Executive Order 9066 and open embrace of Japanese Americans.

Day was born in Brooklyn in 1897, into a non-practicing Protestant family. Her father, a sports journalist, repeatedly moved the family across the

United Sates. (The Day family was living in Oakland in 1906 when the great earthquake struck San Francisco, an event that drove Mr. Day's newspaper out of business). Soon after, the family settled in Chicago, where Dorothy spent her teens. In 1916, after having spent two years at the University of Illinois, she left for New York City, where she started working as a journalist for various radical newspapers and magazines like *The Call* and *The Masses*. During this period, she met all the intelligentsia of Greenwich Village—the likes of Max and Crystal Eastman, John Reed, Louise Bryant, and Eugene O'Neill.

Even though these people were fighting for socialism and a collectivist society, they were also profoundly individualistic. Dorothy Day, conversely, yearned to forge a community and foster genuine solidarity and kinship between people. Blocked from her goal, she engaged in various unhappy love affairs, underwent an abortion, and wrote an autobiographical novel, *The Eleventh Virgin*. After a Hollywood studio bought the rights to her novel, Dorothy Day was able to use the money to buy a small cottage close to the beach on Staten Island. It was there that she spent some of the happiest days of her life, living in a common-law marriage with Forster Batterham, by whom she bore a daughter, Tamar.

In 1927 Dorothy Day chose to convert to Catholicism, which put an end to her relationship with Batterham. Under the influence of Catholic thinker Peter Maurin and in collaboration with him, she devised a radical mix of spiritual thought and social action. The organizational product of their efforts was the Catholic Worker. Founded on May 1, 1933, its goal was to help people affected by the aftermath of the 1929 stock market crash and to offer a humane alternative to capitalism. Throughout the 1930s, Day remained in New York and ran the organization's newspaper and its hospitality center, in the process braving the skepticism (and at times outright hostility) of the city's Catholic hierarchy.

During the prewar years, Dorothy Day had warm contacts with Japanese Americans. In 1937 Day welcomed a Japanese immigrant, Kichi Harada, to the Catholic Worker and had to brave the race-based opposition of some members. She meanwhile corresponded with the Massachusetts-based Nisei socialist and pacifist Yoné U. Stafford. Still, Day was taken by surprise by the anti-Nikkei climate following the

Japanese attack on Pearl Harbor. As Anne Blankenship points out, Catholic clergy, despite their expressed sympathy for Japanese Americans, were limited in the opposition they could offer, at least publicly, to Executive Order 9066. Conversely, as a layperson Dorothy Day was freer to voice her disgust about what was being done to the Nikkei. For Day, the United States was no better than Nazi Germany if it treated its citizens in the same way that the Nazis did. It is important to bear in mind that Day was strongly influenced during this period by the theological concept of the "mystical body of Christ." To harm anyone, whomever the person was, was the same as to injure the body of Christ. She drew on this idea in her firm pacifistic stand during World War II.

During the late spring of 1942, Day spent some weeks on the West Coast. In the June 1942 issue of the *Catholic Worker* she gave a chilling account of the Puyallup Assembly Center in Washington, euphemistically called Camp Harmony, which she had seen and where Nikkei were held before being moved east to other camps. "I saw a bit of Germany on the west coast. I saw some of the concentration camps where the Japanese men, women, and children are being held before they are resettled in the Owens Valley or some other place barren, windswept, inaccessible." Even though she was not able to talk with anyone in the camp, she was well informed about the living conditions that people there were facing thanks to correspondence with Nikkei friends who were detained there. Day didn't hesitate to quote sections of their letters in her article, wanting readers to bear witness to the injustice that was being done in the United States: "There are flood lights turned on us at night," she quoted from one letter. And from another: "There is no privacy. . . . There are long rows of toilets, all facing each other, with no partitions in between, and rows of showers. It is very cold out here, because the building is full of knot-holes. There is no place for the children, we hear their crying all night and all day."[1]

Day continued her reporting in the following issue, telling the shocking story of a young Japanese American boy who was shot to death when he tried to retrieve a ball that had rolled outside the fence of the camp where he lived.[2] All those details about life in the camps brought the Office of Censorship in Washington, DC to send a letter to the *Catholic Worker* warning that it was disobeying the Code of Wartime Practices of the American

Press. Even though Day apologized for not respecting the code, she continued to publicly denounce Executive Order 9066.

The interest of Dorothy Day in aiding Nikkei communities didn't stop with the end of the war. Until her death in 1980 she would often remind her readers that the US government had committed a monstrous crime by bombing the cities of Hiroshima and Nagasaki. Also, during the postwar years she would befriend and work with the famed Nisei writer Hisaye Yamamoto, who spent some years at the Peter Maurin farm in New York City during the 1950s and wrote articles for the *Catholic Worker*.

Brother Theophane Walsh: A Quiet Hero

WITH JONATHAN VAN HARMELEN

In November 2018 the *New York Times* published an article highlighting the work of Father Ruskin Piedra, the priest of the church Our Lady of Perpetual Help in New York City.[3] At eighty-four, the article reported, he busied himself supporting litigation on behalf of immigrants—some from his own parish—to prevent them from deportation. Amid the tearful scenes of deportation and confinement of children in detention centers, Father Piedra's work is a hopeful reminder that despite the callousness of the Trump administration's policies in regard to immigrants and human rights, there are those working to help them and address their troubles.

The story of Father Piedra recalls Catholics who offered support to Japanese Americans during World War II. Dorothy Day defended the rights of Japanese Americans by publishing accounts in the *Catholic Worker* of the anguish of those behind barbed wire. Meanwhile a number of Catholic priests took up responsibility for assisting Nikkei communities during their removal, confinement, and release from camps.

One such figure worth celebrating is Brother Theophane Walsh. Born Edward George Walsh in February 1904 to Irish American parents, he grew

Brother Theophane Walsh. Courtesy of Maryknoll Mission Archives.

up in Boston. A dedicated student, he took night classes while working days as a salesman and clerk. In 1921 the young Edward began a vocation with the Maryknolls, a Catholic missionary order founded in the 1910s whose members evangelized in Asia and elsewhere. He was influenced by his brother Willie, who had previously taken a Maryknoll vocation and had entered Maryknoll's Venard seminary in Pennsylvania. The young Walsh took the name Theophane after Saint Jean-Théophane Venard, a French Catholic missionary and martyr in Indochina.

After leaving the seminary, Walsh was sent to Los Angeles to work in the Little Tokyo Parish, where he was ordained in 1930. During his time in Los Angeles, Walsh was limited in his activities by chronic health problems, which required extensive treatment and hospitalization. Still, he worked with Japanese American youth in various ways. He was solely responsible for putting together the bazaar run by the Maryknoll Japanese Mission, and he took the lead in organizing the buses that transported students to and from its school. He was most notable for working with the Boy Scouts, in connection with the Ad Altare Dei movement of the Scouts. In 1926 Walsh helped organize one of the oldest Japanese American troops in the United States.

In 1942, in the wake of Executive Order 9066, Brother Walsh committed himself to helping the Nikkei community in any way possible. Together with Masamori Kojima and Setsuko Matsunaga (later Setsuko Nishi), he organized a speakers bureau to make the case for the loyalty of Japanese Americans. Alongside fathers Leopold Tibesar and Hugh Lavery, he proposed to move with Nikkei parishioners to a settlement outside the West Coast, and he furnished to the Tolan Committee (the congressional group studying mass removal) with a list of names of potential resettlers. In a 1971 issue of *Rafu Shimpo*, Brother Walsh was remembered for helping organize temporary shelter for Nikkei families from Terminal Island following their forced eviction by the navy in February 1942.[4]

In the fall of 1942, Brother Walsh went off with other Maryknoll missionaries to Manzanar, where he helped families adjust to camp life. In 1943, as young Japanese Americans began resettling outside the camps, Walsh left for Chicago. There, under the direction of Bishop Bernard Sheil, he helped establish the Catholic Youth Organization's Nisei Center, which assisted the newcomers. The center's development came at a time when families were beginning to resettle in large numbers, with Chicago being the principal destination. In August 1944 Larry Tajiri reported in the *Pacific Citizen* that racist hostility against Japanese Americans was rising due to lies by the Hearst newspapers, which charged that Nisei resettlers were arriving in Chicago without "any investigation by the FBI . . . by simply changing their tune and signing papers to be good."[5] With his supportive work, Brother Walsh encouraged local Nisei and helped foster a sense of community among them.

As he worked in Manzanar and Chicago, Walsh maintained correspondence with Nisei friends dispersed in other camps. In particular, he corresponded with a number of his parishioners from Los Angeles who had been sent to Heart Mountain. In one letter to Mary Theresa Oishi (née Hiratsuka), Walsh sent instructions on how to retrieve family cameras confiscated by Los Angeles police following Pearl Harbor, along with a copy of the police report.[6] Such a letter not only sheds light on the benevolent acts of individuals like Brother Walsh, it also reminds us to what extent the state dominated the lives of Nikkei in this time of war, with local police later participating in the roundup with soldiers.

After the end of the war, Walsh remained in Chicago. His continuing efforts with the Nisei Center, including English instruction and work as scoutmaster, were applauded in Chicago newspapers on several occasions. During the US occupation of Japan he briefly served as a missionary in Japan for Maryknoll, delivering lectures on US-Japanese bonds. In one 1948 lecture cited by the *Nichi Bei Times*, he spoke at the Tokyo Industrial Club about "the future of the Japanese in America" and lauded the potentially favorable future for Nikkei in the United States.[7] Following the conclusion of his mission, he settled in Los Angeles where he continued his labors with Nikkei youth and in support of community institutions. In an article for the *Kashu Mainichi* during the 1950s, he extolled Nikkei youth for forming clubs and called for "more adult active participation in the work of any organization of their choice."[8] He continued his sponsorship of Boy Scouts and in 1956 was awarded the St. George Emblem for his Scout work over thirty years. He ultimately would be named the international Boy Scout commissioner for interracial groups. Theophane Walsh suffered again from poor health in later years. He died at the Maryknoll Center in Ossining, New York, in 1981.

Brother Walsh's wartime efforts in Los Angeles and Chicago offer a lesson in humanity and a chance for reflection by Americans. Today, when racist rhetoric by the Right has grown increasingly normalized in political discourse, Walsh's devotion to interracial justice serves as a beacon. While not everyone can devote one's life to activism like Brother Walsh or Father Piedra, their lives suggest some of countless ways to advocate for those victimized by prejudice and to heal divisions in American society.

Pearl S. Buck, Defender of the Nisei

The Nobel laureate writer and social activist Pearl S. Buck was an outspoken wartime advocate for Japanese Americans.

Born in West Virginia and raised in China, the daughter of Southern Presbyterian missionaries, Pearl Comfort Sydenstricker attended

Pearl S. Buck, 1972. Courtesy of the Dutch National Archives through the creative commons license.

Randolph-Macon Women's College before returning to China, where she married a missionary, John Lossing Buck. During the early 1920s she and her husband lived in Nanjing (with one year in Umzen, Japan), where she taught at Nanking University and cared for a mentally disabled daughter, Carol.

During her husband's sabbatical year Pearl Buck earned an MA degree at Cornell University, and then the family returned to China, where Buck started writing stories and essays. She soon attracted widespread attention for a series of popular novels on Chinese themes. Buck's second novel, *The Good Earth* (1931), the story of a peasant family, became an international best-seller, won a Pulitzer Prize, and was adapted into a popular Hollywood film.

In 1933 Buck, who had separated from her husband, returned to the United States, obtained a second master's degree at Yale University, then settled in Bucks County, Pennsylvania. In the years that followed, she married her publishing agent, Richard Walsh. She and Walsh assumed direction of *Asia* magazine. In 1938 Buck was awarded the Nobel Prize for Literature, the first American woman so honored. Other popular novels such as *China Sky* (1941) and *Dragon Seed* (1942) followed, as did a collection of feminist essays, *Of Men and Women* (1941).

Buck worked extensively in the years before World War II as a civil rights activist, with such groups as the American Civil Liberties Union and the National Urban League. She became a public supporter of China against Japanese invasion and raised money for Chinese war relief. In 1941 she and Richard Walsh formed the East-West Society to encourage Asian-American dialogue. During these years Buck had little exposure to Japanese Americans, but in 1940 she met pro-Chinese Issei writer Haru Matsui (Ayako Ishigaki), whose book *Restless Wave* she had reviewed positively. The two women became friends, and Buck encouraged Ishigaki to contribute to *Asia*. Following the Japanese raid on Pearl Harbor, Buck wrote to Ishigaki, offering aid in case of trouble.

As the United States became embroiled in war with Japan, Buck warned in speeches, letters, and articles that victory could not be achieved without the collaboration of Asian peoples and that undemocratic treatment for racial minorities at home, especially Asian Americans, imperiled such alliances. In the process, Buck became virtually the only nationally known figure to oppose mass removal of Japanese Americans during the spring of 1942. Buck forwarded letters from West Coast friends opposing removal to government officials and notably to First Lady Eleanor Roosevelt, and she scheduled meetings with the ACLU's civil rights committee to discuss assistance. Buck also joined the advisory board of the Japanese American Committee for Democracy. At a JACD meeting in April 1942, Buck spoke out about the loyalty of Japanese Americans and declared that rather than excluding them the US government should welcome their participation in the war and train them to help build democracy in postwar Japan. She repeated this proposal in her book *American Unity and Asia*, calling on Japanese Americans to recognize that there were fair-minded people who supported them and asking them not to be swayed in their loyalty by insults or mistreatment. "I beg you, Japanese Americans, that you will not despair of democracy or of America." In October 1943, Buck appeared before a California state senate fact-finding committee investigating Japanese

Americans. Facing hostile questioning, she testified publicly on behalf of the loyalty of Issei and Nisei and insisted that they had the right to a fair trial to determine whether they should be confined. She warned the committee that the nation's treatment of Japanese Americans was being watched throughout the world.

In addition to her speeches and lobbying efforts, Buck encouraged discussion of Japanese Americans in the pages of *Asia* magazine (by then known as *Asia and the Americas*). In 1943 she commissioned an article by Larry Tajiri, "Democracy Corrects Its Own Mistakes," encouraging resettlement. In January 1944 she published an article in the magazine warning Californians of the need to keep their wits and use common sense in their treatment of "Orientals," especially Japanese Americans, and she repeated that the eyes of Asia and the world were on them. In February 1944 she agreed to add her name to a list of "national sponsors" that the JACL put together to help raise money for its programs.

Following the end of World War II, Pearl S. Buck ceased publication of *Asia* and reduced some of her activism, concentrating on her other writing. She nonetheless continued her interest in Japanese Americans. In 1945–46 Buck sponsored the Chinese Theatre, a troupe of Chinese actors with whom she produced a theatrical adaptation of her story "The First Wife." When the production went on tour, she hired Hollywood actor Teru Shimada, then unemployed, to take up the leading male role. (In a thin attempt to obscure his Japanese origins, the actor was billed under the Chinese name Shi ma-da.) In 1947 Buck became a member of the Philadelphia branch of the JACL and publicly supported the granting of citizenship rights to Japanese immigrants.

Buck continued interracial activism in her later years. In 1949, outraged that many adoption agencies refused to place Asian and mixed-race children, Buck founded Welcome House as an international and interracial adoption agency. To help encourage adoption of Asian children, in 1964 Buck created the Pearl S. Buck Foundation. By the time Buck died in 1973, she had published over seventy books. Although she had less to do with Japanese Americans during these years, community leaders remained grateful for her wartime advocacy.

First Lady of the World? Reconsidering Eleanor Roosevelt and Japanese Americans

Eleanor Roosevelt, wife of President Franklin D. Roosevelt and celebrated activist First Lady, spoke out publicly on behalf of loyal Japanese Americans, citizens and aliens alike, before and after Pearl Harbor. She attempted to dissuade the president from ordering mass removal, which she regarded as a violation of human rights and American ideals, spoke publicly of the loyalty of Japanese Americans, and invited Japanese Americans to the White House. In April 1943 she toured the Gila River camp to show her support. At the same time, though, and after the war, she defended the forced dispersion and assimilation of West Coast Nikkei communities, saying it was designed to protect them from mob violence.

Until World War II, Eleanor Roosevelt had virtually no contact with Japanese Americans. While she was a notable supporter of equal rights for black Americans, she seldom addressed the problem of anti-Asian discrimination during her first eight years in the White House. However, in October 1941, editor Togo Tanaka of *Rafu Shimpo* and Gongoro Nakamura of the Central Japanese Association came to Washington, DC to inquire about the fate of Japanese Americans in case of war. Eleanor agreed to meet them and promised her assistance. At a press conference following the meeting, she praised the patriotism of the Nisei, who had joined the army in large numbers, and added, "The Issei may be aliens technically, but in reality they are Americans and America has a place for all loyal persons regardless of race or citizenship."

After Pearl Harbor was attacked, Eleanor immediately flew to the West Coast to assess the situation and coordinate civil defense efforts. When she discovered that Treasury Department orders freezing "enemy alien" bank accounts were causing unnecessary hardship to Issei farmers, she quickly contacted Treasury officials and had the orders relaxed sufficiently to permit Issei to withdraw $100 per month to pay living expenses. While on the West Coast, Eleanor publicly defended Japanese Americans, posing for pictures with Nisei that were released to the press. In a national radio broadcast on January 11, 1942, she also spoke out on behalf of the Issei,

"Gila River Relocation Center, Rivers, Arizona. Representatives of Councils Greet Mrs. [Eleanor Roosevelt], Gila River, April 1943." War Relocation Authority portrait. Bancroft Library, University of California, Berkeley.

whom she reminded her listeners were longtime residents legally prevented from becoming citizens. However, she seems to have believed baseless rumors about Japanese American fifth columnists. Author Louis Adamic later wrote in his book *Dinner at the White House* that on January 13, 1942, Mrs. Roosevelt invited him to dinner at the White House to speak to the president about his ideas on "two-way passage" of cultural interchange with Europeans. When the question of public hostility toward Japanese Americans came up at dinner, Adamic defended Issei and Nisei. Eleanor responded harshly by referring to Japanese Americans arrested for espionage. Her attitude, he said, seemed to him uncompromising and foreboding.

Eleanor was taken by surprise by Executive Order 9066 (partly because she was preoccupied responding to political attacks on her work in the Office of Civilian Defense). When she protested to her husband, he told her peremptorily that he did not wish to discuss the subject. She tried to get around this by meeting with FDR's friend Archibald MacLeish, director of the Office of Facts and Figures, and his aides (including Alan Cranston, a native-born Californian and future US senator) to put together arguments to use against mass removal, but without success.

The mass removal threw her into a quandary that she was unable to resolve. Her options were limited by the fact that she was the president's wife, and part of the administration, even if she was not an elected or appointed official. She publicly supported her husband's policy but privately apologized for it. In a letter to Bill Hosokawa published in the *Japanese American Courier* she expressed her sympathy and said that she was sure the government would do all it could to make evacuation as decent and comfortable as possible. Similarly, she responded to a private letter of protest from author Pearl Buck by stating, "I regret the need to evacuate, but I recognize it has to be done." She added that she hoped to visit the camps. She wrote to an old colleague, Flora Rose, "This is just one more reason for hating war, innocent people suffer for a few guilty ones." When black civil rights activist Pauli Murray wrote to FDR in July 1942 proposing that the government relocate southern blacks to save them from lynching, just as it had removed West Coast Japanese Americans to protect them from racist attacks, she unleashed Eleanor's deep frustration and defensiveness. In a rare display of anger (mixed with some odd ethnic categorization) Eleanor wrote to Murray, "How many of our colored people in the South would like to be evacuated and treated as though they were not as rightfully here as other people? I am deeply concerned that we have had to do that to the Japanese who are American citizens, but we are at war with Japan and they have only been citizens for a very short time. We would feel a resentment if we had to do this for citizens who have been here as long as most of the white people."

Once removal was ordered, Eleanor kept herself informed on Japanese Americans and their problems, in order to help where she could. She asked the War Department for permission to visit an assembly center, a request that was declined. She authorized the transfer of money from the special projects fund she maintained with the American Friends Service Committee to pay for emergency programs serving Japanese Americans, and in her newspaper column "My Day" she praised a church in Berkeley that provided food and clothing for the inmates. She supported the creation of the National Japanese American Student Relocation Council to find colleges willing to accept Nisei students so that they could continue their education.

In March 1943 Eleanor received a letter from Harriet Gipson asking about rumors of Issei and Nisei fifth columnists. After checking with Representative John Tolan, who had held hearings on Japanese Americans in February 1942, she discovered, evidently to her surprise, that there had been no actual incidents of sabotage and no Japanese Americans convicted of disloyal acts. This discovery seems to have pushed her into action. In order to refute widespread charges by hostile members of Congress and newspapers that the WRA was coddling Japanese Americans, she asked again to visit the camps. FDR agreed to let her go, though he refused her plea to bring a Japanese American family to live in the White House as a symbolic gesture of trust, insisting that the Secret Service would never permit it. In April 1943, after she traveled to Arizona, accompanying FDR to a border conference with Mexico's president Miguel Avila Camacho, Eleanor visited the Gila River camp, alone and unguarded.

By her presence and with interest she showed, she made clear to the inmates her sympathy for their plight. However, in the speech she gave, she told the confined Japanese Americans that their residence in Japanese neighborhoods, "in communities within a community," had delayed their assimilation into "the American society" and recommended that they scatter and assimilate once released. While this advice was surely well-meant, according to teenaged inmate Michi Nishiura, who heard the speech, it came across as blaming the victims for their own incarceration. Later, under her married name Michi Nishiura Weglyn, she would write *Years of Infamy*, an activist history of wartime confinement.

Once returned to Washington from Gila River, Eleanor campaigned further to assist confined Japanese Americans. In her syndicated daily newspaper column, she lauded the efforts of the inmates to grow their own food, ameliorate the harsh desert conditions and the ugliness of the hastily constructed camps, and police and educate themselves. In an interview published in the *Los Angeles Times* three days after her visit, she was frank. She described the inmates as living in conditions that were not indecent, "certainly not luxurious," but added, "I wouldn't like to live that way." She strongly recommended that the camps be closed as soon as possible. "The sooner we get the young [native-born] Japanese out of the camps the better. Otherwise if we don't look out we will create another Indian problem." It was her most open public expression of opposition during the war.

Following her return to Washington, Eleanor persuaded FDR to meet with Dillon Myer—the first and only time the president did so—in an effort to build support for the beleaguered WRA leader and to push Myer's proposal that the army permit the release of the inmates. She also wrote an article for *Collier's* magazine (which she invited Myer to "correct") in which she publicized the plight of the inmates and the camps' historical background. Calling attention to the sacrifices the Japanese Americans had made, including their often-forced disposition of property, she urged her readers to live up to "traditional American ideals of fairness" in dealing with them once they left the camps. She met with JACL representatives at the White House and accepted a gift of vegetables grown in camp and a Chiura Obata painting. She asked Michio Kunitani, a resettler in Cleveland, to come to Washington to discuss with her the problems of Nisei outside the camps. She also kept tabs on Japanese American soldiers, first the Hawaiian Nisei of the 100th Infantry Battalion and later the members of the all-Nisei 442nd Infantry Regiment. She corresponded with Assistant Secretary of War John McCloy to ask about the treatment of the Nisei soldiers during their training at Camp Shelby in Mississippi and inquired whether it might be better to move them outside the state because of potential racial discrimination. She sent a letter to wounded soldier Jack Mizuha to express her sympathies—the sending of the letter made clear to Nisei soldiers that there were people in high places following them and expressing concern—and then invited him to tea at the White House. After visiting Hawai'i and meeting Hung Wai Ching, a Chinese American YMCA worker who had helped bring about the creation of the 442nd Regiment, she invited Ching to Washington to brief her (and the president) on the condition of Nisei soldiers.

In June 1944, debate arose within the administration over lifting exclusion. Eleanor worked to bring pressure to bear on FDR. She took to him a proposal by NAACP executive secretary Walter White that black Americans publicly demonstrate their support for the immediate return of Japanese Americans to their homes. The president disingenuously told her that the question of closing the camps and having the inmates return to California was entirely in the hands of the military. He added that he thought a public demonstration specifically by blacks on behalf of Japanese Americans would backfire against both minorities, and he advised Eleanor to tell White that blacks should join others in their communities to assure that individual Japanese Americans received "proper and kindly treatment." Though Eleanor failed to persuade FDR to close the camps before December 1944, she did not cease her efforts. As late as February 1945, less than two months before her husband's death, she was still reminding him about helping returning inmates. In December 1945, after leaving the White House, she alerted President Harry Truman to the violence facing Japanese Americans returning to the West Coast, and she pleaded with him to take action.

In the years after FDR's death in 1945, Eleanor Roosevelt took on the role of public custodian of her husband's memory. She avoided commenting on her wartime involvement with Japanese Americans, even in her memoirs. In an introduction to Allen Eaton's art book *Beauty behind Barbed Wire* (1952), her sole postwar discussion of the wartime events, Eleanor praised the contribution and artistic talent of the Japanese American in the camps. At the same time, however, she justified the camps as a protective measure. "Our military authorities had felt that this element of our population might provide some individuals dangerous to our national security on the West Coast. Feeling was running so high against the Japanese, with whom we were at war, that some felt a great many within our borders would have to be placed where they were not in physical danger." In view of her harsh response to Pauli Murray's assertion that the government should engage in protective custody for blacks, the introduction struck an oddly false and defensive note.

Eleanor publicly supported Japanese Americans before and after Pearl Harbor and disagreed sharply with the policy of removal, but she was forced to balance her belief in justice and equal rights with her loyalty to her husband. Although the surviving evidence indicates her sincere public support of Japanese Americans and her considerable efforts on their behalf, her efforts were not untouched by certain biases.

Wartime Solidarity between Chinese Americans and Japanese Americans

One aspect of Japanese American history that has been increasingly explored in recent times is the complex and revealing question of relations between Nikkei and other ethnic and religious minority groups. For example, Scott Kurashige's *The Shifting Grounds of Race* examines the conditions facing Japanese Americans and African Americans in Los Angeles and their varied (and sometimes competing) efforts to overcome discrimination. Ellen Eisenberg's *The First to Cry Down Injustice?* covers the reaction of Jewish Americans in western states to the wartime removal of Japanese Americans.

Rather less seems to have been written about the relations between Japanese Americans and other Asian American groups—most notably Chinese Americans.[9] This is curious, as Nikkei arguably had more contact with Chinese than with other ethnic communities in the early twentieth century. In cities such as Seattle and Los Angeles, the two populations lived and worked in neighboring enclaves. In San Francisco, dozens of Issei merchants opened shops in Chinatown. In small farming towns, Issei laborers spent their money after hours in Chinese gambling dens. All around the region, Japanese families frequented Chinese restaurants (such as the Far East Café in Little Tokyo) where they felt welcomed and where they could find cheap and tasty Asian-style dishes.

Furthermore, people have generally have assumed, without cause, that until the Asian American movement of the late 1960s and 1970s Chinese and Japanese Americans throughout the country remained entirely separate and hostile—mirroring the conflict between their home countries during the period of the Pacific War. In particular, multiple histories of Asian Americans and World War II mention Chinese Americans who wore "I am Chinese" buttons after Pearl Harbor to distinguish themselves from Japanese Americans. Jane Hong has written, "For many Asian Americans, the need to prove their loyalty to America meant turning a blind eye to the wartime incarceration of Japanese Americans, lest they throw their own allegiance into doubt."[10] Hong admits that there were individuals who raised doubts about the morality of mass confinement or expressed solidarity but adds that such people were exceptional.

To be sure, there were widespread tensions between West Coast Chinese and Japanese immigrants in the years before Pearl Harbor. Chinese communities mobilized to support nationalist resistance to the Japanese occupation of China and organized boycotts of Japanese goods, even as Japanese consulates and the Nikkei press backed Tokyo's policy. Nonetheless, many

Issei and Nisei privately expressed support for the Chinese cause, and a few openly backed China. *Shin Sekai* editor Eddie Shimano joined dockside protests against exports to Japan. James Oda, a Kibei (Japanese American educated in Japan) and future Military Intelligence Service analyst, wrote in the short-lived newspaper *News of the World* in the fall of 1937 that Nisei ought to avoid getting drawn into support for Japan's war in China. That same year Ken Nikaido of Honolulu organized local branches of the American Friends of the Chinese People and the United Committee for Boycott of Japanese Goods.

Still, if contesting mass removal was hardly the rule among West Coast Chinese Americans (or any other ethnic communities, including Japanese) there were numerous cases throughout the war of individuals who expressed solidarity with Japanese Americans and worked to make conditions better for them. To begin with, there were first- and second-generation Chinese Americans who defended the patriotism of the Nikkei. In March 1942, after *Time* magazine falsely reported as fact rumors that "Japanese high school boys from Hawai'i" had figured among the pilots in the Japanese raid on Pearl Harbor, a dozen high school students from Honolulu wrote in to rebut the story. *Time* published two letters from Chinese Americans. Colleen Lau wrote, "We, Americans all, study, work, and play with Japanese high school boys here in the islands, and, I am sure, are in a position to know them perhaps a little better than others. They show their feelings, in speech and in deed, that they're behind the U.S.A. to a man."

Next, Chinese American artists and intellectuals supported their friends and comrades. Author Lin Yutang joined the advisory board of the antifascist activist group Japanese American Committee for Democracy in 1941. Journalist Helena Kuo, who fled occupied China for the United States in 1939, joined the Japanese-born feminist and activist Ayako Ishigaki (Haru Matsui) in joint lecture tours. After Pearl Harbor, when Ishigaki and her husband faced curfew as enemy aliens and feared racist violence, Kuo visited them and went on shopping trips to keep them supplied with food.

The celebrated Chinese American artist Dong Kingman (Kuo's future husband) communicated with the WRA during 1942–43, offering to reside in one of the camps. After being granted permission, he proposed visiting Heart Mountain to paint during his teaching stint at University of

Wyoming in July 1943, but for unknown reasons the visit seems to have been shelved. The popular dance duo of Dorothy Toy and Paul Wing left San Francisco so that Toy (born Dorothy Takahashi) would not be incarcerated with her family, and moved to New York for the duration.

Then there were Chinese who collaborated with their Nikkei neighbors to ease the burdens of the mass removal. David W. Lee, a Chinese American in Portland, Oregon, bought the grocery store of a local Nisei, James Kida. Raymond Chew, a trucker in Mountain View, California, who hauled produce for his Issei friend and neighbor Yasokichi Antoku, leased ten acres of Antoku's farm before removal. In both cases the families remained in touch.

Perhaps most poignant were the cases of Chinese-Japanese couples who faced mass confinement. Don Sugai (a wrestler in prewar years) and Benny Higashi were accompanied by their Chinese American wives to the Portland Assembly Center and then to Minidoka. Pil (Polly) Sugai and Lalun Higashi could have been exempted from confinement, but they chose to stay with their spouses and children. In other cases, Nisei wives were separated from their spouses. Nellie Woo, the Nisei wife of Lun P. Woo, a Chinese grocer in Seattle, sent a letter to the Western Defense Command requesting exemption for herself and her daughters Hazel and Grace but was refused permission to remain in Seattle. She was ultimately sent to Minidoka with the children, while her husband remained behind. Rather than move even farther away, Woo remained in camp despite pressure to resettle. In January 1944, a "mixed-race family" exemption was finally granted, and Nellie became the first Nisei officially permitted to return to the Seattle area.

In July 1942 Charles Leonard Won, a Chinese American from San Francisco, agreed to marry his longtime sweetheart Jean Mio Ikebuchi, then confined at Santa Anita, and to accompany her to the assembly center for their honeymoon. According to the *Pacific Citizen*, the two received a license and made plans to wed, but Ikebuchi decided to break off the engagement until after the war, fearing that as the only Chinese in Santa Anita her husband might be mistreated. (Sadly, it would seem that Jean Mio Ikebuchi did not ever marry her fiancé, as she is listed in later records as Mrs. Miyo Kaneda).[11] Louise Liwa Yakai Chew, the wife of a Chinese American grocer in Oakland, felt herself to be so Chinese that she did not even register with the government as a Japanese American in the spring of 1942. Arrested for disobeying military evacuation orders and brought before Judge Adolphus St. Sure, she reported in tears that she felt completely Chinese and would "rather die than be sent to a Japanese assembly center." She was convicted nevertheless, then immediately paroled to the Topaz camp. After a month there, she was released for temporary labor outside camp but soon fell ill and was permitted to leave. She applied for a permit to rejoin her husband, but it was refused, so she moved instead to stay with family in Cleveland and New York. During this period, her husband sent money to help support her.

In contrast, Kay Kiyoko Horikawa Chinn did not even wait for permission to return to the West Coast after leaving camp in early 1943. Rather, she rushed back to Seattle to be reunited with her husband Harry Chinn (also known as Chin S. Lin). After spending just two months at home, however, Chinn was arrested by FBI agents and jailed. After pleading guilty to violating military exclusion orders, she was offered a suspended sentence if she relocated outside the excluded area, and she moved with her husband to the city of Spokane.

Although ethnic Chinese actors in Hollywood such as Richard Loo became known for portraying evil Japanese in wartime propaganda films, columnist George Schuyler reported that many refused to play treacherous Japanese Americans, for fear of stirring up anti-Asian racism. For example, in the 1942 propaganda film *Little Tokyo, U.S.A.*, the part of a loyal Japanese American killed by his fellows was played by a Chinese actor, but the Nisei traitors were played by whites.

When in early 1943 a white reader wrote a letter to the *Sacramento Bee* opposing the WRA's plan to permit loyal Japanese Americans to resettle outside camp, two Chinese Americans responded by taking their side. Robert Kwot lauded the loyalty of the "American Japanese" he had known, in particular a Nisei friend in camp who had confided in a letter his desire to join the American army and fight the Japanese empire. Walter A. Lum called for liberation of loyal Japanese Americans and implored readers to promote "democratic principles." Shortly afterward, Walter Ching, a graduate student at the University of California, publicly denounced white supremacy and race-baiting attacks on Japanese Americans: "My people have suffered the most from Japanese activities, but I cannot condone United States persecution of American-born Japanese who are in this country through no fault of their own. . . . If you persecute the American-born Japanese in your nation now; if you exercise hatred toward the negro and begin to criticize the Jew, perhaps you will then turn against the Chinese 30 years hence."[12]

In mid-1943 a Chinese Christian Youth Conference meeting at Lake Tahoe under the direction of the redoubtable Beulah Ong (later a well-known actress under the name Beulah Quo) issued a resolution supporting "fair play for Japanese-Americans" and denouncing racial hatred. Reverend Harold Joh, a minister from Oakland, labored at the Topaz camp during the summer of 1944 in a Protestant church program. Henry Shue Tom, YMCA secretary in San Francisco, wrote a letter of appreciation to *Pacific Citizen*, praising the paper. In the fall of 1944, before the US Army lifted its wholesale exclusion of Japanese Americans, numerous Chinese Americans expressed support for their return. A second Chinese Christian Youth Conference, meeting at San Anselmo, called for a cordial welcome to returnees. UCLA student Hazel Wong spoke up at a public meeting in Santa Barbara to endorse their presence: "I believe a loyal Japanese American is not half so dangerous as a prejudiced American."

After war's end, various Japanese Americans found housing and employment among Chinese Americans. (Many Nikkei returned to San Francisco Chinatown, which had been hit hard economically by their removal.) In 1946 Chinese American Post 638 of the American Legion devised the idea of presenting washing machines to hospitalized soldiers, and post commander Harry Lee suggested honoring a wounded Nisei GI. As a result, the post offered Rokuro Moriguchi, a Nisei veteran being treated at Birmingham General Hospital in Van Nuys, with a new washing machine. The Japanese American Citizens League likewise offered support to Chinese American veterans facing discrimination, most notably in *Amer v. California*, a case challenging restrictive housing covenants.

The existence of numerous cases of solidarity between individuals and groups means that we must nuance the received story of people of Chinese ancestry as invariably hostile to ethnic Japanese during the World War II era. Such incidents of support and collaboration, even if they did not represent majority attitudes, helped foster the goodwill and understanding of shared interests that made later alliances possible.

Woody Guthrie

Japanese Americans were not able to find many outside supporters during the early days of World War II. Even in cosmopolitan New York, Socialist Party leader Norman Thomas, the only national political figure to oppose Executive Order 9066, later stated that he had never known a position to which it was so difficult to attract his usual liberal and labor allies. However, throughout the war years, Japanese Americans could count on the vocal support of one exceptional *hakujin* ally living in Brooklyn, the folksinger and activist Woody Guthrie. Guthrie wrote a memoir in which he boasted of defending Japanese Americans; he subscribed to the JACL organ *Pacific Citizen*, corresponded with its editors, and ultimately contributed articles to it himself; and he sang for Nisei groups, including his own songs, many of which would soon become known from coast to coast.

Woodrow Wilson Guthrie was born in Okemah, in the new state of Oklahoma, on July 14, 1912, the second son of Charles and Nora Belle Guthrie. The family faced a number of financial and personal difficulties in the coming years. Woody's sister Clara died young, and Nora Belle Guthrie was institutionalized after contracting a then-unknown degenerative nerve disorder, Huntington's Disease. She died in an asylum for the insane in Norman in 1930. In 1931, in the depths of the Great Depression, Guthrie left Oklahoma and settled in the town of Pampa, Texas. There he met and married a young woman, Mary Jennings, with whom he had three children.

The onset of the great Dust Bowl of the mid-1930s forced Guthrie to abandon his home. Like so many Okie refugees, he migrated west to California, riding the rails or hitchhiking. While Guthrie had already worked

Yuriko Amemiya. Photography by Tom Parker. War Relocation Authority portrait. Bancroft Library, University of California, Berkeley.

in Texas as part of a singing trio, it was during his wanderings that he found his voice, singing in saloons and camps along the road. After arriving in California, he secured a job as a broadcaster for radio station KFVD in Los Angeles, singing "old-time" traditional songs. These he supplemented with his own compositions. His songs and radio commentary showed a strong social consciousness, especially over the plight of the Okies and the need for union organization. He also grew close to the Communist Party and began a regular column, "Woody Sez," for the party newspaper *People's World*. With his partner Cisco Houston, Guthrie toured migrant worker camps to sing and build support for unionization.

Even as he fought prejudice against Okies and Arkies, Guthrie became conscious of discrimination against nonwhite Americans, including Chinese and Japanese Americans. As he later put it, "I met and seen the Japanese farm families, watched them crawl on their knees through the worst patches of land, and turn that land into the richest land by hard work.... They gave me water and wine to drink. I played my guitar in ten dozen Japanese taverns and cafes all over Frisco, Sacramento, Stockton, Los Angeles."

Guthrie became controversial for his uncritical support for the Communist Party following the signing of the non-aggression pact between Nazi Germany and the Soviet Union in August 1939. He left California in early 1940 and moved to New York. There he was taken up by leftist and progressive intellectuals. He recorded a series of ballads for Alan Lomax, the celebrated folklorist at the Library of Congress, and released an album, *Dust Bowl Ballads*, for RCA Victor. It was at this time that he wrote "This Land is Your Land," which would become an unofficial, alternative national anthem. Guthrie joined a loose group of politically informed folksingers, the Almanac Singers, who produced songs about current events. Another prominent member was Pete Seeger, with whom Guthrie would develop a lasting partnership.

In 1941 Guthrie spent several months sojourning in the Pacific Northwest (hired by the New Deal–era Bonneville Power Administration, he produced the classic songs "Roll on Columbia" and "Grand Coulee Dam"). After a brief stop in Texas, he made his way back to New York. During World War II Guthrie was based in New York but did singing tours and served in the merchant marine and the army. In 1942 he met Marjorie Mazia. In the ensuing years, they would marry and have four children, among them the folk musician Arlo Guthrie.

It was during the war years that Guthrie deepened his relationship with Japanese Americans. He was attracted by the Nisei newspaper *Pacific Citizen*—and by its dynamic editor Larry Tajiri, though they would never meet. In June 1942, in his very first issue, Tajiri lamented that Nisei did not have the same folk music tradition as groups such as blacks or Okies, who could turn the adversity of forced migration into song. Tajiri cited Guthrie as his model. "Woody Guthrie, an evacuee out of the parched lands of the Dust Bowl, sang 'I'm Going down the Road Feeling Bad,' wrote his 'Dust Bowl Ballads' which are already as much a part of American music as the spirituals from the deep south." Guthrie, impressed by the plight of the Nisei, became an early *Pacific Citizen* subscriber. He also got to know members of New York's antifascist Japanese American Committee for Democracy, presumably through Toshi Aline Ohta, the wife of his friend Pete Seeger. Guthrie and the well-known folksinger Leadbelly would later perform at a JACD dance.

Meanwhile Guthrie found another way to demonstrate his solidarity. In his fictionalized 1943 autobiography *Bound for Glory* he reported that on the evening of December 7, 1941, he was singing in a bar in Los Angeles's Skid Row when he heard glass breaking. When he rushed out to investigate, he discovered that a mob, infuriated by the Japanese attack, had broken the plate-glass window of a neighboring Japanese restaurant. Guthrie's partner Cisco Houston, aware of the loyalty of Japanese Americans, defended them to the mob, saying "These little Japanese farmers that you see up and down the country here, and these Japanese people that run the little old cafés and gin joints, they can't help it because they happen to be Japanese." With help from a group of passing soldiers and sailors, they made a human barricade to protect the restaurant from the mob. Or so Guthrie's story went. As Larry Tajiri later reported, "The incident never happened. In just that way, anyway. Woody says he made it up just so he could show people how he felt about the mass evacuation of Japanese Americans and prejudice against them there on the coast."

Even after joining the army, Guthrie remained interested in Japanese Americans. In January 1946 he published an editorial in the *Pacific Citizen* entitled "Take It Easy—but Take It!" In the article Guthrie wrote with passionate sympathy about the continuing struggle against "racial fascism" in America and the central importance of folk music as a tool for unity. "My accent is Negro and Indian and Scotch, heavy on the last, but I am just as proud of my Negro and Indian ways as I am of the Scotch." Guthrie challenged the Nisei to write songs that would serve as an authentic expression of their struggles and experiences. "So you see. You see how your story of the Japanese American workers, soldiers, artists and scholars, blends and molds into the union struggle to go ahead and wipe all traces of racial fascism out of our nation's eye, and out of the whole world. I don't know of anybody anywhere that has got a better story to sing than you folks, Japanese Americans everywhere. If you had five albums of hard-hitting records out on the shelves of the music stores or in books a thousand songs, I would buy and sing them all."

In 1946, after being discharged, Guthrie returned to Brooklyn and continued his writing, singing, and activism. He continued subscribing to the *Pacific Citizen*—a 1949 article on Guthrie noted that it was part of his regular reading. He also corresponded with Larry Tajiri and his wife Guyo. In a 1946 letter Guthrie thanked Tajiri for sending him material about Joe Hill, the martyred labor organizer who was subject of the famed 1939 Earl Robinson song. Guthrie enclosed the lyrics of his own song about Hill.

Two years later the *Pacific Citizen* ran Guthrie's brief review of a recital by Nisei dancer Yuriko Amemiya (later Kikuchi), a member of Martha Graham's troupe. (Guthrie was likely inspired to attend by his wife Marjorie, herself a onetime Martha Graham dancer.) The review, couched in folksy, almost Mark Twain–like prose, may have originally formed part of a letter: "Yuriko did a fine job in front of a set made up and lighted for her by Isamu Noguchi. The set needed to change around, light up, or do something instead of stay lit one way through her whole dance. Yuriko is little and quick as a cat and moves by habit in this way. She can squirm and twist around on the floor in her fits and seizures and make you like it as a dance. I like any move she makes."

In the early 1950s, even as he faced McCarthy-era blacklisting, Guthrie's behavior became increasingly erratic. In November 1952, in one of his last public appearances, Guthrie performed at a folk festival at the First Unitarian Church in Los Angeles. Among the others on the program was Sue Kunitomi Embrey—the future founder of the annual pilgrimage to Manzanar. In 1954 Guthrie checked himself into a hospital. There he was diagnosed with Huntington's Disease, the degenerative nerve disorder that had struck his mother. Guthrie passed his last years in the hospital and died in 1967. By that time, he had become a spiritual godfather to the folk music movement, including such notables as Bob Dylan and Phil Ochs. His support for Japanese Americans, long obscure, provides yet another dimension to his humanitarian interests and love of democracy.

Forrest LaViolette and the Paradoxes of Wartime Confinement

Forrest LaViolette (sometimes written La Violette), a sociologist and product of the famed Chicago School, was one of the first scholars to focus on Japanese Americans. This led him to involve himself in various ways with Japanese communities, but the relation between theory and practice led him to some paradoxical actions.

Forrest LaViolette, circa 1960.
Courtesy of Tulane University.

LaViolette was born in 1904 and grew up in Oregon. His older brother was Dr. Wesley LaViolette, a noted jazz composer and teacher. After serving several years as a radio operator in the merchant marine and on a trans-pacific ocean liner, Forrest LaViolette enrolled at Portland's Reed College, where he received a BA in anthropology in 1933. After entering the graduate program in sociology at University of Chicago, he turned his focus to Japanese Americans. His West Coast background doubtless influenced this, as did professors such as Robert Park. Chicago's Sociology Department was the brain center of research on "Oriental Americans." LaViolette began a doctoral thesis on "the assimilation of the American-born Japanese."

In the fall of 1936 LaViolette was named instructor in sociology at the University of Washington (UW). In order to absorb his subject firsthand, he became active in Seattle's Nisei community. LaViolette was drawn to a UW graduate student in sociology, Shotaro Frank Miyamoto, on whom he relied for community contacts and insights into Nisei life. The two became such close collaborators that Miyamoto rented a house together with LaViolette and his wife. The unorthodox arrangement was productive: during this period LaViolette wrote his dissertation, while in 1939 Miyamoto published "Social Solidarity among the Japanese in Seattle," arguably the first scholarly article by a Nisei. In the summer of 1938 LaViolette published his own first scholarly article of sorts in the *Japanese American Courier*. The article urged the government to repeal unequal laws against Japanese Americans and to fund social service organizations to reduce social stigma and encourage racial and cultural pluralism.

LaViolette completed his dissertation in January 1940. His thesis was that social integration of Nisei was not only an interracial problem, like that of blacks, but also an international one. US-Japanese relations, he contended, would determine progress toward the ultimate (and implicitly desirable) goal of absorption of Japanese Americans into mainstream society. Once his dissertation was accepted, LaViolette started transforming it into a book. However, as war loomed and suspicion of Japanese Americans increased, two publishers who had agreed to publish the book canceled his contract, one after another.

In the fall of 1940 LaViolette was named assistant professor of sociology at McGill University in Montreal. Local newspapers reporting his arrival described him as an expert on "the yellow peril." In interviews and scholarly articles LaViolette warned that a Pacific war would be deadly for the Nisei. "By Japanese novelists the second generation has been portrayed as a tragic character, neither fully Japanese nor accepted by Americans . . . yet expected to fight for America. Rumors have it that the *Nisei* would be the first to be sent to the front; others say they will be sent to concentration camps. One *Nisei* told the writer that he was 'fattening' himself up for the 'long lean days behind barb wire.'"

LaViolette was midway through his second year at McGill when war broke out. He made no public protest during 1942, as ethnic Japanese on the Pacific Coast of the United States and Canada were rounded up and confined, though he continued to correspond privately with Nisei friends. In mid-1943 LaViolette took a leave of absence from McGill and spent six months at Heart Mountain as an administrator and community analyst for the WRA. He remained oddly silent and defensive about the camps. After returning to Montreal, he claimed, "Conditions are now so good in relocation centers that there are practically no grievances." Food conditions were "highly satisfactory," and barracks provided "adequate shelter during even the most extreme weather conditions." In a book review published in 1944, LaViolette praised government efforts to atone for the wrong of "evacuation" by concentrating on assimilating Japanese Americans. Nowhere did he mention that Japanese Americans were still confined en masse. LaViolette's silence about this was especially palpable in his 1945 book *Americans of Japanese Ancestry*, adapted from his dissertation. The book concentrated entirely on prewar Nisei life, even though the war had completely transformed Japanese communities; LaViolette did not even mention the camps.

He was similarly cautious in confronting the wartime exile of Japanese Canadians. In 1942 and 1944 LaViolette published largely factual articles on Canadian evacuation for *Far Eastern Survey*. Both described the history of anti-Japanese prejudice in British Columbia and the pressures that led the federal government to issue the Orders in Council exiling Japanese Canadians from the Pacific Coast. However, LaViolette refused to criticize the exclusion of Japanese Canadians or the government's notorious confiscation and sale of their property—a policy that left those already victimized by persecution financially destitute. When McGill publicly refused admission to Nisei students in fall 1944, LaViolette apparently encouraged student resistance measures behind the scenes, but he made no recorded protest.

Yet despite this silence LaViolette soon emerged as a major supporter of Japanese Canadians and their citizenship rights. In February 1945 he gave a public lecture in which he criticized the government's seizure of the property of Japanese Canadians. The following year, LaViolette helped found the Montreal Committee on Canadian Citizenship, a civil rights group that helped defeat the government's plan to deport to Japan ten thousand Japanese Canadians in western provinces who refused to relocate east. LaViolette also helped find jobs and housing for Nisei in Montreal and published a groundbreaking sociological study, *The Canadian Japanese and World War II* (1948).

In 1949 LaViolette moved to Tulane University. He remained there until retirement in 1969. He subsequently returned to Oregon, and his later work focused on Native peoples in British Columbia and housing for African Americans. (In a prophetic 1957 article he warned of the flood risk to that low-lying black districts in New Orleans.) He ceased writing on Japanese Americans and Japanese Canadians, apart from several book reviews. These were marked by his old defensiveness. In one piece he commented that the "momentous and egregious" wartime removal had been fueled by West Coast prejudices but denied that "the Relocation Centers" were concentration camps, saying, "Administrators quickly came to appreciate the social psychological personal expressions of evacuees [and worked] correcting the errors of the democratic process."

LaViolette died in 1989, and I learned about him after I moved to Montreal to teach history. I was amazed to learn that LaViolette, a US sociologist who wrote about Japanese Americans and Japanese Canadians, had taught at McGill. This made him a kind of intellectual ancestor in my mind. I have spent the years since reflecting on his contribution. LaViolette's work on Japanese Americans remains innovative and informative, but his silences on their wartime removal are mysterious.

CHAPTER FIVE

Political Activism and Civil Rights

Clifford Uyeda and Ben Kuroki: Nisei Conservatives

One extraordinary trend in recent years is the eclipse of Japanese Americans in the Republican Party. Alan Nakanishi, the sole Nikkei Republican in the California Assembly, left office in 2008. Beth Fukumoto of Hawai'i, who was the state's House Minority Leader from 2014 to 2017, ended up resigning from her position and quitting the Republican Party, whose leaders she denounced for intolerance of interparty dissent (most notably her opposition to Donald Trump's treatment of women and minorities). In 2018 Fukumoto ran unsuccessfully for Congress as a Democrat (she was defeated in the primary election). Although Bob Sakata, an elderly Japanese American farmer from Colorado, was invited to address the Republican National Convention in August 2012, there were no Japanese American delegates present. Francis Fukuyama, a renowned and visible neoconservative intellectual of the 1990s, publicly supported Barack Obama in 2008 and subsequently announced that he was withdrawing his Republican affiliation from his voter registration. In 2017 he declared that while as a political scientist he was intrigued by the phenomenon of Donald Trump, as a citizen he found Trump appalling.

Sgt. Ben Kuroki making a post-war speech in 1945, sharing the podium with Gen. Omar Bradley, Lt. Gen. Jimmy Doolittle, and others. San Diego Air and Space Museum Archives.

It must be stressed that this was not always the case. Rather, throughout the long twentieth century, Japanese Americans remained active in the Grand Old Party. In Hawai'i numerous Nisei built their careers through it. Tasaku Oka, who in 1930 became one of the first two ethnic Japanese in the Hawai'i territorial legislature, was a Republican. So was Wilfred Tsukiyama, elected to the territorial senate in 1946, who became the first chief justice of the Hawai'i Supreme Court in 1959. In 1986 Patricia Saiki was elected to the first of two terms in the U.S. House of Representatives.

In prewar California, where the Democratic Party was long dominated by anti-Asian newspaper mogul William Randolph Hearst, there was also a heavy Republican bent among educated and upwardly mobile Nisei professionals. In Washington State Clarence Arai, a founder of the Japanese American Citizens League, ran unsuccessfully for the state legislature on the Republican ticket in 1933. And in 1940 Saburo Kido of San Francisco, who later became the JACL's wartime president, headed the Nisei Republicans who supported Wendell Willkie's failed presidential candidacy. Straw polls (admittedly unscientific) conducted by Nisei newspapers in 1936 and 1940 showed a decided preference for Republicans among their readers.

In the years after World War II, however, Democrats became more prominent among Japanese Americans, despite the stain of Franklin Roosevelt's signing of Executive Order 9066. Nisei in Hawai'i (led by 442nd Regiment veterans), working in alliance with labor unions, provided a transformed Democratic Party with a mass electoral base, and their march to power crested with the election of Daniel Inouye as US senator in 1962. On the mainland the JACL found Democrats generally more sympathetic to its civil rights agenda.

Nevertheless, some outstanding figures, such as attorney John Aiso and activist lawyer Minoru Yasui, continued to endorse Republicans. The GOP, in turn, sponsored various community members, first for positions on city councils and school boards, then for higher office. In 1961 Seiji Horiuchi of Colorado became the first mainland Nisei elected to a state legislature. Twelve years later, drawing on heavy community support, Paul Bannai became California's first Japanese American assemblyman. In 1976 S. I. Hayakawa of California became the first—and so far only—mainland Japanese American elected to the US Senate. However, he generally remained aloof from Japanese communities, and many Nisei criticized his outspoken opposition to redress.

It was during the 1960s that a rightward movement became visible among Republicans, a shift symbolized by Barry Goldwater's presidential candidacy in 1964 and by the election of Goldwater's supporter Ronald Reagan as California governor two years later. While some Nisei were alienated by the conservative drift in the GOP, two legendary figures in the Japanese community reaffirmed their Republican allegiance and expressed conservative positions during these years.

The first was Clifford Iwao Uyeda. Born in Olympia, Washington, Uyeda grew up in Tacoma. He attended the University of Wisconsin, then enrolled at Tulane University in New Orleans. Uyeda intended to transfer to Boston University's Medical School, but his offer of admission was rescinded after Pearl Harbor, and he remained at Tulane for his medical education. After interning in Boston and serving as a medical officer during the Korean War, he settled in San Francisco and rose to the position of chief pediatrician for the Kaiser Permanente Medical Group.

After 1960 Uyeda undertook a larger community role, first as researcher for the Japanese American Research Project, then as president of the JACL's San Francisco chapter. In the late 1960s he became a prominent champion of the founding of Asian American studies. During the civil rights movement, however, he took public positions in support of Republicans and against racial integration. In November 1961 he stated dubiously that

Japanese Americans had overcome far greater discrimination than present-day "Negroes" without sharing blacks' "excessive crime rate," and he asserted that "the re-education of the minority groups themselves towards better citizenship" was more important than legislation in fostering equality.[1] In June 1963, after *Hokubei Mainichi* editor Howard Imazeki stirred controversy by calling on African Americans to improve their own communities before asking for equal rights, Uyeda wrote to the newspaper in support. Given what he called "the sordid record of violence and crime" in black communities, he questioned whether blacks could be trusted to be good neighbors if housing was integrated.[2] In early 1967 he criticized the JACL's then-president Jerry Enomoto, who had called for supporting human rights of other minorities. Uyeda complained that, as he saw it, the crusade for human rights (and implicitly civil rights for African Americans) was a matter of minorities vengefully striking out with hate and resentment of the majority group, in the process "pushing for one's own human dignity and rights by destroying the same for others."[3] The following month, the JACL denounced the University of California proposal to abandon its free tuition policy, as it might limit Nikkei educational achievement. Uyeda wrote in support of Republican proposals for tuition charges and criticized JACL leaders for interfering as Democrats in partisan battles. The tuition question, he insisted, could not be considered a civil rights matter of the kind that JACL was empowered to handle.[4]

The other prominent Nisei conservative was Ben Kuroki. Born in 1917 in Gothenburg, Nebraska, Kuroki grew up in nearby Hershey. Following the Japanese attack on Pearl Harbor in December 1941, Kuroki enlisted in the US Army. Though warned that Nisei would not be accepted for overseas service, Kuroki fought successfully, first to be shipped to England, then to attend gunnery school. He flew thirty missions in Europe as a turret gunner on B-24 Liberators. In recognition of his heroism, he was awarded the Distinguished Flying Cross. In 1944 Kuroki was shipped back to the United States. When the draft resister movement threatened to impede Nisei enlistment in the army, Kuroki toured the WRA camps to promote military service. He requested transfer to the Pacific Theater, and permission was granted by special order of Secretary of War Henry L. Stimson.

Kuroki flew twenty-eight missions in B-29 Superfortress bombers over Japanese-held territory. After being discharged, Kuroki immediately launched what he called his "59th mission": displaying a new kind of heroism, he undertook a lecture tour of the United States in which he denounced anti-Semitism and racial segregation and called for fair housing and equal employment laws for blacks and other minorities.

In 1946 Kuroki collaborated with journalist Ralph G. Martin on a biography, *Boy from Nebraska*. The book enjoyed large sales, particularly an armed forces edition. Not only did it win Kuroki further fame, but it also helped inspire him to take up a career in journalism. With his wife, Shige, he enrolled in journalism school at University of Nebraska. Over the years that followed he purchased and edited a series of newspapers, including the *York (NE) Republican*, the *Blackfoot (ID) Daily Bulletin*, and two Michigan newspapers, the *Williamston Enterprise* and the *Meridian News*.

In mid-July 1964, just days after President Lyndon Johnson signed the landmark 1964 Civil Rights Act, the JACL held its semiannual convention in Detroit and focused on civil rights. NAACP leader Roy Wilkins was the principal speaker, and the JACL presented awards to past defenders of equal rights for Japanese Americans. Ben Kuroki, by this time a Michigan resident, received a scroll of appreciation, but the appreciation soon dissolved. Many Nisei were shocked when Kuroki, the old advocate of civil rights, announced his support for Barry Goldwater, who had voted against the Civil Rights Act. Moreover, Kuroki put together a leaflet for distribution in California urging local Nisei to vote Republican. In the advertisement he mentioned his JACL scroll of appreciation.

The timing was especially unfortunate. During the fall of 1964 the JACL was engaged in fighting Proposition 14, an ultimately successful initiative to repeal fair housing legislation. The initiative was backed by the California Republican Party and by Goldwaterites. The JACL devoted massive resources to the "No on 14" campaign and even published a special issue of the *Pacific Citizen* devoted to persuading its members to oppose it. While Kuroki did not explicitly mention Proposition 14 in his Goldwater endorsement, the JACL leadership demanded that Kuroki remove all mention of his award from the leaflet. Kuroki, in turn, complained that JACL leaders had breached their duty to be nonpartisan, saying, "I thought the JACL was for Nisei getting involved in politics."

In 1965 Kuroki sold his Michigan newspapers and moved to the West Coast, where he was hired by the *Ventura County Star-Free Press*. In February 1967 Kuroki was invited to address a meeting of the JACL Pacific Southwest District Council. Kuroki boasted of his Republican Party affiliation and reiterated his previous support for Goldwater. Moreover, he harshly criticized interracial marriage. "We're losing our Japanese heritage through intermarriage," he stated, and he said that Japanese American college students seemed to prefer dating "blondes" and "were getting a little bit too good for our own kind."[5] Although Kuroki did not speak in favor of legal bans on interracial marriage, his position seemed retrograde, especially when the JACL was preparing legal arguments for the US Supreme Court case *Loving v. Virginia*, which challenged miscegenation laws. His remarks shocked several listeners and provoked uneasy laughter.

After the 1960s Clifford Uyeda and Ben Kuroki had very different subsequent career trajectories. Uyeda became renowned as a progressive community activist. In 1973 he helped direct the movement to win a pardon for Iva Toguri D'Aquino, a Nisei who had worked in Japan during World War II and been convicted of treason as "Tokyo Rose." Uyeda likewise actively supported the Japanese American redress movement, although he did not stand to benefit personally, as he had been spared confinement. In October 1978, in order to further redress, Uyeda won election as JACL national president, and he then served for two years. During the 1990s he became an advocate for the wartime Nisei draft resisters. He lobbied the JACL to release Deborah Lim's 1990 report on JACL wartime actions and to apologize for them. Uyeda died on July 30, 2004.

Ben Kuroki worked at the *Star-Free Press* until his retirement in 1984. In a letter to the *Los Angeles Times* published shortly after Congress passed the Civil Liberties Act of 1988, Kuroki offered public praise for redress (for which he, like Uyeda, was ineligible). Kuroki nonetheless remained out of the public spotlight. Many years later, amid celebrations of World War II soldiers as "the Greatest Generation," Kuroki's wartime exploits were newly celebrated, most notably in a 2005 documentary film, *Most Honorable Son*. Kuroki died in 2015.

Japanese Americans and the McCarran-Walter Act

The McCarran-Walter Act was enacted in the summer 1952, at the height of McCarthyism. A product of Cold War xenophobia and exaggerated concerns over "security," it gave the federal government new powers to exclude or deport aliens suspected of subversive tendencies. Conversely, it overturned the exclusion of Japanese immigrants, providing Japan a token immigration quota, and granted naturalization rights to Issei, allowing them for the first time to claim American citizenship. Because the latter two were the primary postwar goals of the Japanese American Citizens League, the organization's leaders gave the bill their support. The JACL's position provoked a rare moment of large-scale debate in the Japanese community over civil rights for all versus individual group advancement.

In January 1950, Minnesota Republican congressman Walter Judd (who had sponsored a series of unsuccessful measures to liberalize immigration) teamed with conservative Pennsylvania Democrat Francis Walter to introduce a resolution abolishing race and ethnicity as factors in naturalization. After passage by the House and in modified form in the Senate, it was ultimately twinned with a bill, sponsored by conservative Nevada senator Pat McCarran, that placed numerous restrictions on civil liberties. Soon after, the New York Nisei weekly *Hokubei Shimpo* printed an article by Abner Green of the left-leaning American Committee for Protection of Foreign Born. Green strongly opposed the bill, noting that one measure enabled the Justice Department to hold noncitizens without bail for an unlimited period, while another excluded all immigrants who belonged to organizations on the attorney general's list of "subversive organizations" created under the 1950 McCarran Internal Security Act (notably the Communist Party USA) and gave the federal government authority to strip naturalized US citizens of their citizenship if they belonged to any of those organizations.

Soon after, Mike Masaoka, chair of the JACL's Anti-Discrimination Committee (ADC), responsible for civil rights legislation, announced that the ADC would wait to take a position on the bill until its legal counsel had had a chance to study it. In May 1950 JACL counsel Edward Ennis delivered his analysis. Ennis pointed to several objectionable features of the bill. One of the worst provisions was that it changed immigration policy to incorporate preferences for entry by skilled immigrants and for family reunification (preferences that have ruled immigration law ever since). Not more than 10 percent of a country's overall quota could be used for any immigrant outside these preferred classes. This automatically disadvantaged Asian immigrants. Despite the critical report, the JACL failed to take an official position.

The bill passed both houses of Congress, but in September 1950 President Truman vetoed it, charging that the security provisions added in conference were so "vague and ill-defined" as to weaken the nation's immigration laws and endanger the right of naturalized citizens. Truman explained that he supported removal of discrimination against Asian immigrants but proposed that Congress reconsider the resolution stripped of the objectionable security provisions. The *Hokubei Shimpo* reported that Washington JACL counsel I. H. Gordon immediately wired President Truman the organization's support for his proposal. The House voted to override the president's veto, but the Senate failed to act before Congress adjourned, and the Walter-Judd resolution was killed for the 81st Congress.

In January 1951 the new 82nd Congress was convened. The former Walter-Judd resolution and parts of the McCarran bill were folded into a larger omnibus bill on immigration and naturalization, HR 5678 (for partisan reasons, Speaker Sam Rayburn insisted that the bill carry only Walter's name rather than Judd's too). In addition to opening up naturalization for the first time to Japanese aliens, the bill provided a tiny immigration quota to Asian immigrants (135 from Japan, 100 from other nations). However, the bill reinscribed the existing "national quota" system, devised in the 1920s, by which nationals of foreign countries were assigned differing immigration quotas in what amounted to a racist hierarchy of desirability, with Great Britain and other "white" western European nations having the highest quotas and Asian and African nations the smallest. Indeed, the bill imposed quotas for the first time on immigration by West Indian blacks, who had formerly been completely unrestricted, and counted all immigrants of Asian ancestry by race rather than citizenship (so that Hong Kong Chinese and other British nationals of Asian ancestry could not come in under the UK's spacious and largely unused national quota).

Worst of all, the bill denied entry to all present and former Communist Party members and allowed the US government to deport and bar from reentry those it identified as subversives. The bill also authorized the government to strip aliens of their citizenship if within five years of naturalization they were found to have been members of "or affiliated with" any proscribed organizations.

In April 1952 *Hokubei Shimpo* criticized the McCarran-Walter Bill in a stinging editorial, presumably written by then-editor Dyke Miyagawa, a former union activist. Miyagawa recommended that his readers study Alex Brooks's article in *The Nation*, "McCarran's Iron Curtain," an extended analysis of the bill's provisions. In considering the relegating of all people of Asian ancestry to "racial" quotas, the editorial remarked, "The hand of racial prejudice shows here." It concluded, "A bill that has aroused so much opposition and controversy remains suspect."

The bill proceeded through a long set of hearings. Liberal opponents of the restrictive clauses, led by Hubert Humphrey and Herbert Lehman, proposed an amendment to strip the bill of the denaturalization provisions. The Humphrey-Lehman Amendment, while not doing away with discriminatory national quotas, would have at least eliminated expressly race-based and sex-based quotas and allowed for pooling of unused visa slots. (McCarran rejected any liberalized version of the measure, though as a sop he agreed that mixed-race children could be charged against the national quota of either parent). On April 26, 1952, the House voted 206 to 68 to approve the bill. It was then sent to the Senate, which passed the McCarran version in mid-May 1952. The two bills were then once more merged, and then the bill was sent to the White House.

The JACL responded positively to the bill's passage. Mike Masaoka hailed the measure in the *Pacific Citizen* as a major step toward eliminating Japanese exclusion, insisting that the ADC's chief interest was in securing passage "without further delay." Five days later, the *Pacific Citizen* reported that JACL national president Randolph Sakada had wired Senator McCarran to pledge the unqualified support of the JACL.

The JACL's action sparked a wave of criticism. One week after Sakada's message, a group called the New York Nisei Progressives published a statement in *Hokubei Shimpo* opposing the bill: "Senator McCarran, Chairman

Walter et al would sell us racism in the name of progress. If these gentle-men were truly dedicated to liberalizing our present immigration laws, why do they not sponsor a simple measure granting immigration and naturalization rights to the peoples now denied them?" The Nisei group initiated a telegram and letter campaign asking President Truman to veto the bill, which its press release described as "racist and reactionary."[6] National JACL vice president Thomas Hayashi responded immediately and negatively, urging passage, claiming, "Half a loaf is better than none." The Nisei Progressives retorted that half a loaf was not better when that loaf was obtained by Japanese and other Asians at a heavy cost to other minority groups.

On June 25 Truman vetoed the new omnibus immigration bill, since it discriminated against people of Asian ancestry and interfered with freedom of religion. Truman called on Congress to abolish the national origins sys-tem and end racial barriers to immigration. Truman likewise stated that the deportation provisions were so vague as to amount to "thought control." Both major party presidential candidates, Democrat Adlai Stevenson and Republican Dwight Eisenhower, likewise expressed their public opposition to the bill.

Following Truman's veto, *Chicago Shimpo* editor Ryoichi Fujii published an editorial congratulating the president on his "courageous" action. How-ever, JACL fixer Mike Masaoka issued a public statement: "We are bitterly disappointed. The President's action shows that he has been misguided about the measure." In the succeeding days, the JACL, which was holding its biennial convention in San Francisco, sent messages lobbying Congress to override the president's veto. They were joined by the American Legion and other conservative groups (some with openly anti-Semitic platforms, critics charged). In contrast, several liberal and civil rights groups with which the JACL had long been associated—the AFL, the CIO, ACLU, the National Council of the Churches of Christ, the Quaker Friends Commit-tee on National Legislation, and others—strongly opposed the bill.

On June 27, 1952, the McCarran-Walter Act was enacted by Congress, overriding Truman's veto. According to an account by New York City JACL chair Aki Hayashi, the group's national council was meeting when word came that Congress had overridden the president's veto and enacted the law. Hayashi recounted how the members of the council unashamedly shed tears of joy. Mike Masaoka received a hero's welcome at the convention—and stated that the job he had set out to do was complete; he announced that he was resigning from the ADC. Masaoka later admitted that he felt inner conflict over the bill: "We had to wrestle with our conscience." His legislative assistant Richard Akagi, in contrast, remained more sanguine. In a speech to the Institute of Human Relations in Washington, DC, he announced, "We are faced with two alternatives. Either we accept the remedial change offered by the omnibus bill or get no improvements at all in the immediate future, since the Congress of the United States has clearly indicated that the reforms advocated by those opposed to the Walter-McCarran bill are unacceptable."

JACL support for the final bill, it must be said, was a rather negligible factor in its passage, but the organization's action remained controversial. The social democratic journal *New Leader* remarked, "The JACL can dispense with future support from those liberals who would be aghast to learn they have been supporting new racist bars and breaking down old constitutional rights." In the Nisei press, there was likewise dissent. In the August 1952 issue of the Chicago-based *Scene* (the Nisei knockoff of *Life*), editor Togo Tanaka accused the JACL of taking an expedient action. Tanaka gladly acknowledged that its strategy was brilliant for short-term gain, but he said that it might have been too high a price if it meant that the Nisei damaged their relations with the groups that had helped them emerge from "mass evacuation." Tanaka's editorial sparked a storm of letters to the editor in the October 1952 issue, with about half congratulating him on his stand but questioning (with good reason) whether liberal groups would actually remain estranged. The other half attacked him. His critics did not distinguish themselves by their arguments. One insisted, "To say the anti-Semites were lined up with the JACL in support of the . . . bill deserves a rebuttal. The communists were lined up against it. So what?" Another writer accused Tanaka of being biased against the ADC and minimizing its achievements. One Nisei from Florida stated (no doubt facetiously), "We shore is mighty proud that we, red-blooded Nisei, now stand with all other red-blooded organizations." Tanaka continued his attacks on the law and the JACL's support in his column in *Colorado Times*.

Meanwhile, in September 1952, gadfly semanticist (and former newspaper columnist) S. I. Hayakawa released to the Nisei journal *Chicago Shimpo* a copy of a letter to the JACL publicly denouncing its support for the McCarran-Walter Immigration Act. Hayakawa accused the JACL of supporting a "heartless," repressive bill and putting its own group interest ahead of those who would be damaged by the law. "To secure the rights to naturalization of Issei at the cost of all the questionable and illiberal features of the McCarran-Walter Bill appears to be an act of unpardonable shortsightedness or cynical opportunism." Hayakawa therefore announced that he would no longer contribute to ADC. "I am afraid the Anti-Discrimination Committee has not lived up to its name. It has purchased the removal of one small discrimination at the cost of legalizing the continuance of many other forms of discrimination, and the creation of a number of new forms of discrimination against foreign-born and second generation citizens of all ancestries." As a Canadian citizen of Japanese ancestry, Hayakawa was barred from US naturalization. His opposition therefore represented an impressive statement of principle. (After passage of McCarran-Walter, Hayakawa rapidly became a US citizen.)

In October 1952 the President's Commission on Immigration and Naturalization held hearings in Washington, DC. Richard Akagi praised the law and termed all criticism of its provisions "premature." He grandly suggested that if subsequently any injustice appeared, the JACL would join the protest. He did not, however, target either the cutoff of West Indian immigration or the larger racial aspects of the system. In response to questions about the national origins clauses, Akagi testified, "The national origin principle is clearly racist in conception and the JACL certainly does not approve of it, but it is also obvious that no one has been able to suggest a counter-system which would be workable and equitable at this time." Hayakawa again criticized the law in *Chicago Shimpo*, noting its expanded provisions for denaturalization, and deplored Akagi's failure to call for correction even of the undesirable features the JACL had swallowed in order to attain passage. "If he felt that the act was not perfect, he had then the opportunity to point out its imperfections and to suggest improvements. Instead he spoke in favor of the act, while 12 or 13 other witnesses appearing that day representing important scientific, religious, and nationality groups testified against it."

Akagi rather lamely responded that he did not speak in favor of the act but had simply said that he supported it.[7]

The McCarran-Walter Act proved wildly popular among Japanese Americans—one Nisei couple even named their newborn son McCarran Walter Ono. In the next years, Issei came in droves to acquire US citizenship. Togo Tanaka soon regretted his quixotic opposition to the law, but S. I. Hayakawa remained steadfast. Publicly questioning how the JACL could henceforth consider itself a civil rights organization, he withdrew from involvement. (Ironically, Hayakawa would reconnect with the JACL in the late 1960s when he was president of San Francisco State University— and opposing student protesters.)

For Japanese Americans, passage of the McCarran-Walter Act finally extinguished most legal discrimination against them (though laws against white-Asian intermarriage remained in some states until the Supreme Court's *Loving v. Virginia* decision fifteen years later). For the JACL, support for McCarran-Walter represented a break with the organization's liberal allies in the ACLU and pro-immigrant groups, and especially with the NAACP, which was bitterly disappointed by the closing of the nation's doors to African and West Indian immigrants. The break marked an important stage in the JACL's evolution toward an essentially conservative and accommodationist stance during the 1950s, based on patriotic values and cultivation of moderate and even conservative allies.

Loren Miller: African American Defender of Japanese Americans

Loren Miller (1903–67), an African American attorney and newspaperman from Los Angeles, worked to build American democracy during a career that spanned almost forty years. Although Miller worked with the National Lawyers Guild and numerous other organizations, he made his most lasting contributions as a civil rights lawyer during the 1930s and 1940s in association with the National Association for the Advancement of Colored People

(NAACP) and the American Civil Liberties Union. In addition to his primary work on behalf of African Americans, Miller's efforts as a defender of Japanese Americans deserve extended study.

Born in Nebraska and raised in Kansas, Loren Miller arrived in California in 1930 after his graduation from Washburn College of Law in Topeka, Kansas. Despite the privations of the Great Depression, he launched a successful law practice in Los Angeles's growing black community. Miller's activism was not restricted to legal matters but also extended to journalism and other writing. Miller was a regular contributor to the local African American weekly *California Eagle* and served as city editor. He also assisted his cousin Leon Washington in launching a rival newspaper, the *Los Angeles Sentinel*, and produced articles for journals such as *The Nation* and the NAACP's *Crisis*. Miller likewise wrote poetry and moved in literary circles. After visiting the USSR with his close friend Langston Hughes in 1932, he coedited an anthology of Russian-language translations of African American poetry.

During World War II Miller became a nationally recognized specialist in the field of housing discrimination law, with a focus on restrictive residential covenants—private agreements not to lease or sell houses to minority groups. These agreements closed off much of urban areas to nonwhite residents and led to overpopulated ghettoes. In the 1944 California case *Fairchild v. Raines* and the 1945 "Sugar Hill" case in Los Angeles, Miller brought the first successful legal challenges to the use of restrictive covenants against African Americans. As a result, national NAACP counsel Thurgood Marshall invited Miller to join the NAACP's legal team. Miller served as NAACP chief counsel in *Shelley v. Kraemer*, the landmark 1948 Supreme Court case in which the court struck down legal enforcement of restrictive covenants as unconstitutional. Not only was the case a blow against housing discrimination, the court's reasoning also served as a major precedent for the *Brown v. Board of Education* case six years later. After the victory in *Shelley*, Miller was named head of the NAACP's West Coast Regional Legal Committee, where he continued to fight housing segregation and employment discrimination cases. He also served as counsel in the landmark 1948 *Perez v. Sharp* case, which struck down California's laws against interracial marriage.

At the same time, like his older colleague Hugh E. Macbeth, Miller threw himself he into defending Japanese Americans, in the face of widespread wartime hostility against them. His first major contact with Japanese Americans was in the 1943 federal court case *Regan v. King*, which involved a suit by white nativists to strip Nisei of voting and citizenship rights. Miller signed the ACLU's amicus brief. He also signed the habeas corpus petition of Ernest Kinzo and Toki Wakayama, a Nisei couple who in mid-1942 challenged their confinement under Executive Order 9066. In the years after World War II, Miller worked to ensure harmonious relations between Japanese Americans returning to Los Angeles and their black neighbors in areas such as Little Tokyo/Bronzeville.

During this period, Miller joined JACL counsel A. L. Wirin to build an effective alliance for civil rights. Miller was of counsel on *People v. Oyama*, the case that challenged escheat suits to take land away from Japanese American owners. The case climaxed in the notable 1948 Supreme Court case *Oyama v. California*. The court's ruling in the case not only struck down alien land laws but also established the court's doctrine of "strict scrutiny" of racial classifications. Miller also served as counsel in *Takahashi v. California Fish and Game Commission*, which challenged discriminatory fishing license laws. The case led to another landmark Supreme Court case, which banned legal discrimination against so-called "aliens ineligible to citizenship." Meanwhile, on behalf of the JACL, Miller and Wirin brought suit in *Amer v. Superior Court* and *Yin Kim v. Superior Court*, two challenges to restrictive covenants (with, respectively, Chinese American and Korean American plaintiffs). After losing the cases in California courts, the two attorneys sought an appeal to the US Supreme Court, on the theory that such cases would help buttress the NAACP case in *Shelley v. Kraemer*. The court declined to take up the cases, but after its *Shelley* ruling it summarily reversed the state court decisions.

In 1951 Loren Miller bought the *California Eagle* newspaper from longtime editor Charlotta Bass. Under Miller's direction, the *Eagle* remained a stalwart voice for civil rights, challenging police brutality, discrimination in city hiring, and, of course, housing segregation. In later years Miller undertook a historical study of the Supreme Court and civil rights. Published in 1966 as *The Petitioners*, it became a standard reference work. Because of his writing and journalistic responsibilities, he reduced his legal work, though in 1956 he was appointed to the NAACP national board of directors.

Miller retained his connection with Japanese American communities. He collaborated with JACL activists on panels to further equal employment opportunity. His children attended the Nisei church school of the Hollywood Independent Church, a Japanese American congregation. In 1963, after *Hokubei Mainichi* editor Howard Imazeki published an editorial suggesting that African Americans organize to improve conditions in their own communities before demanding civil rights legislation, Miller wrote a letter complaining that Imazeki had been "brainwashed" and reminding readers of African American support for Japanese American equality.

In tribute to his civil rights record, in 1958 Miller was appointed executive clemency secretary by California governor Edmund ("Pat") Brown. After the nomination was challenged on the basis of Miller's alleged "subversive" activities, he was forced to withdraw his name. However, in 1964 Brown appointed Miller as a California superior court judge. Miller served only a short time before his untimely death at age sixty-four. In 1977 the California Bar Association created the Loren Miller Legal Services Award to honor attorneys who have demonstrated a long-term commitment to public service. In San Francisco he is honored by the naming of the Loren Miller Homes, a low-rent housing development, and in Los Angeles by the Loren Miller Elementary School.

Aiko Herzig-Yoshinaga

Aiko Herzig-Yoshinaga, who passed away on July 18, 2018, was not a household name, even among Japanese Americans. Yet her place in history as "godmother of Japanese American redress" seems secure. A one-woman research team, she spent years combing through the National Archives and

Aiko Herzig-Yoshinaga, circa 1945.
Courtesy of Herzig-Yoshinaga family.

other government document centers in search of material on the wartime confinement of Japanese Americans.

Aiko's life can be considered a marvelous set of paradoxes. Though she spent her active years outside the West Coast, she began and ended her long life in California. After being confined by the US government under Executive Order 9066, she spent her young adult years in New York. When she later turned to political activism, she used historical research as her main arena of activism. While Aiko had no formal training or experience as a scholar, she brought the meticulous organizing skills she had developed through office work to the accumulation and classification of documents.

Born into a family of Japanese immigrants in 1924, Aiko was preceded by her elder sister Ei and her brother John, then followed by younger sister Amy. In later years Aiko recalled attending dance classes in girlhood and dreaming of being a star performer. While still in her teens, she was sent to Manzanar, where she joined her new husband. While at Manzanar she gave birth to their first child. Ultimately Aiko was able to leave camp and join her family in New York, where her older sister had relocated before the war.

(Aiko always found ironic the fact that that she, a citizen born in the United States, had been confined, while Ei—an alien due to her Japanese birth—had remained at liberty.)

Following the war's end, Aiko lived for a time in Japan with her husband, a Nisei serving the US occupation, then returned to New York. During these years she had two more children. As a young wife and mother, she had little opportunity for leisure or education. Instead she found work as a secretary and office staffer (and later also encouraged her eldest daughter, Gerri, to pursue a career in show business; under the name Lani Miyazaki she would perform on Broadway and on TV in the 1960s).

Aiko turned to political activism in middle age, joining the progressive group Asian Americans for Action (AAA) alongside progressive Nisei such as Yuri Kochiyama (whom Aiko always referred to by her original name "Mary"), Kazu Iijima, and Minn Masuda. Aiko organized AAA protests against discrimination, sending letters and contributing articles to the AAA newsletter. She also became close with Michi Nishiura Weglyn. Weglyn's researches into wartime treatment of Japanese Americans, which were transformed into the book *Years of Infamy* (1976) inspired Aiko to investigate the government's policies. During the 1970s Aiko married John ("Jack") Herzig, a retired military officer. Unlike her previous marriages, this union would prove durable and happy. The newlyweds moved to the Washington, DC area, where Aiko began her crusade for redress. She began to go to the National Archives every day it was open, spending fifty or sixty hours a week going through official documents and then copying and classifying some of them. Jack offered Aiko driving and logistical support and partnered with her in studying documents. As an ex-counterintelligence officer, he would later refute in authoritative fashion false claims by David Lowman and others that the government's MAGIC intercepts represented proof of prewar Japanese American spying.

In 1980 Aiko joined the National Council for Japanese American Redress (NCJAR), led by William Hohri, supporting a class action suit for reparations. Following the appointment of the US Commission on Wartime Relocation and Internment of Civilians (CWRIC), Aiko was engaged as a researcher. She brought the documents she had already reproduced and organized, and she continued her efforts. The masses of documents that she accumulated formed the basis of *Personal Justice Denied*, the CWRIC's official 1983 report, whose recommendations of an official apology and payment to individuals affected by Executive Order 9066 ultimately led to the Civil Liberties Act of 1988. Meanwhile, in partnership with lawyer and scholar Peter Irons, she uncovered the central "smoking gun" documents—notably the original censored version of General John DeWitt's Final Report on Japanese Evacuation from the West Coast—that laid bare the government's fabrication and manipulation of evidence in justifying mass removal. These finds would prove essential in the *coram nobis* petitions of Gordon Hirabayashi and Fred Korematsu, whose convictions for violating the military orders undergirded by Executive Order 9066 were overturned in federal court.

Even after 1988, Aiko continued her activism. Working with the Office of Redress Administration, she advised former inmates about obtaining redress and helped make the case for individuals who had been affected by Executive Order 9066 but had not gone to a camp. She championed the wartime Nisei draft resisters and supported the JACL's 1999 apology. She also worked with the group Japanese American Voice, which pushed for public diffusion of the Lim Report, a critical study by attorney Deborah Lim of the JACL's policies during World War II. Japanese American Voice also challenged the creation of the National Japanese American Memorial to Patriotism in Washington, DC, both on grounds of the design of the monument and the version of history it presented, both of which she thought distorted. Aiko was interviewed in Emiko Omori's landmark 1999 camp documentary *Rabbit in the Moon*.

After twenty-five years in Washington, Aiko and Jack decided to move west in the early 2000s. Sadly, Jack's health began failing, and he died of colon cancer in 2005. Aiko spent her last years helping organize her and Jack's archives, which she offered to the UCLA Asian American Studies Center. She was the subject of various articles and tributes, most notably Janice D. Tanaka's 2018 biographical documentary *Rebel with a Cause*.

It is hard for me to write about Aiko, because I loved and admired her—and because writing about her also requires me to deal with the fact of her passing. We first spoke in 1997. As a budding researcher into Japanese

American history, I contacted Peter Irons, who directed me instead to Aiko and to Michi Weglyn. I had a brief phone conversation with Aiko, who gave me some pointers on sources. (Aiko also told me not to bother Michi, who was ailing; fortunately for me, Michi learned of my research and proceeded to call me and offer me valuable insight during our extended phone chat.) As I did the research for my dissertation, which eventually morphed into the book *By Order of the President*, I discovered the microfilm rolls of the CWRIC papers—the thousands of documents that Aiko had so patiently put together and organized. It was a major find for me, which (along with Roger Daniels's multivolume document collection *American Concentration Camps*) made it possible for me to write an informed study. It was for this reason that I noted in the acknowledgments that my work would have been inconceivable, let alone impossible, without Aiko's compilation efforts.

I met Aiko and Jack in person for the first time in Washington, DC in 2000. Because of my acknowledged scholarly debt, I felt both excited and apprehensive speaking to them. Aiko immediately put me at ease and related to me more in motherly than in academic fashion. (It didn't hurt that my mother had grown up in the same neighborhood in New York where Aiko had lived, though they had not known each other, and was a contemporary of her kids).

From the beginning, I learned important lessons from Aiko and Jack, not just about Japanese American history but also about life in general. Aiko touched me with her generous and unassuming character. She did not minimize the work she had put in but was careful to offer credit to others, and she was quite modest about her own importance. When I told her that I would be insufferably arrogant if I were to ever accomplish a fraction of what she had, she laughed and said, "Oh, Greg, I have so much to learn from you." I vainly sputtered that she had surely already forgotten more than I would ever know. When I spoke of her as a role model, she would scoff, "but I have had three husbands!" and talk about the years she had labored under the disapproval of more conservative family members. Once I escorted Aiko to a staged reading of *A Divided Community*, Momo Yashima and Frank Chin's play about the wartime draft resisters, which was drawn in part from my book *By Order of the President*. At the end of the play, the cast saluted Aiko's presence in the audience and asked her to take a bow. She did so but generously stated that they should also have me take a bow.

I also learned from Aiko about building community. Aiko excelled at the task of bringing people together. She and Jack put me in touch with members of their circle of friends and colleagues, and I benefited from the contacts I made through them with diverse scholars and activists: Leila Meyerratken, the Indiana teacher whose class made a quilt commemorating Japanese American confinement; Yeiichi Kelly Kuwayama, a New York–born veteran of the 442nd Regiment; and professors Rita Takahashi of San Francisco State and Scott Sandage of Carnegie Mellon. Aiko introduced me to Takeya Mizuno, then a graduate student at University of Missouri and later a distinguished professor of journalism at Toyo University, who became a longtime friend. When I first visited Japan in 2006, I discovered that Aiko's appeal was truly international. At her request, scholars from Nara, Kyoto, and Tokyo all made time to take me out to eat and share information. Aiko in turn introduced me to her daughter GerriLani, and we became friends in our own right. Similarly, once when I was in New York I stopped by the house of Aiko's brother Johnnie, to pick up a package she had left for me, and had a lovely time speaking French with Johnnie and his Haitian-born wife Lucienne. These family connections further solidified my bond with Aiko.

One area where Aiko was of supreme help to me was in connection with the artist Miné Okubo. Aiko had known Okubo in her New York days, and they had attended together the Supreme Court hearings on the NCJAR lawsuit. Aiko had lobbied successfully for University of Washington Press to undertake a reprint edition of Okubo's graphic camp memoir *Citizen 13660*. Okubo was famously prickly about selling individual artworks, but she so admired Aiko that she permitted William Hohri to buy one of her paintings as a wedding present for Aiko and Jack. After Okubo died in 2001, my partner Elena Tajima Creef and I coedited a special Okubo issue of *Amerasia Journal*, and later an anthology book, *Miné Okubo: Following Her Own Road*. We faced a major problem in that Okubo's own collection of her papers and artworks was stuck in probate, and we were unable to gain access. Aiko stepped in and saved the day. She granted us permission to reproduce her wedding present, which became the cover of our *Amerasia* issue, and she entrusted me with her extended files of Okubo material. In gratitude, Elena and I dedicated our book to Aiko and Jack. Aiko was so touched by the dedication that she presented me with a small piece of Okubo's art that she had acquired.

Throughout Aiko's last years, I would visit her whenever I was in Los Angeles. At first we met for lunch in Little Tokyo (Aiko attended several of my public events at the Japanese American National Museum), and then, after she grew more frail, I would stop by her house. She liked to reminisce about her girlhood years, and she always pressed me for details of my latest researches. I will miss her presence and her warm kindness.

Jean Sadako King

Jean Sadako King was a powerful advocate for peace and environmental issues in Hawai'i. Born Jean Sadako McKillop on December 6, 1925, she was the daughter of William Donald McKillop, the Canada-born postmaster of the town of Captain Cook (a small town on the Big Island of Hawai'i), and Chiyo Murakami, the Nisei daughter of a coffee-growing family in Kona. Jean and her brother Alan were raised in the Kaimuki neighborhood of Honolulu. The McKillop family was close—a friend later described Mr. and Mrs. McKillop washing dishes together and singing to each other. After graduating from the Sacred Heart Academy, Jean attended the University of Hawai'i. During her student days, she was active in a political organization, Hawai'i Youth for Democracy, and became active in the labor movement, going door-to-door to persuade workers to join unions.

After received a BA in English in 1948, Jean moved to New York, where she received an MA in history from New York University before returning to Hawai'i. There she married James King. She was hired as an assistant by Harry Bridges, leader of the International Longshore and Warehouse Union, and, because of her reputation for attention to detail, King was given the job of transcribing Bridges's interviews with the FBI. In 1950 King audaciously campaigned for a position as delegate to Hawai'i's territorial constitutional convention, the only women candidate. She ran on a platform of equal rights for women, individual and minority group rights, and a free unsegregated school system. She attracted attention but was defeated in the election.

In the years after 1950, King took time off to raise her children and then returned to the University of Hawai'i, where in 1968 she received an MFA in theater arts. Around this time she returned to the political arena as an aide to Tadao Beppu, Speaker of the Hawai'i house of representatives. In 1972 she was elected to the house as a Democrat, representing the Fourteenth District. Two years later she won election to Hawai'i's state senate. King served as chair of both the house and senate environment committees and was a leader in pushing for stricter environmental protection and land-use laws, and she sponsored a bottle bill to promote recycling. Another of her priorities was transparency in government, and she sponsored Hawai'i's Sunshine Law, one of the earliest state laws to allow public scrutiny of official actions.

In 1978 King was elected Hawai'i's lieutenant governor. She was the first woman of color to serve as lieutenant governor of a state. Her swift upward climb politically, in the words of one commentator, showed that there was a place for women in local and state politics. She was aware of her status as a role model. In 1980 she told delegates to the first National Asian-Pacific American Women's Conference, "Asian-Pacific women have not been sufficiently visible in this society."

As lieutenant governor, King distinguished herself by her support for progressive causes, opposing even conservative members of her own party. One of her maverick efforts was protecting Hansen's disease patients at Hale Mohalu from eviction, after Hawai'i's state government announced plans to tear down the facility. King's staffer Charles Freedman recalled driving her to Hale Mohalu so that she could meet with residents: "For decades, patients who suffered from Hansen's disease had lived in those old military barracks when they were on Oahu. When we visited, they were using kerosene stoves because the state had turned off the power. I drove Jean in my old beat-up Datsun because she didn't want a state government car out there. Those meetings were secret. . . . Jean would talk with the group's leaders, including Bernard Punikaia." Although King managed to suspend forced eviction and official demolition, the facility was torn down by the state after she left office in 1983.

During her term as lieutenant governor, King clashed repeatedly with Governor George Ariyoshi over environmental issues and policies to promote affordable housing. In 1982 King audaciously decided to challenge Ariyoshi for the governorship. According to a later account, when Ariyoshi went to sign his papers to run for reelection, it was King, as lieutenant governor, who was the election official who took his paperwork. With the entire Capitol press corps watching, King got up to shake his hand, grasped it firmly, and said, "I would like to formally ask you for a debate." Although King received support from various activists, she was unable to match the incumbent governor's popularity and fund-raising prowess and was defeated in the primary election, though she garnered nearly 45 percent of the vote.

Following her loss, King retired from electoral politics and switched her focus to community affairs, becoming one of Hawai'i's most visible and prominent political activists. Meanwhile, she remained active in the Honolulu Friends Quaker community. In later years, she cofounded and served on the board of Interfaith Alliance Hawai'i, which was designed to encourage cooperation among members of different religious faiths. In 1990 she served as delegate to a Soviet-American women's summit. She also served as a leader of Save Our Star-Bulletin, a grass-roots community group that successfully pushed to keep Honolulu a two-newspaper town after Liberty Newspapers announced in 1999 that it planned to close the *Star-Bulletin*. She also was actively involved in trying to find housing for homeless people. In 2005 she led a movement to sponsor a series of concerts nationwide to mark the eighty-sixth birthday of singer-songwriter and progressive activist Pete Seeger. Among the conditions placed on the concerts was that they had to be free, open to the public, and that those in attendance had to sing "Happy Birthday" as a tribute to Seeger. Ultimately, a series of four concerts was performed in Honolulu.

Jean Sadako King died on November 24, 2013, a few days before her eighty-eighth birthday. In tribute to her memory, Hawai'i governor Neil Abercrombie ordered all flags in official buildings statewide be flown at half-mast.

In the summer of 2006, I first visited Hawai'i and participated in a program at the Japanese Cultural and Community Center of Honolulu on Japanese Americans in wartime Hawai'i. An elderly but striking woman spoke from the audience to relate her story of the impact of war: she had been promised she could obtain a driver's license once she turned sixteen. However, her sixteenth birthday was on Saturday, December 6. The day after, the Japanese military attacked Pearl Harbor, closing down all of Hawai'i's civilian offices. I thanked her afterward for her story. I only later learned that it was Jean Sadako King—it was my only meeting with her.

Diverging Paths: Redress in the United States and Canada

On August 10, 1988, following almost two decades of political organizing, lawsuits, and lobbying by Japanese Americans and their supporters, the Civil Liberties Act of 1988 was enacted. It granted an official apology and a $20,000 tax-free payment to surviving members of the group of 120,000 Japanese Americans who had been confined without charge in government camps during World War II.

Six weeks later, following a settlement brokered by the National Association of Japanese Canadians (NAJC) and the government of Prime Minister Brian Mulroney, Canada's Parliament approved redress legislation for survivors of the 22,000 Japanese Canadians who had been removed from their homes during World War II under Order-in-Council 1486, and who had been stripped of their property by the Canadian government and forced to pay for their own confinement. The Mulroney government offered victims an official apology and a payment of $21,000 each.

Superficially, the redress struggles in the two countries closely resembled each other, and it goes without saying that the Japanese Canadian campaign was heavily influenced by its counterpart south of the border. Certainly, had not the US Congress acted in the summer of 1988, it is likely that the final settlement of Japanese Canadian redress would have been granted much later—if at all.

Still, the evolution of redress was quite different in the two countries. At the risk of rigidly oversimplifying, we can note that in the United States the movement for reparations started out with rather universalistic goals and motivations and grew progressively narrower as time went on. During its initial organizing in the early 1970s, which occurred in the wake of the civil rights and Black Power movements, the push for reparations by Japanese Americans formed part of a larger multigroup movement against white supremacy. Activists frequently referred to their wartime confinement as an episode in a larger history of racial discrimination, especially that against black Americans. Meanwhile, the movement's chief early outside supporters were African Americans, notably black political leaders in California such as Los Angeles mayor Tom Bradley and Representatives Augustus Hawkins, Yvonne Braithwaite Burke, and Mervyn M. Dymally (who in 1982 introduced in Congress the first iteration of the redress legislation that would ultimately be enacted).

During the 1980s, however, the Japanese American redress movement shifted "from protest to politics" (to paraphrase black civil rights activist Bayard Rustin). JACL leaders and Nisei members of Congress focused on the passage of special remedial legislation. In the process, the redress movement lost much of its initial universalistic quality. Rather than connecting their experience with that of other nonwhite groups, redress supporters underlined the exceptional nature of the wartime internment. Indeed, one reason that Japanese Americans requested reparations only for surviving individuals, and not the families of the deceased, was to ease fears by conservative legislators that any posthumous award would set a precedent for demands by African Americans for reparations for slavery. Similarly, redress advocates underlined the wartime loyalty and patriotism of Japanese Americans by reference to Nisei soldiers—the civil liberties bill was deliberately registered as H.R. 442 in tribute to the 442nd Infantry Regiment.

In Canada, in contrast, the movement for reparations started small and then grew more universalistic over time. In the generation following 1949, when Japanese Canadians were finally granted voting rights and permitted to return to their West Coast former home region, they generally devoted themselves to recovering from the psychological impact of the war, getting an education, working, and raising families. Japanese Canadians sponsored a handful or newspapers and formed the National Association of Japanese Canadians to lobby for political reform. Unlike in the United States, where the JACL cosponsored reform legislation and gained a national platform in support of civil rights for all (and where Nisei from Hawai'i and later California were elected to Congress) the Canadian groups operated on a rather small scale and did not form strong alliances with other groups, though in select cases local individuals and communities formed with members of diverse ethnic and racial groups.

By the beginning of the 1970s, as Canada reopened its doors to Asian immigration on an equal basis and the government instituted a policy of official multiculturalism, Japanese Canadians began to organize remembrances and educational campaigns on the model of those taking place south of the border. The NAJC and other groups organized to lobby for redress. Even more than in the United States, former inmates divided bitterly over both strategy and tactics, notably the size of a proposed redress package and whether to claim individual reparations or accept a lump-sum payment, as well as over the larger question of who could claim the right to speak and negotiate in the name of the community.

Redress advocates in Canada met with strong resistance, both official and unofficial. Canadian war veterans who had been captured in the fall of Hong Kong in December 1941 and placed in Japanese POW camps opposed reparations for Japanese Canadians. Liberal prime minister Pierre Elliot Trudeau, for his part, remained hostile. While Trudeau admitted during a speech in Tokyo during 1976 that the wartime treatment of Japanese

Canadians represented a deprivation of civil rights, he publicly rejected the principle of reparations for past injustices.

Partly in response, Japanese Canadians began reaching out to members of other groups. They were thereby able to gain important supporters for the movement. For example, in early 1984, just before Trudeau resigned as prime minister, the Canadian Jewish Congress's national executive, including its president Milton Harris and national chair Dorothy Reitman, sent him a telegram expressing firm support for "moral and material restitution" to Japanese Canadians. "We cannot do justice to visible minorities in Canada today," the CJC added, "if we do not rectify the injustices of yesterday." The CJC and other Jewish groups would repeatedly raise the issue of redress in Ottawa in the years that followed. Indeed, the Japanese Canadian case dovetailed with Prime Minister Trudeau's larger campaign for the creation of a Charter of Rights and Freedoms (ultimately enacted in 1982): if a group of citizens and legal residents could be stripped of their basic rights at will by the government, nobody could be truly safe.

In 1984 the Conservative government of Brian Mulroney was swept into office. Mulroney was sympathetic to claims by Japanese Canadians, but he hesitated to place a dollar amount on a settlement. The NAJC responded by commissioning a study from the esteemed accounting firm Price Waterhouse. It estimated that the official actions had cost Japanese Canadians some $333 million in revenue and $110 million in property (in 1986 dollars). In 1988, even as the US Congress voted on H.R. 442, a final round of negotiations was scheduled between Japanese Canadians and the Mulroney government on a redress package. When the parties became deadlocked, the prime minister named his close collaborator, Secretary of State Lucien Bouchard, to lead the government's team. Bouchard used his influence to broker an agreement on a redress package, and the plan was voted into law in September 1988, six weeks after redress was enacted in Washington.

The history of redress in both countries was marked by a central tension between multiracialism and exceptionalism, universalism and narrow political interests. In the United States, even as the redress movement achieved its goals, it grew less attractive and relevant to other minority groups, though they remained engaged with the principle of reparations. In Canada, redress evolved into a more universal question. Like the civil rights movement in the United States, though on a much smaller scale, it was a deeply morally engaged movement by a minority group that made citizens of all backgrounds view their government and their rights differently. The Canadian experience provides an important case of recognizing the importance of preserving fundamental rights of minorities from oppression by transient majorities and their elected representatives, and thereby it serves as a reference point for Native peoples seeking to defend their historic rights, immigrants needing protection from arbitrary treatment, or same-sex couples seeking equal access to marriage rights.

CHAPTER SIX

Arts and Sciences

Taro and Mitsu Yashima

WITH VALERIE MATSUMOTO

One remarkable and little-known Japanese American story is that of the epic and tragic partnership of Taro and Mitsu Yashima, an extraordinary couple of artists and freedom fighters. Together they survived many years of hardship—imprisonment, exile, poverty, and illness—and made a name for themselves as authors and illustrators before they reached a point where Mitsu was unable to continue with her husband.

Taro Yashima was born Atsushi Iwamatsu on September 21, 1908, the son of a doctor and art collector in the seaside town of Nejime (now part of Minami Ōsumi-cho), in Kagoshima prefecture in southern Kyushu. The young man (known as Jun) later recalled that his childhood was a happy one. "My parents' house was full of patients," he recalled, remembering his father's medical practice. "When the people were cured, they were happy toward my father." From his boyhood, the young Jun demonstrated a passion for art, as well as a strong social conscience. At age thirteen he

Taro Yashima, March 1953. Courtesy of the *Pacific Citizen*

New York JACL Hears Talk by Artist

NEW YORK CITY — Taro Yashima, well-known author and artist, brought dolls from his own large collection when he spoke on "The Folk Art of Many Nations" at a recent meeting of the New York JACL. Yashima is the author of "The New Sun" as "Horizon is Calling." His oils have been shown in many art galleries.

published satirical manga in *Kagoshima Shimbun* (later known as *Minami Nihon Shimbun.*)

At nineteen Jun entered the Tokyo Academy of Fine Arts in Ueno (now the Tokyo National University of Fine Arts and Music). However, as a pacifist, he refused to participate in the military training course required in all Japanese schools, and as a result he was expelled for insubordination. Instead of changing schools, he became active in antifascist activities and joined the left-wing Japanese Proletarian Artists' League, where he taught drawing and cartooning. (He sketched a death mask of proletarian writer Kobayashi Takaji, who had died of torture in prison). While at the Artists' League, he became involved with Mitsuko Arai. Born Tomoe Sasago, she was the daughter of a shipbuilding engineer from Kobe. She first had attended Kobe College, a Christian girls' school, then enrolled at the Tokyo women's college Bunka Gakuin. After being attracted by the student arm of the Japanese Communist Party, which led resistance to Japan's ruling military clique, she joined the "research institute" of the Art Students League. The two were married in 1930 and joined together in political organizing.

In the following three years, Jun was arrested nine times for antigovernment activities. The official harassment climaxed in 1933 when both partners were put in prison, where they were housed in a six-foot square cell with five to fifteen other prisoners. As Yashima later described in his graphic memoir *The New Sun*, both were tortured while in prison. Mitsu, who had lost her first-born son and was now again pregnant, feared losing the baby. Ultimately they were released but only after signing "confessions" in which they formally disavowed their political activities. Two months after their release, in December 1933, Mitsu gave birth to their son Makoto, known as Mako.

In the following years, the Iwamatsus lived comfortably with Mitsu's family in Kobe. While they reduced their more visible political activism, Jun produced a set of cartoons in the political-economic monthly *Keizo* and other publications in which he satirized the militarists. Eventually they decided they had no future in Japan, which was in the hands of the militarists and moving toward war. In 1939, they applied for permission to travel to the United States, on the pretext of visiting the San Francisco World's Fair and writing about America. Once they received their visas, they departed, leaving Mako behind with his grandparents, and went into exile in New York.

The Iwamatsus settled in Manhattan, where they both enrolled at the Art Students League of New York. They were forced into dire poverty, living in a cold-water flat in East Harlem (where they slept on the floor for many weeks until they could secure a single mattress) and working to scratch out a living. Jun scrounged through wastepaper baskets for paper, canvas, and art materials. In desperation, Jun attempted to organize a *koenkai* (organization of sponsors) among New York's Japanese community. However, especially in the wake of his pro-democratic reports from North America in *Keizo*, he was opposed by the pro-Tokyo community leadership, and his efforts to enlist help from the Consulate General of Japan, the Japanese commercial attaché, and the head of the Japan Institute all met with unanimous refusal. The Iwamatsus did receive patronage from editor Shigetsu Sasaki of the *New York Shimpo*. Sasaki solicited support for Jun and commissioned him to produce artworks (including fashion sketches of hats) for the *Japanese American Review*.

After the Japanese attack on Pearl Harbor, the Iwamatsus were hired as freelancers by the Office of War Information (OWI). They took the names Taro and Mitsu Yashima in order to shield their family in Japan from reprisals. Both also worked with the antifascist Japanese American Committee for Democracy. In mid-1942, for example, Taro organized a JACD blood drive for the US Army and donated some of his own blood.

In 1943 Taro Yashima published his first book, *The New Sun*, a graphic memoir of his imprisonment in Japan that detailed his and his wife's mistreatment by the Japanese secret police. Despite his opposition to Japanese militarists, he also hoped to convey in the book what he considered his message to Americans at the time: that all Japanese were not "wild monkeys." While *The New Sun* was widely and positively reviewed, and was even adopted by the OWI as a useful tool in the war against Japan, it sold poorly. In 1944, together with fellow artists Miné Okubo and Yasuo Kuniyoshi, Taro was commissioned to produce drawings of Japan for *Fortune* magazine's special Japan issue. The issue was so successful that the government organized an exhibition tour of the artworks.

Soon after, the Yashimas were hired by the Office of Strategic Services (OSS). Mitsu worked as "America's Tokyo Rose" (as she was later termed), producing and narrating radio broadcasts to the women of Japan, urging them to commit sabotage and do what they could to stop Japan's military machine. Taro wrote and illustrated handbills in Japanese that were dropped on battlefields, bearing the phrases "Don't Die!" and "Papa, Stay Alive." When he was later charged with being a traitor to Japan, he responded that his sole aim had been to save Japanese lives. "At the time it was easy to say I was one who was against his own country," he explained. "That's the most terrible thing, because my feeling was, I'm doing it because I love my country."

Yashima was in India with the OSS on V-J Day. Soon after, he was sent by the OSS on a mission to Japan, which he had not visited since 1939, as a member of a US strategic bombing survey team. According to his later account, Yashima had seen films of bombing raids on Kobe, during which he saw his studio—where his son and parents were living—ridden with bullets from a fighter plane. He had no way to discover whether his family was alive or dead. After arriving in Japan, he visited his old house. Although it was indeed ruined, Yashima located his twelve-year-old son, whom he was relieved to find in good shape.

After Yashima's discharge, both partners' legal status in the United States remained tenuous. With sponsorship from their wartime government superiors, a special bill was enacted in Congress in 1948 to permit the Yashimas permanent residence in the United States, as a reward for their wartime work. They were also granted permission to bring Mako to live in the United States. He arrived in 1949, shortly after the birth of the Yashimas' daughter Momo. In later years, Mako became a celebrated stage and screen actor and was nominated for an Oscar for his performance in the 1966 film *The Sand Pebbles.*

Once the war ended, both Yashimas threw themselves into writing and art. Both began working for the new *Chicago Shimpo*, edited by progressive Issei Ryochi Fujii. Mitsu contributed an essay titled "Women in Japan," while Taro produced a regular Japanese-language column, "Taro's Miscellany," that discussed art, literature, and democracy. He also wrote a play based on the Momotaro legend. Both Yashimas helped found an artists' group, the Japanese-American Art Studio, which held a joint exhibition of their work in 1949. In the summer of 1950, the Yashimas spent two months at the artists' colony Yaddo. That fall, Taro had his first solo exhibition since the war, showing thirty paintings at the 6 Fifth Avenue Gallery. During these years, the Phillips Collection in Washington successively bought three of Taro's paintings, and the Yashimas produced their first significant joint production, the graphic memoir *Horizon Is Calling.* A sequel to *The New Sun*, it was an episodic account of the family's life in prewar Japan. Although Taro was credited as sole author, Mitsu's contribution is tangible in the descriptions of her family as well as the narrator's sensual and loving description of playing with baby Mako and his beautiful nude form.

Unfortunately, once the long trauma that the Yashimas had undergone finally ended and the family was reunited, the emotional time bomb that had been gaining momentum within Taro exploded. "I held everything inside," he later recalled. "When it was all over, I couldn't keep it any longer." He developed a crippling ulcer and was largely unable to work. Mitsu scrambled for commercial art work to support the family. Stuck at home during his long recovery period, Taro formed a close bond with his young daughter Momo, who provided him needed companionship and joy. In turn, the tales that Yashima told his daughter inspired him to go into children's book writing and illustration as a career. His first picture book, *The Village Tree* (1953), was a success. It would be followed by *Crow Boy* (1955), *Umbrella* (1958), *Youngest One* (1966), and *Seashore Story* (1967), among others. Taro also provided illustrations for several books by other authors. Ultimately three of his works would be noted as Caldecott Honor Books, and he would be awarded the 1974 medallion from the University of Southern Mississippi for his outstanding contribution to children's literature and given a lifetime achievement award from the Southern California Council on Literature for Children.

In 1954 the Yashimas moved to Los Angeles, settling in the city's Boyle Heights neighborhood. There they established the Yashima Art Institute and worked as painters and educators. In 1965 Taro did scene and costume design for the production of the Japanese classic *Rashomon* that Mako produced for the Asian American theater company East/West Players. He also painted a notable mural for the Kagoshima science museum. After suffering a stroke in 1977, Taro Yashima limited his activities. Glenn Johnson's film documentary *Taro Yashima's Golden Village* recounts his journey late in life back to his hometown of Nejima. Taro died in Los Angeles in 1994.

Mitsu continued her work and activism during the couple's years in Los Angeles. She was coauthor with Taro of the books *Plenty to Watch* (1954) and *Momo's Kitten* (1961). In the late 1960s, after Momo graduated high school and left the house, the couple separated. Taro's physical abuse of his wife, which had persisted for many years, had grown intolerable for Mitsu, who left him and moved to San Francisco. She gave a lecture, "People's Art in Japan," at the University of California, Berkeley, and during the 1970s she taught art at Kimochi, a Japanese American community center. She remained active in Women Strike for Peace and opposed the Vietnam War. She made her screen acting debut in the 1976 TV movie *Farewell to Manzanar*, opposite her son and daughter, and subsequently appeared in such films as *Foul Play* and *Oh, God! Book II*. She died in 1988.

Yoichi Okamoto

Since the early days of the camera, photography has enjoyed a particular vogue in Japan. Long before the stereotyped tourist groups snapping pictures arrived on the international scene, Japanese photographers had

Yoichi Okamoto, the official White House photographer, taking a picture of himself in the mirror at the LBJ Ranch in Stonewall, Texas; President Johnson seated at left. Courtesy of Lyndon B. Johnson Presidential Library.

demonstrated their talent. Japanese brands such as Olympus, Nikon, Canon, Minolta, Pentax, and Fujifilm, all firms originally founded during the interwar years, came to dominate the international film and camera market by the end of the twentieth century.

While it is not clear how direct an influence Japanese shutterbugs exercised on overseas Nikkei communities, photography remained a prominent interest of Japanese Americans. Numerous Issei operated photo studios, including Toyo Miyatake of Los Angeles and Frank S. Matsura in Okanagon, Washington. (The career of Matsura, who managed to produce thousands of images of frontier life, including striking portraits of Native Americans, before his early death from tuberculosis, is highlighted in ShiPu Wang's 2017 book *The Other American Moderns*.) Manabu and Saki Kohara settled in Alexandria, Louisiana, in the 1920s and opened a photo studio that remained in the family for decades. Various individual Issei and Nisei worked in art photography or practiced photojournalism. One remarkable artist, Yoichi Okamoto, distinguished himself in both areas.

Yoichi Robert Okamoto was born in 1915, in Yonkers, New York. His father, Chobun Yonezo Okamoto, emigrated from Japan to the United States in 1904 and settled with his wife Shina in the New York area. A wealthy Japanese exporter and real estate magnate, Yonezo was also an art patron, publisher of Japanese textbooks, and author of a dozen volumes, including *Bara no Kaori* (Fragrance of Roses), a set of capsule biographies of leading Americans, and *Nyuyokushi naigai no jisho*, a guidebook for Japanese travelers to New York. According to various newspaper stories, Yonezo's book expounding Buddhist philosophy became a best-seller in Japan.

The young Yoichi spent three years in Japan during his early childhood, then returned for a visit in mid-1923, only to be caught up in the giant 1923 Kanto earthquake while out walking with servants. After being evacuated on an American warship and returned to the United States, the eight-year old toured the United States with a Red Cross unit and recounted his observations of the calamity. Yoichi (known to his friends as Oke) grew up in Yonkers, becoming known locally as a skilled amateur magician. At some point in the 1930s, Yonezo and Shina moved back to Japan and divorced. Yonezo remarried and moved to Sierra Madre, California. Shina returned to New York and worked as a domestic servant. Yoichi settled in Scarsdale, attended Roosevelt High School, then enrolled at Colgate University. While at Colgate, he was selected as head varsity cheerleader for the school and editor of the student magazine *Salmagundi*. (Known on campus as a fancy dresser, he also wrote a men's fashion column for the student newspaper, the *Banter*).

During his Colgate years, Okamoto began concentrating on photography. He may have been influenced by his father, who owned a photography business in Japan. After graduation he moved to Syracuse, where he worked as a candid camera photographer in local nightclubs and studied photographic technique on the side. In 1939 Okamoto was hired as staff photographer by the Syracuse *Post-Standard*, and he remained in that position for three years.

In January 1942, shortly after Pearl Harbor, Okamoto entered the US Army, becoming the first New York Nisei enlistee (he later stated that he was initially refused because of his Japanese ancestry, and it took interventions from the mayor of Syracuse and from a friendly army major to secure his entry). He was sent for training at the Quartermaster School at Camp Lee, Virginia, before joining the army's Signal Corps. In 1944 he traveled to

Europe as a war correspondent. The following year he was sent to Vienna, where he was commissioned as personal photographer to General Mark Clark, the high commissioner in Austria. During this period, Okamoto was responsible for all photographs published in the American occupation zone.

After being discharged with the rank of major in 1946, Okamoto joined the new US Information Service in Vienna, where he headed the Pictorial Section. Thanks to his photos, which documented the rebuilding of the Austrian capital after the ravages of war, he soon became a well-known figure in local social and political circles. He photographed in depth the city's postwar cultural life, including portraits of artists and performers that were featured in a public poster campaign, "Schöpferisches Österreich" (Creative Austria). In 1954 the Art Club of Austria organized a show of Okamoto's photos at Vienna's well-known Galerie Würthle. The same year he was honored by the Austrian Photographic Society with a silver medal for his "contributions to the advancement of photography." During these years, he married a local woman, Paula Wachter, with whom he raised two children, and learned to speak fluent German.

In 1954 Okamoto was recalled to the United States and appointed head of the Visual Materials section of the newly named US Information Agency. He was joined by his wife, who worked as a broadcaster for Voice of America. Okamoto's photographic work became more widely known in the United States during these years. First, he won several prizes in a 1953 contest sponsored by *Photography* magazine, including a snapshot of a boxer dog investigating a tiny cricket. Soon after, the renowned photographer Edward Steichen included Okamoto's portrait of Austrian dancer Harald Kreuzberger in his landmark 1955 photo exhibition "The Family of Man." Okamoto was honored with a one-man show at the Arts Club of Washington in 1958. During these years he remained professionally active. In 1956 he attended a four-week seminar at Indiana University on interpreting photographs. Two years later, he was invited to present the keynote address, which he titled "How to Become a Hack," at the annual meeting of the National Press Photographers Association. In 1961 he was retained as an instructor for the University of Missouri's one-week summer photojournalism seminar.

Okamoto's career underwent a drastic shift in 1961 when he was invited by USIA director Edward R. Murrow to accompany Vice President

Lyndon B. Johnson as his personal photographer on an official tour of Berlin, staged in the aftermath of the Berlin Wall's construction. The vice president afterward admired the photos from Berlin and asked that Okamoto be assigned to him on future trips.

In November 1963, following the assassination of President John F. Kennedy, Johnson became president. Upon reaching the Oval Office, he invited Okamoto to serve as official White House photographer. Okamoto accepted on the condition that he be granted unlimited access to the president, in order to capture candid portraits. During the years that followed, Okamoto spent up to sixteen hours per day at the Johnson White House and managed to capture the highlights of history in the making: meetings with civil rights leaders, conferences on Vietnam, speeches, and so forth. Okamoto received a top secret security clearance and remained the only individual (other than Johnson's appointment secretary Marvin Watson) permitted to walk into the Oval Office without warning. In the end, Okamoto took an estimated 675,000 photos. Thanks to Okamoto's efforts, the Johnson administration is perhaps the best-documented of presidencies in visual terms.

After leaving the White House in 1969, at the close of the Johnson administration, Okamoto opened a photofinishing business, Image Inc., in Washington and pursued a career as a freelance photographer, alongside his wife Paula Okamoto. In 1972 he took photographs of the aging FBI director J. Edgar Hoover for the *Nation's Business* magazine. His images drew a public expression of appreciation from Hoover. In 1977 he produced photographs for a special edition of *Smithsonian* magazine on the Supreme Court. Four years later, along with writer Bill Brock, he produced *A New Beginning: A Photo Documentary of the 1980 Republican National Convention*. Okamoto ended his own life in 1985, when he was sixty-nine. Two years later, his book *Okamoto's Vienna: The City since the Fifties* appeared. Published with the assistance of his widow Paula, it showcased Yoichi's photos of postwar Austria.

The work of Yoichi ("Oke") Okamoto merits further attention and study. He set the standard for White House photographers by demanding unfettered access to the president and documenting the daily events of the Johnson administration. His powerful portraits show the president in a variety of moods and reveal the burden of the office on the man, especially during the Vietnam War. They go beyond political propaganda and shine as both art and history.

Prewar Nisei Films and Filmmakers

In recent times, numerous directors of Japanese ancestry have made their mark on the silver screen, including Cary Joji Fukunaga, Karyn Kusama, Gregg Araki, Lane Nishikawa, and Destin Daniel Cretton. There have also been diverse film and television productions that have featured Nikkei community stories. Emiko Omori's *Hot Summer Winds* and Chris Tashima's *Day of Independence*, both television dramas, and Desmond Nakano's feature film *American Pastime* are some notable works about the Japanese American experience.

Some might think that Nikkei filmmakers and cinematic portraits of Japanese communities are rather a new thing. In fact, a set of films made in Southern California during the 1930s provide some interesting historical precedents.

The first feature film to depict the lives of the Nisei was the 1930 Japanese-language sound film *Chijiko wo mawasuru chikara* (literally "The Force that Turns the Earth around Its Axis" but translated variously as *The Inevitable Urge, Eternal Passion,* and *Tragedy of Life*), brought out by the Hollywood Nippon Talkie Company. According to one source, it was put together by Japanese writer and scenarist Teruo Mayeda, who raised $20,000 for it. According to another, it was produced by famed Chinese American artist and cinematographer James Wong Howe, who financed it partly through his own funds and partly with the aid of Japanese investors. Howe codirected it with Thomas Hayashi and served as director of photography. It was shot on location in Southern California, using amateur actors such as Ruth Washizu and Henry Okawa. Taruyo "Jack" Matsumoto portrayed an Issei father. The Nisei actors reportedly had problems with the Japanese-language dialogue. The film was screened in the Fox Brooklyn Theater in Los Angeles in June 1930, then transferred for further showings at the Nishi Hongwanji Temple in Little Tokyo a few months later. In the end, the film failed to attract a large audience, either among Japanese Americans or in Japan (where audiences reportedly found the Nisei actors' accents humorous).

Chijiko wo mawasuru chikara was succeeded in the next years by a trio of Nisei-produced silent films. The first of these was *Taichi ni Shitashimu* (Love of the Soil). Released in October 1934, it was the first (and likely only) motion picture completed the Hollywood Japanese Picture Association, a new production company. The story involved a Nisei from the countryside who goes to the big city but ultimately grows disillusioned and returns to the farm. It was written by Jakuyo Matsumoto, with George Mitsuhata producing the titles. Yujin Takamatsu was the director and Buhachi Suzuki acted as cameraman. The cast was made up of local Nisei Eiji Takeshima, Miyako Numata, Miyeko Matsui, Kimiyo Morishima, Takeo Kikuchi, Kusuo Yanasc, Yukiko Miyakawa, Riyosui Sugihara, and Jakuyo Matsumoto. After being previewed during an event held at the Miyako Hotel, it was screened at the Japanese Union Church in Little Tokyo. It seems to have had little or no exposure outside of Los Angeles.

Another feature that expanded on this same theme was *Nobite Yuku Nisei* (The Growing Nisei), produced by the Pan-Pacific Motion Picture League (also called the Pan-Pacific Motion Picture Society), headed by Kazuo Nakayama of Los Angeles. Kido Kurimoto and Jiro Abe directed the production, which featured actors Kunio Morishima, Kazuo Sumida, Reiko Tsuki, Yuriko Arikawa (a former Long Beach Nisei Beauty Contest winner), Tomoko Yoshii, Tetsuko Miyahara, and Kiyo Arikawa. The film dealt with a brief but turbulent phase in the life of a Nisei youth who faces some of the harder facts of life. These include a quarrel with his Issei farmer father, followed by an unsuccessful search for work in the city; a scene portraying a benefit dance, with a drunken Issei; scenes of gambling; and an interracial love affair that ends in disappointment. Ultimately the hero realizes that his place is "back on the farm," and the film ends with him organizing a cooperative movement among the younger farmer and shows a cooperative meeting in action.

The film was screened in Los Angeles in mid-1937. In his column "Smoking Room," in the newspaper *Shin Sekai* (*New World Sun*), columnist Iwao Kawakami praised the attractive cast of Nisei men and women and expressed pleasure at the sequence with the Nisei farm cooperative. However, Kawakami complained of the poor cinematography and the heavy-handed "back to the land" message. Furthermore, he stated that the film reflected a Kibei point of view, which reflected a poor understanding of Nisei psychology. Following the release of the film, the producers announced that they were making another silent film, titled *Too Many Girls*. They also announced a plan to launch a statewide project to take intimate pictures of Nisei life, both on the farm and in the city, with the idea of compiling a documentary to take to Japan and show to the Japanese people. Neither project seems to have been realized.

A more ambitious and certainly more warmly received project was the film *Nisei Parade*, released in 1935. While this was the most complete cinematic portrait of prewar Nisei life in California, it was produced by the brothers Ikuo and Sueo Serisawa, both of whom were Japan-born. Just how they came to direct the film is uncertain, but in 1934 they began making up a scenario and bringing their cameras into local communities in Southern California. They put together the film on 16mm stock in their studio, a little space in the Ohio Building on Little Tokyo's East First Street.

Nisei Parade takes place in the celery farms of Southern California, the vegetable marts of Los Angeles, and the waterfronts of San Pedro. The story follows the lives of three Nisei youths working at a vegetable stand. The story is centered on Jiro, who is employed in one of the many huge produce markets in Southern California, and his pals George and Shig. Jiro is torn between the choice of a career as a photographer, necessitating years of study, and his love for Sumi, the sister of one of the other youths, who returns to California after attending school in Japan. (To trace the dialogue among Nisei and Kibei, the film used both Japanese and English titles). The Serisawas recruited Tadashi Kamayatsu, Alice Iseri, Peter Takahashi, and James Suishi for the leads. Several local Nisei had cameos—one source notes that future pharmaceuticals tycoon Wesley Oyama was among them.

After months of shooting and final cutting, the film previewed at the Miyako Hotel in December 1934 and then had its official premiere in Los

Angeles in January 1935. In March 1935 it received its first Northern California showing, at the Sokoji Hall in San Francisco. The film won praise from Nisei critics for its cinematographic excellence. Columnist Jimmie Omura complained of the morbid love story "a la Orientale," which lacked realism. Still, he added, "[As] a sidelight on the life of the second generations and a pioneer venture in the cinema field . . . although the picture has many defects, its aim is laudable." The film's San Francisco showing was sufficiently successful that it was then screened at a Methodist Episcopal church in Alameda, under the auspices of the Alameda JACL chapter, and a week later in San Jose under sponsorship from the Nitto Club. In April 1935 the Monterey-Watsonville JACL sponsored a screening, and there was another at the Japanese Presbyterian Church in Salinas, in cooperation with the local branch of the Young People's Society of Christian Endeavor.

Despite the initial buzz generated by these films, they seem to have sunk rapidly into oblivion. Neither *Love of the Soil* nor *The Growing Nisei* had any recorded showing after their initial screenings. *Nisei Parade* was featured at a benefit performance in Stockton in February 1939 and then disappeared from view. Sueo Serisawa went on to have a long and successful career as a painter and printmaker. However, when he died in 2004, no obituaries mentioned his early film. It is not clear whether any of these films survive. Historians and Nikkei film buffs can only hope that a stray print will someday be rediscovered in some vault.

Sueo Serisawa

Publication of my article on prewar Nisei films led readers to question what happened afterward to the young filmmakers, notably *Nisei Parade* director Sueo Serisawa. In fact, Serisawa's work on the film came at the outset of a long and distinguished career in art and design.

Serisawa was born in Yokohama in 1910, two years before his brother Ikuo. Their father, Yoichi Serisawa, was a painter who had studied with

Hashimoto Gaho at the Japan Academy of Fine Arts. Some years thereafter, the elder Serisawa moved the family to Seattle and then on to Long Beach, California, where he worked as a calligrapher and commercial artist. After Yoichi Serisawa's early death from lung cancer in 1927, Mrs. Serisawa returned to Japan, leaving the teenage Serisawa boys alone. Both turned to art, Ikuo to photography and Sueo to painting. While studying at the Long Beach Polytechnic High School, Sueo was taken up by his art teacher, George Barker. Barker (who had trained with Laurie Wallace, a disciple of the master American realist Thomas Eakins) schooled his pupil in European classicism and the techniques of the old asters. In 1932 Serisawa enrolled at Otis Art Institute, where he trained under the New York realist Alexander Brook, a specialist in figure studies.

After completing his courses, Sueo joined with his brother during 1934 in shooting a documentary-style film of Little Tokyo and crafting a scenario. The result, a two-thousand-foot silent film, *Nisei Parade*, was previewed at the Miyako Hotel in December 1934 before opening officially early the following year. While the film did not achieve great commercial success, its photography was praised in Hollywood (notably by celebrated director Fritz Lang), and it was awarded an honorable mention for documentaries in the 1935 *American Cinematographer* Amateur Movie Awards. According to Larry Tajiri, writing ten years later, the only print of the film went to a photo supply dealer who had provided film and other materials to the producers. Serisawa reaped an extra dividend from the film when he married Mary Tanaka, one of the film's leads (her sister married Ikuo Serisawa). Mary would serve as one of her husband's principal models, as their daughter Margaret did later.

During the 1930s Sueo worked as a painter and portrait artist in Los Angeles. In 1934 one of his works appeared in the invitational exhibit of contemporary American painting held at the University of Illinois. In 1937 he had his first solo show, in his hometown of Long Beach, a set of portraits and landscapes done in oil. Serisawa's *Backstreet*, a Little Tokyo scene, won first prize at the Laguna Beach art salon and then honorable mention at the Pomona County Fair. (Drawing on his experience in Little Tokyo, Serisawa also produced *A Second Generation*, a portrait study of Issei and Nisei). In 1937 his work was featured in an exhibit of art by "California oriental painters" at the Foundation of Western Art. Two years later, his still life *The Three Pears* was featured in an invitational Southern California art exhibit in San Diego's Balboa Park.

In 1939 the first Los Angeles solo exhibition of Serisawa's art was held at the city's Tone Price Gallery. The esteemed *Los Angeles Times* art critic Arthur H. Miller said of the show, "[Serisawa] is the most promising artist and especially his improvement and advancement in quality of many of his paintings in the last two or three years are very noticeable." The show brought increased exposure to the young artist. In April 1940 Serisawa's work appeared alongside that of Benji Okubo and Hideo Date in a show at USC's Harrison Gallery. Soon after, he held a solo exhibition at the Dalzell Hatfield Galleries, located in the city's Ambassador Hotel. Hatfield would remain a prominent dealer and supporter of his work.

In October 1940 Serisawa's painting of a church in a summer landscape was featured in the eighth annual Foundation of Western Art's *Trend* show. Another painting won second prize in a show at the California State Fair. In December Serisawa was awarded the Foundation of Western Art's medal as the most promising young Southern California artist. Serisawa remained similarly active in 1941. In February he held a solo oil painting exhibition at Scripps College. The following month he joined in the annual exhibit of art at the Oakland Art Gallery (today's Oakland Museum of California) alongside such artists as Miné Okubo and Henry Sugimoto. In September his painting *A Portrait of a Singer* (a study of Nisei soprano Tomi Kanazawa) was displayed at an invitational art exhibit of California paintings at the Los Angeles County Fair in Pomona. One of his watercolors won first prize at a San Diego exhibition. Serisawa's work attracted the attention of MGM composer and producer Arthur Freed, who commissioned him to do portraits of performers Ann Sothern and Judy Garland for the studio.

In fall of 1941 Sueo Serisawa was granted a large-scale solo exhibition at Los Angeles's Museum of History, Science, and Art (today the Natural History Museum of Los Angeles), which honored him as its artist of the month. However, the exhibit opened on December 7, 1941—the day Pearl Harbor was bombed. While the *Los Angeles Times* respectfully reviewed the exhibition, it was all but ignored in the ensuing crisis.

In the spring of 1942, following Executive Order 9066, both Serisawa brothers made the difficult decision to move their families away from the West Coast in order to escape mass confinement. After settling in Colorado and then Chicago (where Sueo Serisawa studied at the famed School of the Art Institute of Chicago), Serisawa moved to New York City in 1943, settling in bohemian Greenwich Village. According to Los Angeles critic Miller, Serisawa was not keen on life in New York. "Great place to find stimulation. Bad place to live. Artists there eat each other. One develops a trick and everybody rushes to copy it." During all this time Serisawa shipped his work to Los Angeles for storage and handling.

Serisawa's involuntary exile from California paid dividends artistically. While in New York he made contact with sculptor Isamu Noguchi, and he was invited by Yasuo Kuniyoshi to work at Kuniyoshi's house in the Woodstock art colony. His work attracted favorable attention from East Coast galleries. After attending a show of the German artist Max Beckmann, Serisawa was inspired to adopt a more radical expressionist style that mixed Asian and Western elements. In 1945 he participated in two exhibitions at the Lilienfeld gallery in New York City. The gallery offered him a solo show, but it was later postponed indefinitely due to difficulties in transporting his work from Los Angeles.

In 1947 Serisawa and his family returned to the West Coast. He was hired to teach art at the Kann Institute of Art (1948–50) and later at Scripps College (1950–51). He also offered private art lessons to Hollywood actors and writers such as Edward G. Robinson, Claire Trevor, and Frances Marion. During this period Serisawa studied the religious teachings of J. Krishnamurti and became absorbed in Zen Buddhist art and philosophy, which would exercise a lasting influence on his painting. He and Ikuo teamed up again to produce *Bunka* (1953–54), a short color film about Japanese culture in Southern California.

In the following years Sueo Serisawa became one of Southern California's best-known artists. In 1948 he enjoyed a second solo show at the Dalzell Hatfield Galleries and later participated in others at the Wildenstein Gallery and Felix Landau Gallery. In 1949 one of his paintings won the $1,000 first prize at the California State Fair competition. In 1952 his painting *Trees* appeared in a show at the Los Angeles County Museum of Art and was heavily praised.

Serisawa also participated in exhibitions farther afield. In 1947 his oil painting *Pierrot* was featured at an exhibition at the Pennsylvania Academy of Fine Arts and won the Carol H. Beck medal for best portrait. Three years later, his painting *House of Cards* was also featured at the academy. In 1950 his painting *Puppet and Child* (described by *New York Times* critic Howard Devree as "successfully infus[ing] occidental abstract approach with oriental spirit") was shown at the Metropolitan Museum of Art, whose directors then acquired the painting for $1,000. In 1958 he showed his semi-abstract painting *Mountain* at the annual of the Whitney Museum in New York. He also branched out to commercial art, designing greeting cards for Hallmark and record album covers for Pacific Jazz Records.

In 1955 Serisawa returned to Japan for the first time since his childhood and visited Tokyo and Kyoto, where he studied traditional Japanese art and design. In response, he began to embrace a more spiritual mission. As he later explained it, "The deeper meaning of art is the expression of universal themes and truths." Upon his return to California, Serisawa was commissioned by the Huntington Library to refurbish the landmark teahouse in its Japanese garden and open it as a permanent display of Japanese design. In the ensuing years he altered his style from European-style expressionism to heavy reliance on use of abstract Japanese elements. During the 1960s he began using calligraphic forms and producing gold- and silver-leaf sumi ink paintings. In subsequent years he began producing wood-block prints as well as creating acrylic and oil paintings that integrated elements of traditional screen painting.

In the mid-1970s Serisawa remarried and moved to Idyllwild, California, a small mountain community, and taught art at the University of Southern California–Idyllwild. Nature and natural forms became predominant subjects in his work. As one critic later termed it, Serisawa's style, which the artist termed "Humanistic Expressionism," sought to evoke humanity's shared emotional and spiritual connection to nature and the cosmos. A retrospective of his work was held at the Occidental College in Laguna Beach, and his work was held in the collections of the Museum of Modern Art, Los Angeles County Museum of Art, Santa Barbara Museum of Art,

Smithsonian Institution, and San Diego Museum of Art. Serisawa remained in California, creating works of art and teaching until he died on September 8, 2004, at the age of ninety-four. His unsung career, with its many highlights, wartime interruptions, and durability, expresses many of the themes of the Japanese American experience.

Dr. Newton Wesley: Inventor of the Contact Lens

One fun aspect of history is discovering the unheralded inventors of everyday products. There is the streetlight, developed by African American inventor and engineer Lewis H. Latimer. Or the Bing cherry, developed by Ah Bing, a Chinese immigrant horticulturist in Oregon. There is the case of Frank Zamboni, the son of Italian immigrants in Idaho, who developed the ice-resurfacing machine that bears his name. One particularly intriguing figure in this respect is Dr. Newton K. Wesley, a Nisei inventor and optometrist who played a leading role in the development of the contact lens.

He was born Newton Uyesugi on October 1, 1917, in Westport, Oregon. According to family lore, he was named for the physician who delivered him. Eight years later, the Uyesugi family moved to Portland, Oregon. The young Newton first made his name not in science but in sports. In 1934 he was named president of the Osei Asahis, the basketball team of Portland's Osei Athletic Club, and he was reelected in 1935. In 1938–39 he starred for the Busseis in an Oregon Japanese basketball league—and in January 1939 was leading the league in scoring. In June 1939 he was elected president of the local Japanese Methodist church's Epworth League. He meanwhile joined the JACL's Portland chapter, and he was elected its president in 1941. In 1941 he married Cecilia Sasaki, with whom he would have two children.

The question of improving vision concerned the young Newton from his early days since he had eye troubles. Beginning at age nine he wore glasses, but his eyesight continued to decline. In spite of his vision troubles—or because of them—he attended the North Pacific College of Optometry, graduating in 1939. As a college senior, he developed bilateral keratoconus, leaving him with increasingly blurred vision. He was nonetheless able to graduate in 1939 and thereafter opened an optometry practice in Portland. In the years that followed, he changed his name from "Uyesugi" to "Wesley." According to one source, he advertised himself in the Portland telephone directory as "Dr. Newton K. Wesley" (choosing the name to appeal to his devout Methodist parents, with the K. in honor of a brother who died young) because Uyesugi was too difficult for non-Japanese to pronounce. He continued to use the name Uyesugi in the Japanese community during the 1940s—he ran ads for his business under this name in the Japanese American press.

Soon after Wesley's graduation, his former teacher Dr. Harry Lee Fording, the owner of the North Pacific College of Optometry, offered to sell the school to him for $5,000. Wesley was only twenty-two years old at the time, but he and a classmate, Dr. Roy Clunas, managed to arrange the purchase. In 1942 Wesley and his family were confined at the Portland Assembly Center. After a few months, he left confinement and enrolled at Earlham College, a Quaker institution in Richmond, Indiana, before settling in Chicago. While Wesley refused to return to Portland, he retained his interest in the North Pacific College, which in 1945 became the Pacific University College of Optometry. Thanks in part to Wesley's campaigning, the OD degree became accepted as a standard postgraduate degree.

In 1944 Wesley began wearing a pair of contact lenses. The lenses arrested the progress of his keratoconus and saved his sight. Around this same time, he accepted a faculty position at Monroe College (later the Illinois College of Optometry). Along with a student, George Jessen, Wesley entered the field of contact lenses. In 1946 the two men formed the Plastic Contact Lens Company of Chicago (later known as Wesley-Jessen Corporation). They sought to improve on existing models. Early contact lenses distorted the cornea, harming vision, and were so uncomfortable that they could only be worn for short stretches. Wesley and Jessen spent six years of intensive research designing plastic lenses that would correct keratoconus and permit the wearer improved vision but still be comfortable. Wesley coined the term orthokeratology (OK) for gas-permeable contact lenses that flatten the cornea. Their first lenses were produced using a sewing machine treadle.

By 1956 Wesley and Jessen had developed a very small lens that would fit onto only the spherical portion of the cornea and not harm the wearer's vision. Wesley meanwhile began working on the photoelectric keratoscope, a diagnostic instrument, which Wesley-Jessen began manufacturing a decade later. Ultimately Wesley left his faculty position to run the contact lens manufacturing business and advocate for the use of contact lenses. Wesley bought his own airplane and flew all over the United States to lecture to eye doctors about contact lenses and to train optometrists to fit them, and he did media interviews. His efforts were crowned with notable success in 1970, when contact lenses were approved by the American Medical Association.

Around the same time as they developed their first commercial lenses, Wesley and Jessen developed sets of bifocal lenses. Although Wesley was unable to obtain a patent for the bifocals, as inventor John de Carle had beaten him to it, the two ultimately joined forces in 1959 to form the Sphercon Lens Company (initially as a British branch of Wesley's company), which used de Carle's patents and Wesley's technology. In 1963 the Plastic Contact Lens Company of Chicago went public as Wesley-Jessen. Wesley meanwhile sold off Sphercon, which became known as Contactalens. Wesley also opened joint ventures in other countries, beginning with Argentina and Japan. Eventually he owned shares in companies in thirty-three countries. In the late 1970s Wesley-Jessen began manufacturing soft contact lenses, including colored lenses.

In 1955 Wesley started the Contact Lens Association of Optometry and the National Eye Research Foundation (NERF) to promote research and clinical studies specifically regarding contact lenses and their applications for improvements in vision and health. NERF provided grants for research to doctors and schools of optometry, notably the Illinois College of Optometry and the Pacific University School of Optometry. Through the NERF, Wesley opened an eye research clinic in Northbrook, Illinois, using techniques devised by his brother, Dr. Edward Uyesugi. Wesley's son, Roy Wesley, became involved on a full-time basis from 1981 to 1992 as president and director of the clinic. Wesley served as chairman until he retired from optometry in 2000. Dr. Newton K. Wesley died on July 21, 2011, at age ninety-three, from congestive heart failure.

Eugenie Clark

Internationally famous as "the Shark Lady," Dr. Eugenie Clark was a leading ichthyologist and conservation advocate in the public sphere.

Clark was born in New York City on May 4, 1922, to Charles and Yumi Clark. Charles was a Pennsylvania native, while Yumi had immigrated from Japan in 1907, at the age of ten. Charles Clark died shortly after his daughter's birth. Yumiko later married a local Japanese, Masatomo Nobu, who owned New York's Chidori restaurant.

The young Eugenie (known as "Genie") grew up in New York. The 1930 census reports the young Eugenie and her mother living in Queens with Yumi's younger brother Walter Mitomi, an architectural draftsman, and their mother Yumiko Nagahara. In her early years Genie spent a good deal of time with her grandmother at the beach in Atlantic City, New Jersey, where she learned to swim. Genie encountered prejudice during her school days, when her Japanese ancestry made her stand out from her school classmates. As she later recalled, "I'm half-Japanese, and in those days, people didn't understand the Japanese—they thought we were the mysterious people of opium dens and long fingernails." A drawing of hers was vandalized with the word "Jap" scrawled over it. Clark responded by being outrageous: when other children would ask about the sheets of black seaweed she would bring for lunch, she would say, "I'm eating carbon paper."[1]

The young Genie had a life-changing event one Saturday morning when she was nine years old. She accompanied her mother to Manhattan, where Yumiko worked, and was left alone all morning in the New York Aquarium (then at Battery Park). Clark recalled how she spent hours there, pressing her face against the glass of the fish tanks, imagining that she was swimming

Dr. Eugenie Clark (*center*) with Otto H. Oren (*left*) and Adam Ben-Tuvia, 1962. Collection of Heinz Steinitz

in the water surrounded by such mysterious and beautiful creatures. From that time on, she decided to work with fish. She bought a mini-aquarium with some tropical fish to raise at home and eventually filled "rooms and rooms" with them. She spent countless Saturdays at the aquarium studying the movements and interactions of the fish. Clark also attributed part of her interest in the ocean to her Japanese ancestry and cultural background, in which the sea plays a large part.

In 1942 Clark earned a BA in zoology from Hunter College. Shortly afterward she married Hideo Roy Umaki, a Hawaiian-born Nisei airline pilot. The marriage ended in divorce in 1947. During the war years, Clark was unable to find a job in her field and instead worked for a plastics company, Celanese Corporation of America. Meanwhile she enrolled at New York University, earning her master's in zoology in 1946. (While she considered studying at Columbia University, she was discouraged by a professor's sexist comments during her interview.)

After receiving her MS, Clark was invited by oceanographer Carl L. Hubbs to serve as research assistant at the Scripps Institute of Oceanography in La Jolla, California. Here she learned how to dive—she almost drowned on one occasion when a hose in her diving helmet became blocked and the air failed to reach her. After leaving Scripps, she was hired as a research associate by the American Museum of Natural History in New York, which allowed her to complete a PhD in zoology at NYU in 1950. Her dissertation was on the mating behavior patterns of xiphophorin fish.

After graduating, Clark began doing field research around the world, including in Micronesia, Hawaiʻi, and the West Indies. One of her earliest research sites was the South Pacific island of Palau, where she studied poisonous fish. Since compressed air was not available on these islands, located far from populated countries, she had to learn to free-dive. It was while she was in Palau that she learned the technique of consulting with local fishermen, whose experience gave them expertise on the characteristics of fish in their environments.

In 1951 Clark married Ilias Themistokles Papakonstantinou (Constantinou), an orthopedic intern. The couple had four children in the following six years. Even as she raised her children, Clark's career took off. In 1951 Clark used a Fulbright grant to embark on a ten-month study of poisonous fish at the Ghardaqa marine biological station on the Red Sea. Armed with goggles, a snorkel-type breathing tube, and an elastic speargun, she remained in the water for an estimated twelve hours per day. She later related that she shocked local Muslim women and men when she wore a two-piece bathing suit. Clark found nearly three hundred species of fish, including forty poisonous and three never before discovered.

Following her return, she settled in Buffalo and wrote a memoir of her experiences, with assistance from a Eugene F. Saxton fellowship. It was published in 1953 under the title *Lady with a Spear*. The book earned Clark widespread publicity, both as a researcher and as an attractive young woman in a male-dominated field. A British edition appeared the following year, and numerous foreign-language editions followed.

In the wake of her memoir, Clark was invited by the Vanderbilt family to move to southwestern Florida, where the Vanderbilts financed the construction of a lab and research station. The Cape Haze Marine Laboratory (later the Mote Marine Laboratory) opened in 1955, with Clark as founder and executive director, plus one assistant. Its mission was to do research on sharks and to acquire sharks for other researchers. Clark continued to travel the world. In Eilat, Israel, during the 1960s, she conducted a "poisoning" operation and discovered new species of fish. She met then crown-prince Akihito of Japan, taught him how to snorkel, and gave him a nurse shark.

In 1967, after separating from her husband, Clark moved to New York. The following year, she was named professor of marine biology at University of Maryland and relocated to Bethesda, Maryland, although she retained her connection with the Mote Laboratory. She was briefly married twice more. In 1969 she published her second autobiography, *The Lady and the Sharks*. She wrote numerous popular articles for *National Geographic* magazine over the following years. In addition to her study of fish, Clark worked as a conservationist. Her deep concern for protection of marine environments led Egyptian president Anwar Sadat to protect the reefs of Ras Muhammed, which in 1983 became Egypt's first national park.

While Clark continued research on various fish during these decades (and had multiple species named for her) she achieved her greatest renown as an expert on sharks. She traveled to Mexico's Yucatán Peninsula in search of the so-called "sleeping sharks" that remain immobile in the water. Her discovery challenged longstanding scientific theories that sharks died if they ceased moving. She also discovered that sharks were nauseated by the secretions from the Moses sole, a flatfish living in the Red Sea, and used her discovery to develop the first effective shark repellent. She became an expert on the whale shark, the world's largest fish. In 1973 she located a dead specimen in a net in the Red Sea, which she was able to study. In the 1980s she encountered live sharks. On one occasion she grabbed the skin under a whale shark's dorsal fin and was carried along on a ride with the shark until she finally decided to let go. She also rode jockey-style on the back of a female whale shark off the coast of Baja California.

Clark devoted herself to dispelling public fears about sharks, which were magnified by the popular 1970s novel and film series *Jaws*. Indeed, one of her *National Geographic* stories on them was titled "Sharks: Magnificent and Misunderstood." Clark maintained that, despite public misconceptions, sharks were neither dumb animals—they were intelligent enough to learn to press buttons on command—nor generally dangerous to swimmers, whom they avoided. It was for this work that Clark received her "Shark Lady" moniker.

Clark retired from University of Maryland in 1999, although she continued teaching. She continued diving into her nineties, even after being diagnosed with non-smoking-related lung cancer. She died in 2013 at the age of ninety-one.

CHAPTER SEVEN

The Queer Heritage
of Japanese Americans

The Archaeology of Queer Nikkei History

The annual series on queer Japanese American history that I have under-taken to mark LGBT Pride Month is one of the parts of my work of which I am the proudest. Throughout the years these entries have shed light on the nature of sexuality in Japanese communities, the rise and decline of homo-phobia, past gay activists, and community debates over LGBT civil rights.

One thing that is important to discuss is the question of evidence, as it forms perhaps the greatest problem in studying the history of sexuality. It is a truism that scholars are only as good as their sources. Yet sexual desire and relations—of any kind—involve the most intimate kinds of feelings and vulnerabilities, all of which makes getting a clear picture of past practices troublesome. Inquiring into queer Nikkei sexuality is especially tricky and uncomfortable, because of both the difficulty of asking for information and the sorts of responses one gets. Same-sex desire and practice long remained stigmatized in Japanese communities, as in mainstream American society. Because of the illicit nature of the subject, signs of its existence were denied, destroyed, or at best lay half-concealed amid rumor and hearsay. Thus, the available pool of evidence is fragmentary, and even what exists is not always reliable, all of which makes interpretation hazardous.

Indeed, in dealing with data in this area, I find a certain kinship with my colleagues who specialize in ancient history. They reconstruct the past based on tiny sets of primary materials, using archaeological and philological tools. They must grasp subtleties of meaning in scattered pieces of text written in dead languages—fragments of poems, inscriptions, and the like. In the same way, as a scholar of queer sexuality I must deal with texts phrased in slang and coded language, with no ready system for detecting irony or euphemism. Like a traveler encountering a foreign country with different language and social codes, I face a situation ripe for misunderstanding and sometimes comic error.

Let me offer two examples of the pitfalls of interpreting the incomplete, ambiguous sources that I come across. The first case is that of a short composition, "A Nisei in the U.S. Army." I came across the text some years ago while on a research trip to Honolulu (and yes, I *do* really spend a lot of time researching when I am in Hawai'i—the state has many archives relating to Japanese American history, and there is much to study and absorb). One day I was in the special collections room of the Hamilton Library at the University of Hawai'i-Manoa, looking through the papers of the Romanzo Adams Social Research Laboratory for the World War II era. In a file marked "AJAs" (Americans of Japanese Ancestry), I found a composition by one Kimei Kawahara, who was listed as a "freshman in Mr. Shepardson's class." It was undated but clearly a product of the war years.

The story told of a Nisei soldier from California, Sergeant Frank Goda, who had been sent to Hawai'i and now faced a decision as to whether to volunteer for a dangerous mission. The reason for Goda's hesitation was the treatment of his family on the mainland. His father had been "interned at a detention camp in Arizona," while his mother and siblings had been sent to "an evacuation camp in the interior" dubbed "Shangri-la" in the newspapers. My eye was caught by the passage that followed:

> His thoughts were also with Butch Watanabe who was stationed at
> Fort Bliss, Texas and whom he missed as much as he did the family. He

remembered how Butch and he used to haul vegetables to Los Angeles at such ungodly hours of the morning as one or two. And how they came home at early dawn to make delicious hamburger with as little noise as possible and to steal into his room upstairs to eat it and to read each other's love letters which usually emerged at the end rumpled and dotted with catchup and mayonaise [*sic*].

How could I interpret this tantalizingly ambiguous tale? What is clear from the text is that Frank's feelings for Butch were strong, as strong as for his immediate family, but is this a case of romance or male bonding? Equally uncertain is whether Frank and Butch wrote to each other the love letters they exchanged or whether they came from others. The text does not mention Frank missing anyone else, even someone who might have felt close enough to write him love letters. In either case, the text suggests that the boys shared their letters primarily to impress each other and were quite cavalier about the feelings of the writers whose tokens of affection were crumpled and stained with the boys' condiments.

It is tempting to do a queer reading. Certainly there is a touching intimacy about the boys stealing quietly together up to Frank's room at daybreak to have private time together, rather than eating downstairs. The odd phrase about "making delicious hamburger with as little noise as possible" has a powerful erotic subtext—as can be seen by how natural the phrase sounds if the word "love" is substituted for "hamburger." The problem is that any such reading risks launching countervailing charges of over-interpretation. Critics might dispute whether a Japanese American college freshman in Hawai'i, inventing a story about mainland Nisei, could have intended such a meaning or even been aware of it. External evidence was useless here. I was unable to find biographical information on "Kimei Kawahara"—to discover even whether the student was male or female.[1]

Conversely, there is the case of "Helen Ito." I recently came across copies of *ONE* magazine, posted online at University of Southern California. *ONE* was the journal of the Mattachine Society, the first and most important "homophile" group. (In the 1950s, before Stonewall and gay liberation, small numbers of "homophile" activists organized to fight police repression and call for decriminalization of homosexual acts.) On reading the very first issue of *ONE*, from January 1953, I was stunned and excited to see a poem called "Proud and Unashamed." The narrator dreamed of a time when gay people could share in the world's great love poetry, be associated with other historic loves—in sum:

That we, too, might be proud and unashamed
To bring our love out into the sunshine
And proclaim to the world, "We love!" "We love!"
And proclaim to the world "We love"

Even greater was my enthusiasm when I saw that the author of the poem was listed as "Helen Ito." Of course, I knew that in those days, when homosexuality was illegal in the United States, many contributors to *ONE* used pseudonyms (the Mattachine Society got its name, after all, from a medieval figure who spoke truth from behind a mask). Yet I thought that surely Helen Ito, with her call for pride, would not have hidden behind a false identity. At the very least, I thought, she was brave not to conceal her Japanese ancestry in her pseudonym. I determined to trace her career, the more so as so few women were connected with *ONE*.

Imagine my disappointment when, in the course of perusing later issues, I found an obituary for Elizabeth (Betty) Purdue, and discovered that *she* was Helen Ito. Fearing the loss of her job as a schoolteacher if her lesbianism was discovered, Purdue, a white woman from the South, had protected herself by adopting a Japanese pseudonym—possibly in tribute to a Nisei girlfriend. Betty Purdue was still inspiring for her dream of unashamed love, and I could not blame her for protecting her identity in a time of mass repression, but my thrill at finding an out and proud Nisei lesbian were dashed. Meanwhile, I could only guess at the identity and intentions of Kimei Kawahara. Such are the trials of working on the queer side of the Great Unknown!

The Evolution of Community Opinion
and the Rise of Homophobia

This column was published in June 2015, as the Supreme Court was poised to decide whether states could constitutionally deny equal marriage rights to same-sex couples.

All eyes nationwide rest on the Supreme Court. Its forthcoming ruling on marriage rights will not only have a significant legal impact, at least in the short term, but also an enormous political and symbolic value. Still, in a larger sense, the issue will continue to be litigated in the court of public opinion. In the last years, even as the federal government and a large majority of states have been obliged to accept marriages contracted within their borders (often following rulings of judges appointed by Republican officials), diverse polls have signaled an emerging supermajority in favor of marriage rights for same-sex couples.

More importantly, the rapid turnaround of public opinion has left those who oppose same-sex marriage—and equal rights for gay people generally—on the defensive. Far from the days when most Americans regarded homosexuality with open loathing and derision, conservatives now complain of feeling stigma over expressing their opposition to homosexuality.

I confess that, as a citizen, I view such claims with skepticism, especially when conservatives demand license to discriminate in the public sphere on the basis of "sincere" religious (i.e., Christian) belief. Yet as a historian of Japanese North Americans I am glad to discover any past statement on homosexuality in the Nikkei press, positive or negative, in order to help trace the nature of opinion on the subject within ethnic communities in the United States and Canada. Looking at references to LGBT in some earlier pieces, which were generally quite negative in their tone, certainly tells us how far things have evolved since.

One early fragment of evidence I have found of attitudes toward homosexuality in the Nikkei press dates from June 1965, when Carole Terada, a Sansei (third-generation Japanese American) teenager, complained in the

New Canadian that local teenage guys, notably in Toronto's Village, were all dressing and acting in effeminate style and thereby revealing themselves as frivolous and immoral. As an example, she complained of a singer, Monti Rock III, who kept his hair long, sported earrings, wore outrageous clothes, and "pranced about the stage." Although Terada did not explicitly refer to homosexuality in her diatribe about effeminacy, her implication was clear enough to a male reader, Stan Kondo. Kondo slammed Terada as sensationalistic and intolerant in associating long hair and modern dances with effeminacy and queerness—though he agreed that the latter were indeed deplorable: "You paw through a ton of apples until you finally seize upon one rotten one (there is always one). . . . Take any group of 500 teen-age boys and you'll inevitably find one homosexual among them. And consider that there are 300,000 male teenagers in Toronto."

Another early piece is an unsigned article that appeared in the November 5, 1971, issue of *Kashu Mainichi*. Despite its title, "Japanese Travelers Warned of Homosexual Attacks Overseas," the article did not discuss gay-bashing. Instead it focused on the arrest of two teenagers from a Tokyo high school who had been caught having sex with men in a Shinjuku hotel. "The school authorities suspended the two boys concerned, but it is said the unhealthy practices are rife even among students. Such unnatural perversions have a long history in Japan as well as in foreign countries." The author, seeming to forget this "long history," then implied that homosexuality was a foreign practice, warning Japanese men who traveled abroad, especially if they were handsome, "to be careful of men who pass them by in corridors of hotels." While ostensibly this article concerned only Japan and Japanese travelers, rather than Japanese Americans, the fact that the text was published without a byline suggests that it was written by *Kashu Mainichi* editor Hiroshi Hatayama or that Hatayama may have shared the author's views of homosexuality as sexual perversion and "unhealthy" vice.

Another instance of homophobia in community media dates from 1982, when Judge William Marutani, longtime JACL national counsel, broached in his column in the *Pacific Citizen* the subject of community attitudes toward homosexuality. Marutani stated bluntly that he opposed civil rights for "Queers," such as the right to teach in public schools, in order to ensure that the practice of homosexuality "not be encouraged or advanced." He added that, like most Nisei he knew, he found the whole concept of homosexuality to be personally and emotionally abhorrent.

After Marutani's column appeared, he was challenged by a reader who sent a private letter (not published) with a detailed refutation of his views. Marutani responded by explaining that while intellectually he could accept that gays and lesbians should not be persecuted, he had felt "emotional obstacles . . . since childhood" to their existence. He made a distinction between fairness and equality, the latter of which he deemed endorsement. "Thus, for example, while we fully subscribe to teaching our children the virtues of civil rights, we are not prepared to include in that teaching the 'positive rewards' (our term, whatever that may mean) of a life of homosexuality." He added that he did not know any Japanese Americans who "engaged in homosexual activity," and while he did not doubt that there were some, he could not imagine that they could amount to even 1 percent of the total ethnic population—and thus by implication could not be considered of importance.

The fact that such a distinguished member of the community, one known for championing the civil rights of minorities, held such negative views is striking. Even more so is his bald statement that he was unaware of any Japanese Americans who even had gay sex, which suggests a willful blindness on his part. It is difficult to know whether in 1982 such negative attitudes were as widespread as Marutani presumed. By that time, public discussion of homosexuality had begun, if haltingly, within Japanese American circles, as an offshoot of larger debates over homosexuality in the United States.

On June 26, 2015, the Supreme Court announced a decision in the case of Obergefell v. Hodges. *By a 5–4 majority, the court struck down all state laws forbidding marriage rights to same-sex couples.*

Japanese Americans Coming Out in the 1970s:
The Community Forum

During the 1970s, lesbian and gay communities spread throughout the country, with San Francisco, Los Angeles, and New York as national centers. Their members built alternative social institutions such as bookstores, dance clubs, health clinics, women's music concerts, theaters, and bars. There were also assorted men's saunas and sex clubs, many of which would be closed by official decree in the 1980s amid the AIDS crisis. Community members also turned to political organizing through such groups as the Gay Activists Alliance and the National Gay Task Force (now the National LGBTQ Force). In the wake of the Stonewall Riots, LGBT activists privileged the coming out experience—the public taking on of a queer identity and telling friends and family—not only as an act of personal liberation from shame but also as the core of civil rights politics.

During these years, despite ambient racism in gay communities, whose public face was very white, countless Asian Americans found a home there. A few gay and lesbian Asian Americans discussed their sexual orientation publicly. Kiyoshi Kuromiya, cofounder of the Philadelphia chapter of Gay Liberation Front in 1970, was an early activist. Willyce Kim, a Bay Area Korean-American lesbian writer and artist, published a book of photographs, *Lesbians Speak Out!*, in 1974. Dennis Chiu told his story in the pioneering 1978 documentary *Word Is Out*. As Eric C. Wat records in his book *The Making of a Gay Asian Community*, in 1980 a circle of activists in Los Angeles, led by the late Tak Yamamoto, formed Asian/Pacific Lesbians and Gays, the first official Asian American LGBT group.

In Asian communities, however, homosexuality long remained taboo, and many people were frightened to break the silence to their friends and families. As columnist Edward Iwata noted sardonically in 1982, "There is only one thing that most Asian Americans fear more than speaking in public or finding bad skiing conditions, and that is homosexuality. It is the last taboo, it is tainted ground. If one is religious, homosexuality is a filthy sin. If one is a Nisei, it is verboten to discuss. If one is a Sansei, it is a netherworld full of lisping, limpwristed men."

Still, despite these formidable burdens, at the tail end of the 1970s there were two notable attempts by queer Nikkei, with help from outside allies, to speak out in community media. The first was by the interviewees of an article, "Japanese American Lesbians Reach Out for Understanding and Acceptance," by Gardena, California, journalist Judy Tachibana. In the article, Tachibana told the life stories of a quartet of Japanese American lesbians. None of these women, she explained, was particularly "butch" or distinctive in appearance, and they felt they did not differ from other middle-class Japanese North Americans whose goals, values and backgrounds they shared. Their special problem lay in explaining their sexual orientation to their families. They had agreed to be interviewed in hopes of changing negative community attitudes toward homosexuality, but each included only the initial of her family name out of concern for privacy, especially at work. The article reminded readers that the "Briggs initiative," a California state ballot referendum to deny gay people the right to teach in public schools, had been defeated at the polls only one year previously, and people still were wary of going public out of fear for their jobs.

The first of Tachibana's interviewees, Carol, a twenty-eight-year-old Sansei, was a recreational counselor who was generally open about her sexuality. She had felt inspired to come out by the example of a Nisei uncle, an artist who had been openly gay for eighteen years and whose white partner was accepted at family gatherings. Carol nevertheless encountered friction from her family over her sexuality. She related that when she came out to her mother, the mother remarked, "What are you getting yourself into?" and had afterward continued to ask whether she had changed her mind—both Carol's mother and older brother seemed to consider her lesbianism a "phase." Carol had never spoken about her sexuality with her father, with whom she had a difficult relationship. She felt uneasy bringing her Anglo girlfriend of two years home, because of the tension it provoked.

The second interviewee, Sharon, a thirty-five-year old Nisei working in the medical field, felt unable to discuss her sexuality with her Issei parents, partly because of the language barrier, partly because of her sense that they would be unable to handle it on cultural grounds. Her strict father, in particular, would feel "dishonored" by a lesbian daughter, she thought. Because of her own negative feelings about her sexuality, Sharon had initially consulted a psychotherapist to fight her attraction to women. Using an English-Japanese dictionary, she had explained to her parents that she was seeking professional help but not told them why, and they had offered financial help but did not ask. Sharon had largely cut herself off from the Japanese community, both in rebellion against her parents' focus on ethnic group activities and because she did not want her parents to learn through "the grapevine" about her lesbianism. Interestingly, Sharon added that if she did ever come out to her parents, they might find it easier if she had a Japanese American girlfriend.

The third subject was Nancy, a twenty-two-year-old Hawaiian-born Sansei working as an auto mechanic. Though she had long been aware of her attraction to women, it was attending a meeting at the Los Angeles Gay Community Center that had led her to live a gay life, and she had since dated several women (including a Japanese American). After being outed to her family by an older Nisei friend, Nancy had tried to make her mother understand her and felt she had succeeded. The rest of the family knew of her sexuality but were less accepting.

The last of the women interviewed by Tachibana was Grace, a twenty-four-year-old Hawai'i-born Yonsei (fourth-generation Japanese American) raised by her grandparents. Grace had previously been sexually involved with Asian American friends, but they had all "turned straight" on her, as a result of feeling the pressure to conform and live as heterosexuals. Grace did not feel ready at that point to speak to her own family about her sexual orientation.

Tachibana's article appeared in *Rafu Shimpo* on October 24, 1979. It caused a certain stir in local Japanese communities. Donald Hata, an educator and then–city councilman in Gardena, later recalled: "The *Rafu*'s English language editor, Dwight Chuman, was a gutsy Gardena Sansei who thrived on publishing stories that made the Nisei Establishment uncomfortable, and Judy's lesbian piece was perfect for that purpose. [Chuman] gave it special attention by lowering the masthead and printing Judy's article above it." Hata added, "Gay and Lesbian issues were evolving topics in mainstream political circles, but totally suppressed in Gardena. This is why so many Nisei parents, as well as Sansei, were shocked when [Tachibana's] Japanese American lesbian article appeared in the *Rafu*."

Just months after Tachibana's article appeared, Jeff Sakuma, then a student at University of Washington, pushed the discussion a step further by publishing a bylined article, "Coming Out," in the Seattle-based Asian American monthly *International Examiner*. Sakuma (who was unaware of Tachibana's piece) began by relating that some months previously his father had remarked that he did not know any Asians who were gay and wondered if such a thing even existed. Sakuma had quickly changed the subject because he felt unable at the time to tell his father about his own gayness. Following the incident, however, he realized that many Asians, like his father, still saw homosexuality as a "white man's disease," a misconception that rested on the absence of visible gay Asians. He was therefore inspired not only to come out to his family but also to take a public stand.

Sakuma's article briefly refuted some of the popular myths about homosexuality, such as that it was a mental illness or a choice. He explained that being gay, in terms of struggles against hostile stereotypes and discrimination, was much like being Asian or part of any other racial minority. Gay Asians had an especially difficult time since they generally lived in close-knit ethnic communities, so coming out not only meant being open to their families but also to the entire community. The fact that so few Asian Americans were open about their sexual orientation made many gay Asians fear that they might be the only one. Sakuma concluded that he had written to offer himself as an example, both to increase community awareness of gay Asian existence and to make it easier for others to come out. He bravely published his home telephone number (plus the hotline number for the LGBT student group at the University of Washington) in case people needed someone to talk to or wished to speak with the Asian community about homosexuality.

Sakuma's article was well received. He later recalled that he found positive responses from all sorts of people, including distant family members whom he had not previously "filled in" about being gay. Interestingly, he was contacted shortly afterward by Japanese American religious leaders and invited to speak before a local Japanese American congregation about homosexuality. Apparently so many people asked how his parents were taking his public revelation, though, that Sakuma's mother ultimately penned a letter to the editor of the *Examiner* to express support for her son. Sakuma did not only speak to Asian American audiences. He produced a piece for *Northwest Oasis*, a fledgling gay-themed journal in Seattle, titled "On Being Asian in the Gay Community."

Two months after his initial article in the *International Examiner*, Sakuma published a follow-up piece. Here he again answered basic questions about gay life: When did he first know that he was gay? (He realized he was "different" by age five.) Were all gay men effeminate and lesbians masculine? (No.) Did he want children (yes) and, if so, would he want them to be gay? Here Sakuma opened up. He had already stated that gay life was rewarding, and he added that he would not wish to change his sexual preference (as it was then termed) any more than his race. However, in the face of society's negative attitudes, being gay was, he admitted, "not the easiest way to live," and he confessed that he would prefer that his children grow up without that burden. Imagine, he explained by way of example, if children had to miss out on the best years of their lives because they could not experience "puppy love, dating, and attending their senior prom with the person that they were truly attracted to."

While the focus on high school proms as the summit of life experiences betrayed the author's youth, the larger question of gay families that Sakuma posed pointed to the turn that LGBT civil rights struggles would take in later decades, during which time legal status for same-sex couples, especially those with children, would take precedence over protections for individuals against housing and employment discrimination.

Pioneering Nisei Lesbians

The 2017 Gay Pride season is upon us. This year there is extra cause for celebration with the selection of professor Amy Sueyoshi, a community activist and leading historian of queer Asian Americans, as a grand marshal of the San Francisco Pride parade. In addition to Amy's own considerable qualities, the choice is gratifying on a symbolic level as a recognition of the important presence of LGBT Nikkei in both queer and Japanese communities.

Amy's selection is also a reminder that a crucial aspect of this evolution, and one that I have shamefully neglected, is the leading role of women. In one sense, this absence is not surprising. Throughout history the grass-roots activism of women, especially outside government, has tended to pass under the radar of media coverage and popular notice. Lesbians in particular have often felt invisible, both in LGBT groups and in the society at large. Indeed, the reason that women insisted on the inclusion of the word "lesbian" in movement language and organizational titles beginning in the early years of gay liberation was precisely that the word "gay," though originally conceived to refer to both women and men, was popularly associated only with men. (The shifts continued further to embrace other less visible populations—for example, the National Gay Task Force, founded in 1973, was renamed the National Gay and Lesbian Task Force in 1985 before later morphing into the National LGBTQ Task Force.)

That said, within Nikkei communities it was most often lesbians rather than gay or bisexual men who took the lead in speaking publicly about their homosexuality in the key period after Stonewall, and in the process they challenged community silence and hostility. We can speculate about the reasons for this: macho social expectations on men that led them to remain hidden; the massive impact of the AIDS crisis in diverting the attention of gay men; greater acceptance of Asian Americans in lesbian communities; high levels of community literacy that promoted women's self-expression; and the impact of the sexual revolution on women generally. Certainly, one central element was the women's movement, which tapped into a genuine if contested strain of feminism in Japanese communities. Throughout the postwar era large numbers of Nikkei women mobilized to seek education and take up careers or community work, all of which in turn encouraged them to be more independent. Whatever the reason, Japanese American lesbians were outspoken in asserting their existence and their goals.

One early activist was poet Michiyo Fukaya (Michiyo Cornell), who in 1979 attended a conference of Third World gays and lesbians and delivered an address, "Living in Asian America: An Asian American Lesbian's Address before the Washington Monument." (The title alluded to the first national gay rights march, which took place that year.) In the address, she linked her experiences as an Asian American lesbian with larger antiracist struggles of Third World people and spoke about racism in LGBT communities. (Fukaya died at age thirty-four in 1987. Her writings were later collected in *A Fire Is Burning, It Is in Me: The Life and Writing of Michiyo Fukaya*.)

Some of the first recorded public statements by Nikkei lesbians came in feminist circles. For example, in 1983 the feminist journal *Off Our Backs* reported on a women's studies workshop in Los Angeles. There Pamela Hamanaka, then a student at UCLA and organizer for Los Angeles Asian and Pacific Lesbians and Gays, spoke poignantly about the plight of Japanese and other Asian lesbians. Asian women as a group, she noted, remained dominated by their families and were generally not allowed to deal with their sexual identities. Hamanaka added that some black and Latin lesbians in Los Angeles saw Asians as white and excluded them, even as there were white lesbians, particularly old-style lesbians, who saw Asians as passive or even as servants. Hamanaka concluded that even if groups such as the JACL were willing to listen to Asian lesbian and gay speakers, she still felt the burden of educating Asians about gay life and of explaining about Asian identity in gay circles.

Six years later, at a conference, Lil, a fifty-seven-year-old Nisei lesbian from San Francisco, spoke as part of a panel on older lesbians. Lil described her experience, explaining that she had been married with children but had left her husband when she came out of the closet. When asked about her parents' reaction, Lil stated that her mother didn't speak to her for seven years after finding out.

Meanwhile, north of the border in Toronto, Mona Oikawa—who labeled herself as a "Sansei lesbian feminist"—wrote an article in the journal *Fireweed* describing her experience of feeling excluded from both LGBT and Asian communities. On the one hand, in taking a petition to Lesbian and Gay Pride Day supporting reparations for Japanese Canadians, she was told by some individuals, "We are not interested in that." Conversely, among Nikkei she faced the burden of assumptions that she was a single, straight woman.

In 1989 the government of Orange County, California, sought to overturn the city of Irvine's human rights ordinance, which banned discrimination on the basis of sexual orientation. (The bigotry of Orange County officials drew a stinging rebuke in the *Los Angeles Times* from renowned poet-activist Mitsuye Yamada.) Local gays and lesbians mobilized to speak in support of the ordinance. In an article in the *Orange County Register* Ann Uyeda recounted her experience as a lesbian. Though she had realized from the time she was little that she was different from others, Uyeda recounted, she denied her homosexuality until she was in college. The first open homosexual she had ever met was a gay man who invited her to a meeting of Parents and Friends of Lesbians and Gays in Orange County in the spring of 1987.

While sporadic and largely ignored by mainstream media, these first recorded stirrings of openness and pride in the 1980s were impressive, and they would give way to a much stronger current in the 1990s.

Military Service and the Shift to Equal Rights

In May 1994 the national JACL board enacted a resolution in support of marriage equality for same-sex couples. This made it the first nonwhite national civil rights organization to support equal marriage rights. The national board's action was controversial and led to bitter divisions and a number of resignations by dissenting members (notably JACL legal counsel Allen Kato). The resolution was submitted to a referendum by the national council at that year's JACL national convention and was only confirmed by the narrow vote of 50 to 38. Despite the closeness of the vote, the marriage resolution proved an epoch-making event for the JACL, placing the organization in the avant-garde on the issue of marriage equality (some two decades before the US Supreme Court finally decreed it nationwide) and signaling a new direction toward engagement with larger civil rights concerns that would expand after 9/11.

In fact, the marriage vote was the climax of a series of earlier shifts that had set the JACL and Japanese American activists generally on new paths. During the 1980s, the struggle for redress dominated Japanese American political action. The enactment of the Civil Liberties Act of 1988 and the success of the coram nobis petitions in vacating the convictions of the wartime Nisei defendants were major victories for the community. Once they were accomplished, though, activists and other concerned members were forced to reflect on future directions. (There was also a certain amount of bad blood between members of community factions who had supported differing strategies.)

It was in this climate of uncertain new beginnings and lingering discord that the issue of LGBT rights touched Japanese Americans. It was not a matter on which the organized Nikkei community had ever taken a position or paid a great deal of attention. In 1988, even as redress approached its final stage, the JACL adopted a new constitution that added "sexual orientation" to its list of categories for which it sought equal justice. Although this established the basis for future action, there was zero discussion of the provision in the *Pacific Citizen* or public debate on the question at the JACL national convention that adopted the constitution. Rather, such language was common in nondiscrimination clauses of universities and other private organizations and in municipal laws. It is conceivable that the drafters of the JACL constitution included sexual orientation as boilerplate language and that members did not realize that they were setting a new precedent in enacting it.

There was no immediate result of the new JACL policy. In the fall of 1992, however, voters in Colorado enacted Amendment 2, an initiative to strip gays and lesbians in the state of legal protections by barring local nondiscrimination ordinances. Though the amendment's provisions were stayed pending a court challenge (and ultimately struck down by the US Supreme Court in the 1996 case *Romer v. Evans*), the prospect of discrimination being enshrined in law was enough to spark discussion by civil rights advocates.

Meanwhile, in early 1993 newly elected president Bill Clinton, who had campaigned for office on a promise to end the military's exclusion of LGBT service members, announced his intention to lift the ban. The change was opposed by General Colin Powell, chairman of the Joint Chiefs of Staff, who asserted publicly, "The presence of homosexuals in the military is prejudicial to good order and discipline." Powell dismissed the parallels to exclusion of African Americans by arguing that, "skin color is a benign, non-behavioral characteristic." The president's plan was also opposed by Senator Sam Nunn, the powerful chair of the Senate Armed Forces Committee. Nunn proposed a policy whereby LGBT service members would not be automatically excluded, provided they kept quiet about their sexual orientation, but could be dismissed if their homosexuality became known.

The public debate over antigay discrimination could not fail to interest Japanese Americans, especially given their history of both official exclusion and outstanding military service. In February 1993, the *Pacific Citizen* published an article on the lifting of military exclusion of gays and lesbians. Martin Karu Hiraga, an openly gay man, reminded readers that the ban negatively affected community members. An outstanding proponent of equal service was Bruce Yamashita, whose views carried particular weight because he had himself been the subject of a major civil rights case. After entering a ten-week course in the US Marine Corps officers candidate school in 1989, Yamashita, a Sansei from Hawai'i, had been subjected to racial harassment and then kicked out two days before graduation on grounds that he had exhibited "leadership failure." Following a sustained campaign, he ultimately received an official apology and the offer of a commission in the marine reserves.

The *Pacific Citizen* article on military service was hotly criticized by columnist and JACL stalwart Bill Hosokawa. Hosokawa (who had rather speciously defended the vote on Amendment 2 in his home state of Colorado as a sane measure to eliminate unneeded laws) complained that the article was "tilted" against the ban and gave the appearance of official JACL support for lifting exclusion. Perhaps as a result of Hosokawa's barbs, the *Pacific Citizen* published a piece soon after by Lt. Col. Thomas Mukai supporting the military ban. Mukai argued that the military should not be forced to lead social change and that the JACL should not focus on the rights of "a special interest group so different from what JACL is." Even more strongly opposed to permitting "gays in the military" was Phill Coleman of Lomita, California, a Vietnam War veteran and librarian. In a letter to the *Pacific Citizen*, Coleman noted that, as an African American, he considered it natural that minorities should band together. However, he insisted that biology was the foundation of human morality. Since homosexual couples could not naturally reproduce themselves, he argued, "Homosexuality runs counter to human survival" and should thus never be legalized or regarded as legitimate. Jimmie Kanaya, a retired army colonel, chimed in that service by gays and lesbians threatened indispensable unit cohesion. "If homosexuals are known to be assigned to a particular unit, they have the tendency to congregate and associate by themselves, and openly flaunt their status to the detriment of the organization."

Despite the opposition, in the spring of 1993 the JACL national board adopted a resolution supporting the right of gays and lesbians to military service. Paul Igasaki, executive director of the Asian Law Caucus, welcomed the vote as a symbolic gesture on the critical civil rights matter of LGBT equality, on which he said the JACL still lagged behind. Karen Narasaki, Washington JACL representative, urged Clinton to hold firm and stand by his commitment to lifting the exclusion. However, in the face of hardline opposition, the movement for opening military service to gays and lesbians sputtered. Clinton ultimately agreed to Nunn's proposal, leading to the enactment of the so-called "Don't Ask, Don't Tell" policy. It was a feeble face-saving compromise, which not only maintained the stigma of the closet and limited freedom of speech in dramatic fashion but also did nothing to stop the investigations and mass discharges that plagued LGBT service members. "Don't Ask, Don't Tell" lasted for seventeen years until Congress reversed the ban and opened military service to LGBT Americans without restriction in 2010.

Marsha Aizumi's *Two Spirits, One Heart*

Marsha Aizumi's book *Two Spirits, One Heart* is a memoir about her experience as the mother of a child who comes out as a lesbian, then transitions from female to male. It is a timely book, coming at a moment when no less an observer than Vice President Joe Biden has asserted that discrimination against transgender people is "the civil rights issue of our time."

A note on the book's jacket describes it as chronicling "Marsha's personal journey from fear, uncertainty and sadness to eventual unconditional love, acceptance, and support of her child." I confess that when I saw that blurb I thought irresistibly of Laura Z. Hobson's semiautobiographical 1975 novel *Consenting Adult*, which recounted a mother's twenty-year struggle to come to terms with her son's homosexuality. I first read *Consenting Adult* as a teenager a decade after it was published. Even then it seemed to me not only dated but cheap—it seemed to ask readers to identify and sympathize with a mother going through trauma rather than with the son trying to come out in a difficult environment.

Fortunately, Aizumi's book turned out to be well worth reading. First, she is clearer than her book's own cover about the unconditional love and concern she never stopped feeling for the troubled daughter Ashley who emerged finally as a happy son Aiden. While Aizumi is upfront and unvarnished about describing her feelings, including negative ones, and her developing understanding, she never plays for sympathy. Rather, she balances the worry she went through over her child with insight on what the experience taught her about the larger problems of LGBT youth. Her experience turned her into an activist: Aizumi was selected for the national board of Parents and Friends of Lesbians and Gays (PFLAG) and took a leading role in advocating policies to support LGBT students in Los Angeles public schools. To her credit, she also includes her son as a coauthor and makes some attempt to bring in his voice and viewpoint.

What is more, her book has a great deal to teach us about the experience of transgender people and their families. First, it reminds us that coming out is a process, one that can be far from linear. Aiden Aizumi and his parents go through several different stages on their journey to self-realization. It also gives us insight into the rapidly shifting state of public opinion on sexual minorities. As a butch lesbian, Aizumi's then-daughter was harassed in school and even attacked physically by a group of Asian guys. In contrast, Aizumi's younger child, Stefen, apparently accepted the emergence of his older brother without trouble and had none of his parents' generation's concerns or doubts about LGBT questions.

Without detracting from its overall value, one curious aspect of the book is the author's relationship to her ethnic identity. On the one hand, Aizumi obviously feels a strong bond with her background. She and her Japanese American husband consciously adopted two children from Japan so they would share ethnicity, and she encouraged her son to take a Japanese name, Takeo, as well as Aiden. This background informs her work. She founded a special Asian American Pacific Islander section of PFLAG in 2012 and attended a White House roundtable on LGBT and Asian-Pacific Islander (API) issues. However, she repeatedly speaks of her Asian background in fairly stereotyped or negative ways. She claims that she was raised in an Asian household, which meant that feelings were not always acknowledged; that because of her background she feels pressured to act in ways that her family or ancestors would approve, not those that reflect her own dreams; and that, in writing, she wrestled with the honor of her family name and the dignity of her ancestors. Aizumi makes a single tantalizing reference to being the only Asian in her class in a conservative town and being taunted for being different, which left her yearning to fit in. She is silent on the question of whether anti-Asian racism makes for special difficulties for current-day LGBT Asians and their families.

While Aizumi is clearly (and laudably) interested in reaching out to other API families, some of whom may be conservative, she does not seem to realize that Asian Americans are not simply conformists: they also have a proud history of protest and struggles for equality. Indeed, we may hope that as LGBT Japanese Americans, in particular, achieve greater visibility, more Nikkei will become aware of the evident fact that such people have always been a part of their communities.

Sometime after this piece appeared, I received a message from Marsha Aizumi. It was the first time that an author whose book I reviewed had ever written to me. She graciously congratulated me on my "honest" review and added that it had made her more aware of her own ethnic heritage—she was now more interested in seeking role models among Japanese Americans who spoke out against injustice. I thought that it was very good of her to have taken my remarks in the spirit in which they were intended and to have made positive use of them.

CHAPTER EIGHT

Other Places, Other Lives

Japanese Americans in Mobile, Alabama

I am endlessly intrigued by the discovery of new frontiers, both geographical and thematic, in Japanese American history. One largely unexplored area is the experience of Japanese Americans in the US South. We have had a few glimmers of this history in memoirs, as well as in books such as Thomas K. Walls's *The Japanese Texans* and John Howard's *Concentration Camps on the Home Front*, a study of the Arkansas-based WRA camps at Rohwer and Jerome. Recently a new book appeared on Asian American experience in the South, Raymond A. Mohl, John E. Van Sant, and Chizuru Saeki's *Far East Down South*, which includes Chizuru Saeki's essay on the reactions of whites in Alabama to Japanese between 1941 and 1953 (and my chapter on Japanese Americans in Louisiana). In fact, the presence of ethnic Japanese in Alabama goes back long before World War II, and the Nikkei history of the Gulf Coast city of Mobile is particularly remarkable.

Mobile was founded at the beginning of the eighteenth century. Like New Orleans, it was part of French Louisiana, and one might call the two brother cities, as they were founded by brothers from Montreal. Even after Mobile became part of US territory in 1813, it remained a cosmopolitan city with French-language writers and newspapers and a small free black Creole population whose school attendance and civil rights were protected under the Louisiana Purchase Treaty. After the Civil War its French-speaking population declined, and Mobile became more Americanized in character, though its citizens continue their traditional Mardi Gras parade even today.

It is not entirely clear when the first Japanese came to Mobile. What is certain is that the region was once a center for cultivation of satsuma oranges from Japan, long before orange-growing became concentrated in (and identified with) Florida. Thousands of acres of orange groves were established in the early twentieth century. While the vagaries of the local climate ultimately made orange growing too risky, this history is reflected in the name of the city of Satsuma, Alabama, in Mobile County.

Meanwhile, two notable Japanese families, the Sawadas and the Kiyonos, established themselves in Mobile. Kosaku Sawada, born near Osaka, the son of a satsuma orange grower, was still in his early twenties when he emigrated to the United States in 1906. After arriving, he joined a group formed to grow rice in Texas, but the experiment did not succeed. Instead, hoping to carry on his father's trade, Sawada founded the Alvin Japanese Nursery Company (named for the Texas town where it was located). The nursery offered satsuma orange and pecan trees imported from Japan for farmers to plant orchards. Four years later, after they lost their entire stock of satsuma seedlings during a hard frost, Sawada and his partners opened a branch in Grand Bay, Alabama. (Grand Bay is adjacent to the Creole fishing town of Bayou La Batre, which has become known in recent years for its Southeast Asian immigrant fishing population.) By 1912, the Alvin Japanese Nursery, officially headquartered in Mobile, was advertising heavily in the region's newspapers.

In 1916 Sawada left his partners and returned to Japan, where he met Nobu Yoshioka from Kanazawa. The two married, and Sawada returned to Alabama with her and resumed his work at the Alvin Nursery. However, three years later, a severe freeze and an attack of citrus canker destroyed the orange plants, and his partners returned to Texas. The Sawadas decided to move to Mobile and start a plant nursery. According to legend, Mrs. Sawada's dowry included a few camellia seeds. The climate in Mobile proved ideal for the flowering shrub, and within a few years the camellia became the focus of the Overlook Nursery (later Overlook Nurseries), the Sawadas' business. The couple developed hybrid varieties for the nursery's seed catalogs. The "K. Sawada" and the "Mrs. K. Sawada" were the best-known. Their nursery became the center of a network of flower production that included large deliveries to New Orleans markets. Mrs. Sawada died in 1929, but the couple had four children, all of whom attended college. Tom Sawada studied at Spring Hill College, a local Jesuit institution. (Father James Yamauchi, a Nisei Jesuit, studied at Spring Hill around the same time and would later join the faculty.) Tom Sawada afterward joined the family firm, as did brother George, who attended Alabama Polytechnic Institute. Sister Lurie attended Huntington College in Indiana. After graduating from Emory University, Ben Sawada became a Methodist minister and worked as a missionary in Japan. (Another family, the Imuras, moved to the region along with Sawada, and Mr. Imura worked at the Overlook Nursery. During the 1930s the family's daughter, Sara Imura, writing from Crichton, Alabama, served as a correspondent for the *New World Sun* newspaper in San Francisco.) According to legend, the nursery was threatened with seizure by the government after Pearl Harbor, but local nurserymen and other influential citizens testified on behalf of the Sawadas' loyalty, and their ownership was not disturbed. Kosaku Sawada died in 1968, but his sons continued the business, and today his grandson George Sawada continues to run the family business.

The Kiyonos have a parallel story. In 1907, at the age of nineteen, Tsukasa Kiyono immigrated from Okayama, Japan, to the United States. With help from his wealthy father, he hired a private tutor to teach him English and started a satsuma orchard near League City, Texas. In 1914, following a frost, he closed his business and moved on to Semmes, Alabama, in the Mobile area, where he bought a forty-acre farm. There he again produced satsumas and pecans, though without great success. (He also married a local white woman, but the marriage did not last.) In 1921 Kiyono returned to Japan and met the woman who would become his wife Tomoe. After returning to Alabama, the couple had two children; their daughter Mary later attended Cedar Crest College in Allentown, Pennsylvania. Mrs. Kiyono brought funds from her dowry and also made money through small-scale flower growing and chicken farming. Eventually she persuaded her husband to use the $3,000 proceeds to invest in more flower growing. He bought an additional eighty acres and planted camellias and azaleas. Business boomed so greatly that by 1935 Mr. Kiyono could estimate his net worth at $325,000 (the equivalent to over $6 million in early 2020). Around this time, the couple established a formal partnership, and Mrs. Kiyono assumed control of one-third of the business. The couple made enough money—$100,000 per year according to their partnership tax return—that they were able to hired staff to perform much of the work. Mr. Kiyono traveled to Japan and Europe, where he searched for plants and shrubs for the Kiyono Nurseries. He and his camellias were even featured in an article in *Life* magazine in 1939.

The Kiyonos' success, however, came at a price. Based on a tip from a secret informant (perhaps inspired by envy), in 1939 the Internal Revenue Service opened an inquiry into the Kiyonos' taxes, then charged them with fraud and deliberate under-declaration of income. The Kiyonos' shoddy bookkeeping practices did not aid their case. The case was still pending in the US Tax Court when the Kiyonos traveled to Japan on a buying trip in mid-1941. They had their return tickets and were ready to board in August 1941 when diplomatic conflict between Japan and the United States caused travel between the two countries to be suspended. The Kiyonos remained trapped in Japan during the war years. In early 1942 the Kiyonos' Alabama property was seized by the federal Office of Alien Property Custodian and sold at auction. Most of the proceeds were turned over to the Internal Revenue Service. The Kiyonos returned to the United States in 1945, following the end of the war. Stripped of his lucrative property, Mr. Kiyono took a job as manager of the Cottage Hill Nursery, near Mobile. He hired an attorney to pursue his case in US Tax Court. Finally, in fall of 1949, the court made its ruling. The judge found that while the Kiyonos had understated their income, and thereby owed back taxes and interest, they were also owed money for legitimate expenses that they had not known enough to claim. More importantly, they were not guilty of any deliberate fraud. This meant that the Kiyonos could not be subjected to fines for fraudulent activities, and also that the government could not recover back taxes for the period before 1935, as such was barred by statute of limitations. In the years following the settlement, the elder Kiyonos lived in retirement in Japan. In 1956 Tsukasa Kiyono presented the JACL with a $2,000 donation in gratitude for the organization's work on behalf of Issei and Nisei.

Japanese Americans in Upstate New York

I have long been intrigued by the rich history of Japanese Americans in upstate New York. I realize that this statement immediately leads to some confusion. As a native of the Big Apple, I myself am used to hearing the label "New Yorker" used to refer to those from New York City. Worse, there is no true collective term that encompasses all of New York State outside the five boroughs. (Even as Canadians commonly refer to the English-dominant areas outside Quebec as the "Rest of Canada" or "ROC," perhaps we should speak of the "Rest of New York" or "RONY.")

In fact, there are at least two distinct New York regions outside the city. First, there is Long Island—meaning Nassau and Suffolk Counties, which are the largely suburban areas that lie east of the city limits. (My Brooklyn-born father used to jocularly refer to this region as the "Guyland" because, in the borough's classic brogue, "Long Island" is pronounced almost like "Lawn Guyland.") Then there is the bulk of the state's territory, which lies between the city and the Canadian border. This region is usually encompassed by the term "upstate New York." Even that definition is fluid, as "upstate" sometimes includes Westchester County, the suburbs immediately north of the city, and other times not.

Whatever term we use, there is clearly a historic division between New York City—urban, noisy, and heavily Democratic—and the largely rural and historically Republican remainder of the state. Yet if the rest of the state lacks the cosmopolitan diversity of Gotham, it has nonetheless been home to a startling variety of intriguing Issei and Nisei.

Japanese immigrants began congregating in New York City by the 1880s and continued to enter throughout the prewar era, though the pace of slowed after the 1924 Immigration Act cut off Japanese entry. Affluent Issei quickly spread to suburbs such as White Plains and Scarsdale (Westchester County) and Long Island. Unlike on the West Coast, there were no restrictive covenants or alien land laws to keep the newcomers from settling where they pleased. For example, Fukuzo Arita moved to Rye and Port Chester, where he founded a successful business as a flower gardener. He also earned extra money by providing day care for local children, who played in Arita's grass fields with his children. During World War II, Arita's three sons enlisted as soldiers. Perhaps the most famous of the prewar suburbanites was silent film star Sessue Hayakawa, who bought a house in Great Neck, Long Island. He played golf at the Soundview Country Club and taught fencing at the club to a group of Nisei boys.

A handful of Japanese migrated to other cities around the state. Isaburo Nagahama, who first arrived in New York City in 1885, was hired by H. C. Parks, a fine arts dealer. After marrying Parks's daughter Gertrude, Nagahama relocated to Schenectady at the turn of the century, where he taught art embroidery at Emma Willard School in nearby Troy and opened his own shop to sell art embroidery. The Nagahamas' daughter Augusta studied nursing, then married Brooklyn-based physician Kanzo Oguri. During the 1930s Nagahama apparently gave up the shop and moved to California. Caught in the wartime removal of West Coast Japanese Americans, he was confined at Heart Mountain during World War II and taught embroidery in camp. He returned to New York after the war and died in 1968 at the age of 101.

One outstanding upstate Japanese resident was Yonezo Okamoto, Japanese businessman (he owned the Japanese textbook publisher Okamoto & Company), author, and art collector, who moved to New York from Washington State around 1914 and settled in Yonkers and then Tuckahoe, New York. Okamoto was patron to the Japanese modern artist Takeuchi Seiho and author of the book *Bara no Kaori* (Scent of Roses), an account for Japanese readers about leading Americans in business, art, and philanthropy.

Beginning in the 1930s, younger Issei and Nisei moved into the suburbs. Architect Minoru Yamasaki moved from Seattle and took a house in Mamaroneck (Westchester County). Another Seattleite, photographer

Toge Fujihira, settled in Roslyn Heights, Long Island. During World War II he would work photographing resettlers in New York for the War Relocation Authority, then would be hired by the Methodist Mission Board. Toru Matsumoto, a young Japanese who had trained as a minister at Union Theological Seminary, settled with his wife and son in Larchmont.

A few migrants settled in rural areas. There were a handful of students at Cornell University in Ithaca, and scattered others, mainly agricultural laborers and domestic servants. In 1910, Sotero Chafl was listed as the family butler of Barnes Compton in Millbrook, Dutchess County. Another Dutchess County family later had a more difficult time with their domestics—in 1932, Gentaro Akiyama of Poughkeepsie was convicted of murdering his employer, J. William Smaltz, and sent to the electric chair, while a maid, Sadako Otsuka, was sentenced for twenty years to life in prison for the crime.

Some Japanese Americans settled in Woodstock, in rural Ulster County. There a commune of artists, led by the renowned painter Yasuo Kuniyoshi, became established. Takashi Ohta, who had worked as a set designer at the Provincetown Playhouse in New York City, moved to the area with his wife and two children and was hired as artist and set designer for the Woodstock Playhouse. During the Depression, the Ohta family survived on what they could grow or sell and finally returned to the city. After the war, Takashi lived with his daughter Toshi and her husband, composer and musician Pete Seeger, in the house the couple built in Beacon; the Seegers remained there through Toshi's death in July 2013.

An interesting trade taken up by Japanese migrants was the roadhouse restaurant or speakeasy. Famed comedian-pianist Oscar Levant later wrote that in his youth, circa 1924, he was employed at a Japanese-owned roadhouse in Harmon (Croton-on-Hudson), New York, called the Mikado Inn. There was a rival restaurant, the Nikko Inn, close by. "Japanese restaurants were comparatively scarce," Levant later remarked, "so it was ironic that the leading proponents of Japanese cuisine should have been within a short distance of each other. Consequently the rivalry was keen." Levant played piano in a duo with a violinist (plus a cello on weekends), alternating between classical and popular music. He added, "I shared sleeping quarters with twenty or thirty Japanese waiters in the cellar." The proprietor, according to Levant, was addressed by the staff as "Admiral Moto" but was himself commanded by his dictatorial Irish wife. They originally had a Japanese chef, but, after the chef quarreled with the management and departed, a local Italian American was recruited to make sukiyaki. In addition to the establishments referred to by Levant, there was one owned by Kin Hana (Kenneth Hanada) and his wife Elizabeth, located in the small Adirondack village of Jay, New York. In 1930 the Hanas, their two daughters, and Mrs. Hana's father, Matt Cobb, were held up by a group of four men, who severely beat Cobb when he tried to resist. Seven years later, celebrity golfer John Montague was arrested on charges of being one of the robbers, though a sensational trial ended in his acquittal.

One remarkable story was that of the Asai family of Ithaca, New York. The patriarch, Matsujiro (also known as Monroe) Asai, moved to the United States in 1892 and enlisted in the US Navy. While serving as a messman on the USS *Chicago* during its tour of Europe, Asai waited on the future King George V and on Kaiser Wilhelm. Asai got married in Japan in 1902, and he and his wife returned to the United States in 1903. They settled near Houston, where Asai worked alongside the Saibara family creating the historic community of Japanese rice growers in Texas. In the succeeding years, the couple had nine children. In 1918 the Asais decided to move to Ithaca so that the children could get an education at Cornell University, with its celebrated agriculture college. (According to a family story, Asai could not drive, so the eldest son, fourteen-year-old Joseph, drove a truck with the family belongings, while the eldest daughter, thirteen-year-old Lillian, piloted the Model T car with all the passengers.) Once in Ithaca, Monroe opened a fruit store.

Monroe's ambition paid dividends. In the end, all nine Asai children attended Cornell, then went on to notable careers. The eldest child, Joseph Byron Asai, received a degree in business administration and was employed by the Fujiyama Company in New York. Lillian Isabella Asai (later Mrs. Vincent Raymond) received a diploma in domestic science, joined Ithaca's welfare department as a caseworker, and ran the Nippon Gift Shop. She also became a local Democratic Party committee member. Tazu Elizabeth Azai (Warner) and Hannah Nightingale Asai became experts in floriculture, and Tazu became a stenographer in the College of Home Economics at Cornell. Sim Lincoln Asai took a degree in hotel management. After a stretch in the army, he was hired as chef at the Statler Hotel in Boston (now the Boston Park Plaza). Mary Victoria Asai specialized in entomology. Kito Kaiser Wilhelm Asai joined the army. Brother George received his PhD in horticulture in 1943, then enlisted in the armed forces. He was detailed to the Military Intelligence Service and studied Japanese at Fort Snelling in Minnesota. After serving in occupied Japan, he was promoted to major during the Korean War and later served as a civilian in the Defense Department. He died in 2006, just before his ninetieth birthday. The youngest child, Woodrow Wilson "Woody" Asai, like two of his sisters, received a degree in floriculture. After spending World War II in the US Army, he moved to New York City, where he was a stalwart member of both the Japanese American Committee for Democracy and later the fledgling New York chapter of the Japanese American Citizens League. In 1951 he was hired as a gardener by the New York City Housing Authority, and he then worked in the city in that capacity for thirty years. Following his retirement at age sixty-three, he took up a second career as a screen actor. He won roles in several films, notably *Zoolander*, before his death in 2005.

World War II brought new Japanese American migration and visibility to upstate New York. In 1943, after receiving assurance from local religious leaders and community leaders that Japanese Americans would be welcomed, the WRA opened a resettlement office in Buffalo, on the eleventh floor of the Rand Building. Saki Yonayama of the Buffalo YWCA and Dr. Kiyoshi Sonoda of the International Institute of Buffalo helped coordinate the activities of resettler groups, while Kazuo Mihara and Mrs. Frank Fukuda assisted individuals. With the help of these official and unofficial agents, resettlers began to settle in the Buffalo area. By mid-1944, the *Gila News-Courier*, published at the Gila River camp in Arizona, reported that there were about twenty-five Nikkei in the city, including several students at University of Buffalo, and that local labor shortages made it an attractive destination. (Apparently few resettlers took advantage, as the following year the *Manzanar Free Press* reported that there were hundreds of job offers still available in Buffalo).

One newlywed Nisei couple, Mr. and Mrs. Sadao Baishiki, who resettled in Buffalo in mid-1944, received the surprise of their lives after they came to the large building in which the resettlement office was located. Upon getting off the elevator at their floor, they were greeted by Eleanor Roosevelt, who had been visiting another office on the same floor. The First Lady approached them with outstretched hand and said, "I'm so glad to see you," before entering the elevator and heading off.

Rochester, New York, also became home to a number of Japanese Americans. Thanks to the efforts of an interfaith church group, the Committee on the Resettlement of Japanese Americans, the city was singled out for praise in the pages of the *Minidoka Irrigator* for the "warm welcome" it offered resettlers. Yoshio Sato, who had received his master's degree in chemistry from University of Oregon before the war, enrolled at University of Rochester as a doctoral student and teaching assistant and received his doctorate there in chemistry in 1947. Three Nisei women, Mary Marutani, Fumi Yosaki, and France Yoge, were enrolled as student nurses at the city's General Hospital.

In April 1944 the WRA opened an additional upstate relocation office in Rochester. WRA staffer Miwako Yanamoto, who had resettled from Arizona's Poston camp to New York, was transferred to help run the new office but left soon after to enlist in the Women's Army Corps. Newcomers found employment in fields ranging from nursing to dairy farming. Harry Yasuda, a linotypist who had been confined at Topaz, was able to find housing in Rochester at the Brick Church Institute's dormitory and was hired by the Ledger Printing & Publishing Company, with union membership granted him.

Scattered Japanese Americans in small upstate towns gained attention. In one well-publicized case, a young Nisei, Coolidge Shiro Wakai, graduated from Central High School in Tully, New York, in 1943 before enlisting in the army and becoming a physician in the postwar years. The Ikeda family, who resettled from Minidoka to the little town of Bedford Hills in Westchester County, attracted positive attention. Henry Ikeda was elected president of his class at Bedford Hills High School in 1945. His sister Betty was selected as drum major for the town's Memorial Day parade. Perhaps the most intriguing Nikkei migrants to upstate New York in the period were Minosuke and Tomi Noguchi. During the prewar years they had raised five daughters, all of whom graduated from college and went on to productive careers. In 1948, after spending forty-two years living in Colorado, they moved to Millbrook and lived with their daughter Sugi Noguchi, a doctor.

Not all the wartime experiences of Japanese American New Yorkers were entirely positive. In June 1942, Toro Matsumoto's Victory Garden, part of a larger garden plot in Larchmont, was trampled and destroyed by vandals. In April 1945, the local resettlement committee in Buffalo reported that when a resettler, Mr. Mihara, wished to purchase the rooming house in which he was a tenant from its white owner, he encountered perceptible racial hostility from locals. Congressman Edward Elsasser wrote to the WRA to ask that Mihara forego such a purchase. Shortly after, when WRA officials inquired about resettlement possibilities in the state capital of Albany, Gerda Bowman, an officer of the New York State War Council, reported, "I am afraid I shall have to report that Albany as a whole, would probably be cold to any Japanese who tried to settle here." Despite the warning, some Japanese Americans did settle in Albany, notably the family of Lydia Minatoya, who told stories of her childhood in Albany in her memoir *Talking to High Monks in the Snow*.

Be a Good Sport about It: Nikkei Athletes in Louisiana

Over the several years I have been engaged in large-scale research on the remarkable and largely unknown history of ethnic Japanese in Louisiana, especially in the cosmopolitan city of New Orleans. One particularly noteworthy aspect of the story of Nikkei in Louisiana during the first half of the twentieth century is the record of their participation in sports, especially at the college level. To be sure, only a handful of individuals were involved: with such a tiny and scattered prewar ethnic Japanese population, there was no counterpart to the all-Nisei semipro teams that dotted the West Coast. Still, not only were the achievements of the Japanese athletes in Louisiana impressive in themselves, they also testified to an overall level of social

Ole Miss' Rebels, conference champs of '47, came to Tigertown one week later boasting a great pitch and catch combine in All-Americans Charley Conerly and Barney Poole.

In the best game of the year, the Johnny Reb nosed out the Bayou Tiger 20-18.

Y. A. Tittle, relieved of his play-calling duties by Ray Coates who returned to action after five weeks on the bench with an injured leg, sparked the Tiger attack.

Abner Wimberly won the "Battle of the Flanks" from the vaunted Poole.

The Tigers scored first, marching 49 yards with Rip Collins plunging over from the one. Heard failed to convert, as he did after each subsequent touchdown.

Ole Miss went ahead 7-6 on a drive which featured Conerly's passes and ended when the Reb tailback tallied on a buck. Bob Oswalt kicked goal.

A few moments later Conerly's replacement, Bobby Wilson, intercepted one of Tittle's tosses on the LSU 35 and ran it back to the Bengal 11. Two smacks and Conerly was over again. This time Oswalt failed to kick goal and the Rebels were out in front at the half 13-6.

Early in the final quarter Collins culminated another LSU scoring parade by diving over from the 3-yard line.

BUCK GALLARD
Center

JOE NAGATA
Halfback

Boston College Eagles smother a Bayou Bengal

But Conerly wasn't through; he added another six points to the Ole Miss side of the edger when he rambled 26 years on a fake pass and run play.

Trailing, 12-20, the Bayou Bengals had one more trip to "Touchdown Town" planned; they made connections on a lateral from Tittle to Coates, who passed to Joe Leach, who was alone in the Ole Miss end zone.

Several times the Tigers missed scoring opportunities; with a little extra push this one could have gone into the win column.

Score by quarters

Ole Miss	0	13	0	7—20
LSU	6	0	0	12—18

First Downs—Ole Miss, 9; LSU, 22

Joe Nagata, from the Louisiana State University yearbook *Gumbo*, 1948. Courtesy of Louisiana State University.

acceptance and inclusion that formed a vivid contrast with the situation of West Coasters.

Exactly when Japanese athletes first began competing in Louisiana is not entirely clear. According to contemporary newspaper accounts, in spring 1905 Shumza (or Shumzu) Sugimoto, a Japanese baseball player who had played for the African American Cuban Giants baseball team, was offered a tryout with the National League champion New York Giants by legendary manager John J. McGraw. Had Sugimoto been selected for the team he would have become the first ethnic Asian major leaguer. However, after being rejected (on racial grounds?), he announced that he would spend the season playing with the Creole Stars, an African American team in New Orleans. There is no other documentation about Sugimoto, his immigration, or his baseball career. Citing this fact, some baseball historians have cast doubt on the accuracy of the story.

What is certain, however, is that various Japanese did compete in sports in Louisiana. In 1922 Shizuka Nakamura, a dental student at Tulane, joined the school's wrestling team. In 1937 Roger Yawata, a former East Bay all-star from Oakland, joined Loyola's football team as a guard. In 1938 one S. Yamate competed in the New Orleans Open winter tennis tournament. Three years later, the New Orleans Lawn Tennis Club hosted the annual city tournament. Hajime Naka and George Masuda each competed in the individual matches, and the two teamed up for the doubles competition. In 1943 Audubon Park was the site of the Southern AAU swimming and diving championships. Thanks to financial support from Nisei benefactor Earl Finch, a swimming team from the 442nd Infantry Regiment, training at Camp Shelby in Mississippi, was able to get leave and travel the 112 miles to New Orleans to compete. Led by Takashi "Halo" Hirose, who had been national champion in the 100 meter freestyle in 1941, as well as Charlie Oda and Charlie Tsukanao, the Nisei swimmers competed in various events and walked away with the first-place trophy.

Among Japanese Americans in Louisiana, there were two outstanding Nisei athletes. The first was Herbie Hiroshi Mashino. Born in Kansas City in 1916, he grew up in Oklahoma City and Shidler, Oklahoma, and he attended the Oklahoma Military Academy (now Rogers State University).

There he became known as a featherweight boxer. In April 1936 he won the Missouri Valley bantamweight title. The next year he won the Oklahoma AAU featherweight title by defeating William Tiger, and travelled to Chicago to participate in the Golden Gloves amateur boxing tournament, where he went to the finals before being defeated by Johnny Estrada. He also boxed in that year's tryouts for the US Olympic boxing team, also held in Chicago, but failed to make the squad.

In 1937 Mashino enrolled at Centenary College, a Methodist institution in Shreveport, Louisiana, where he majored in history and joined the school's boxing team, the Centenary Gents. The appearances of the "American-born Japanese" were covered in multiple newspapers from the region. In his first season Mashino won by technical knockout in a match with ace bantamweight Bumps Gormley. While he lost a big bout to Loyola's Sewele Whitney, the AAU champion, in February 1938, Mashino won a great victory the following month when he defeated Tommy Hand, a two-time Oklahoma Golden Gloves champion. As a newspaper account described it, Hand "found Hiroshi Mashino, clever little Japanese and former O.M.A. star, too fast and too tricky. Mashino had the little Indian on the retreat most of the way, and in the third round was dealing out considerable punishment. Hand was game, but no match for the clever Gent."

After leaving Centenary, Mashino did postgraduate work at Oklahoma A&M University. In December 1941 he had just completed a national defense course and was set to work at an airplane plant when he was arrested as a "dangerous Japanese" and jailed with five other men. In 1942 Mashino joined the Army Air Corps. After the formation of the all-Nisei 442nd Regiment, he was assigned to Second Battalion, G Company. At some point he was promoted to private first class. In 1944 he was assigned to Fort Sheridan, Illinois, and returned to boxing. In the South Side Chicago Golden Gloves he knocked out George Holt and then beat Sgt. Joe Kiado. In another bout he knocked out Bill Danzy. There is no record of Mashino continuing his boxing career after World War II. In later years he worked in the financial management division of the Marine Corps. He died in Maryland in 2004.

An even more celebrated Nisei athlete was Joe Nagata. Born in Montgomery, Alabama, in January 1924, he was the son of Yoshiyuki Nagata, a Japanese immigrant, and his Irish American wife Edith. Joe grew up in Eunice, in Louisiana's Cajun country, where his parents ran the Eunice Market, a produce store. Nagata starred as a halfback and fullback on Eunice High School's football team, and in the fall of 1941 he was named to the all-Southwest team. Just days afterward, the Japanese attack on Pearl Harbor launched the United States into World War II. The following Wednesday, while carrying a load of produce, the elder Nagata was arrested by FBI agents and held overnight, while his car and cash were seized. FBI agents then visited the family store, which was forced to close for three days during the investigation. Agents confiscated a short-wave radio, but Mr. Nagata was permitted to return, and the store then reopened.

Joe Nagata enrolled at LSU in 1942 and soon joined its football team, then under the direction of coach Bernie Moore (future major league baseball star Alvin Dark was Nagata's teammate). At 165 pounds, Nagata was too slight for fullback. Posted at halfback and wingback, he played well enough to win a letter. On November 7, in a game against Fordham University at the Polo Grounds in New York, he caught a pass and scored a touchdown.

Nagata began the 1943 season with a hamstring injury, which limited his effectiveness through the balance of the fall. By January 1944, when LSU faced off against Texas A&M in the Orange Bowl in Miami, Florida, he was healthy. Placed as fullback in LSU's Notre Dame Box formation alongside Steve Van Buren (later a pro with the Philadelphia Eagles and elected to the Pro Football Hall of Fame), Nagata's running and handoff skills distracted the defense, and he helped LSU to a 19–14 victory. In 1944 he enlisted in the army, joining the 442nd Regiment and participating in the Po Valley Campaign in Italy. He won eight medals for his military service, including the Bronze Star and the Infantry Combat Medal.

After the war, Nagata returned to LSU and resumed play on the football team, then under the leadership of future NFL great Y. A. Tittle. Meanwhile he met Jen Brown, whom he married in 1949. The couple would have three children. After receiving a degree in agriculture from LSU in 1951, Nagata returned to Eunice. There he became a high school teacher and football coach at Eunice High School and St. Edmund Catholic School. In twenty-three years as head coach, Nagata won 142 games, and his teams twice reached the state finals. Nagata was elected to the Louisiana High School Sports Hall of Fame. Following his death in 2001, Eunice High School named the Joe Nagata Memorial Jamboree in his honor.

Louisiana would continue to be home to Japanese athletes even after the war years, including the weightlifters Walter Imahara and Ted Yenari and footballer Scott Fujita of the New Orleans Saints. A more exhaustive study may prove useful in assessing their contribution.

The Ito Sisters of Chicago

One intriguing aspect of Japanese American history is remarkable families and clans, with generations of siblings and cousins who have achieved renown in varying fields. One such clan is the Itos of Chicago.

The patriarch of the family was Tokumatsu Ito, who arrived in the United States in 1903, at approximately thirty, and settled in Chicago, where he opened a Japanese goods store. (A 1915 Chicago directory lists his shop at 901 North State Street.) Ito became known for selling fine Japanese prints to collectors. He married a Japanese bride, Kameo, after she came to the United Sates in 1908. Daughter Josephine was born soon after, followed by son Howard, then daughters Elizabeth and Eileen and son Wallace. They settled in a house on East Fifty-Fourth Place in Chicago's Hyde Park neighborhood. Tokumatsu spent his later years dividing his time between work in the Anthropology Department at the Field Museum of Natural History, where he worked during the 1930s as a ceramics restorer, and the Department of Oriental Art at the Art Institute of Chicago. In 1940 Tokumatsu was listed as a restorer for a "historical museum," as was his son Howard.

It was Tokumatsu Ito's daughters who each distinguished themselves in various fields. Josephine Joanne Ito, born on September 30, 1908, attended school in Chicago and then enrolled at Northwestern University. In 1937 she moved to Washington, DC, where she was employed as a research assistant on the staff of Secretary of the Interior Harold L. Ickes. On August 13, 1938, she married Walter W. Sanborn, with whom later she had a son, David. During World War II Mrs. Sanborn worked as a secretary to author and historian Saul Padover, who occupied a position in the Interior Department. In the postwar years she worked as secretary to the director of nurses at Monson State Hospital in Massachusetts. She lived to be one hundred years old, dying in 2009.

The second daughter, Elizabeth Carol Ito, known as Betty, was born on June 4, 1913. While growing up, she sang in the Hyde Park Baptist Church choir, but her ambition was to be a doctor rather than a performer. She enrolled at University of Chicago as a German literature major in the early 1930s, and she earned money working as a secretary to professor Philip Schuyler Allen. During her undergraduate years, she was selected Phi Beta Kappa, winning the Carl Schurz Award for excellence in German. She also danced in the campus Mirror Show and worked as a model for artists Paul Trebilcock and Warner Williams. After completing her undergraduate studies, she entered graduate school with the intention of achieving a PhD in German. However, she was selected for a guest shot on a popular radio show, *Myrt and Marge*, and was soon attracted by a career as a radio actress. (To win the guest role she assumed a fake "Oriental" accent at her audition.) Betty's first regular role was in 1936, as Martha Yamoto, a doctor's daughter, on the WGN hospital drama *Delicate Hands*. In January 1937 she performed in a radio version of Chicago playwright Arch Oboler's "Oriental mystery play" *Chinese Gong*, appearing before the live audience in costume and giving the play a note of authenticity by her presence. Soon after, she was engaged as a player on the NBC radio serial *Jack Armstrong*, in which she voiced the role of a Chinese woman.

In August 1937 Ito was signed to a regular contract by NBC—the publicity over her signing lauded the fact that not only did she speak perfect English but also fluent German, Italian and Japanese, plus reading French and Swedish. Publicity materials described her as "sloe-eyed, ebony-haired and ivory skinned" and added that "she likes dancing theater, cosmopolitan food, crazy hats and excitement." After signing with NBC, Ito was engaged as a featured player in the short-lived serial *Young Hickory*, playing a white woman, Alice Carter. She was hired soon after for the radio version of the famous comic strip *Don Winslow of the Navy*. At first she played the bit part of an agent of the Scorpion (Don Winslow's nemesis). However, she proved so popular that she was engaged to play a major role as Scorpion's associate Lotus, an "Oriental" siren who later joined forces with the hero to protect the United States. In 1939 Archer Taylor, Ito's advisor, was named chair of the German Department at University of California, Berkeley. She transferred to Berkeley as a linguistics student, leaving her radio career behind. In 1941 UC Berkeley engaged her as a teaching assistant in the German Department.

After the beginning of 1942 and the signing of Executive Order 9066, Elizabeth Ito was barred from the West Coast and was thus unable to continue her studies at UC Berkeley. Like her sisters before her, she came to Washington. Anxious to contribute to the war effort, she applied for a job as a Japanese translator and enrolled in Japanese classes, since her Japanese was rusty in comparison to her fluency in other languages. With help from a referral by Harold Ickes (who had spoken to Josephine Ito Sanborn about recruiting the family for war work), Elizabeth Ito was engaged by the Justice Department and by Archibald MacLeish, director of the Office of Facts and Figures (OFF). In April 1943 she produced a report for the Justice Department's Special War Policies Unit on "Japanese Activities on the West Coast prior to and Immediately after Pearl Harbor." Meanwhile, the Office of War Information (successor to the OFF) engaged her to write and edit weekly reports on the Japanese-language press after surveilling it for disloyal content. In 1944 she transferred from the OWI to the Office of Strategic Services (OSS), the ancestor of the CIA. The exact nature of her work there is not clear. Perhaps more importantly, during her time at OSS she met a fellow analyst, the sociologist Barrington Moore Jr. The two were married in 1944 (rather to the distress of Moore's elite family) and moved afterward to Boston.

In the decades that followed, Barrington Moore taught at Harvard University. Betty served as a silent partner and uncredited collaborator on Moore's books, notably the classic study *The Social Origins of Dictatorship and Democracy* (1966). As a memorial tribute explained it, the writing of

Moore's books was based on "family labor": "Drafts were handwritten from personally assembled research notes. When a full draft was done, it was turned over to Betty Moore, who subjected it to thorough editing and double-checking." Although she was not listed as coauthor of Barrington Moore's books, the importance of her collaboration is indicated by the fact that she was assigned the author's royalties to them. Betty Ito Moore died on Valentine's Day in 1992.

Eileen (also called Irene) Ito, the youngest daughter, was also the last surviving sister. Born in 1915, she graduated from University of Chicago in 1936 with an bachelor's degree in art. While at college she met a fellow student from Chicago, Robert Weiskopf. After serving as a summer intern at the Art Institute of Chicago, she moved to Washington to attend the Corcoran School of Art and like her older sister was employed by the Department of the Interior. Weiskopf meanwhile moved to Los Angeles and got a job as a writer for the radio comedian Eddie Cantor. In 1940 Robert and Eileen got married and began living together in Los Angeles. However, in the aftermath of Pearl Harbor, both spouses feared for Eileen's safety as a Japanese American on the West Coast, and she felt obliged to return home to Chicago. After six months of nightly long-distance calls with her bereft husband, the couple moved to New York, where Robert found work as a writer for *The Fred Allen Show*. The couple remained in the New York area for nine years, during which time Bob wrote for *The Fred Allen Show* and also served a short stint in the army. In 1947 their son Kim Weiskopf was born.

The Weiskopfs returned to Los Angeles in 1952. Bob Weiskopf soon formed a partnership with another comedy writer, Bob Schiller. The two would distinguish themselves as writers for the classic sitcom *I Love Lucy* and for Lucille Ball's follow-up sitcom *The Lucy Show*, and in later years they would be head writers on the Norman Lear–produced sitcoms *All in the Family, Maude* (which they also coproduced), and *All's Fair*. The couple's son Kim Weiskopf would also go into the business. With his partner Michael Baser, he wrote scripts for and coproduced such shows as *Three's Company* and *What's Happening Now*. He also was a writer-producer for the long-running show *Married . . . with Children*. Bob Weiskopf died in 2001, and Kim passed away in 2009. Eileen Ito Weiskopf died in 2011.

Jitsuichi Masuoka: Issei Sociologist at Fisk University

Jitsuishi Masuoka, a sociologist who studied race relations, taught for many decades at Fisk University, a historically African American institution in Nashville, Tennessee.

Masuoka was born in Yamamoto Mura, Japan (today part of Gion Machi, a suburb of Hiroshima). His father, Yoshizo Masuoka, had gone to Hawai'i in his youth to work on a plantation, then returned and bought a rice farm from his savings. Jitsuichi was the seventh of eight surviving children. Mrs. Masuoka died when Jitsuichi was only three years old. He and his youngest brother were then raised by a grandmother until her death five years later. In 1913 Yoshizo Masuoka returned to Hawai'i, where the family's two eldest sons were already living. With their help, he gradually brought over the rest of the family. Jitsuichi arrived in Hawai'i in April 1917, at the age of thirteen. The family settled on a plantation at Puunene, on the island of Maui. For a time Jitsuichi attended public school, despite his lack of English fluency. However, at age fifteen he was sent out to work in order to repay his eldest brother for his passage to Hawai'i. He spent a few months as a field hand, then found work as a stable hand and carpenter.

During this time, Masuoka converted to Christianity and began attending a Japanese Congregational church. He studied English with a church leader, a Mrs. Tsuda, who persuaded the family to support him in further studies. After attending the Lahainaluna school, an interracial boarding school, he enrolled at Maui High School, commuting daily from his brother's house in Puunene. During his high school years, Masuoka supported himself by making deliveries for a Japanese schoolteacher who ran a private post office.

While Masuoka was in high school, one of his teachers, Esther French, encouraged him to attend her alma mater, the College of Emporia. In 1925, at the age of twenty-one, Masuoka enrolled at the college, majoring in sociology and economics. Even before he arrived in Kansas, he advertised in a local newspaper for a situation as a houseboy or chauffeur, describing himself as "strong, husky, not brilliant, but earnest, ambitious and sincere." He added: "Speaks English imperfectly." He later recalled that he had little time to study because he worked full-time as a busboy in a local restaurant.

However, he not only excelled in his courses but was also elected president of the Cosmopolitan Cub, a student group. In 1928 Masuoka was invited to lecture in nearby Hartford, Kansas, at a reception marking a touring exhibition of Japanese dolls.

After graduation from Emporia in 1928, Masuoka enrolled in graduate studies in sociology at the University of Kansas. During this time he visited nearby Ottawa University to attend the Christian World Education Conference there, and he was invited to address the journalism students on international relations. In his speech, he criticized the popular press for sensationalism and for fueling racial antagonism. While at Kansas, Masuoka devoted himself to studying race relations and the role of minority groups. He undertook work on a thesis, "Race Attitudes of the Japanese People in Hawai'i: A Study in Social Distance," that he would complete for his master's degree at the University of Hawai'i at Manoa in 1931. In it he tried to explore why there was less intergroup prejudice in Hawai'i.

In June 1929 Masuoka returned to Hawai'i to collect data. He worked in a pineapple canning firm during the day and conducted interviews at night, questioning Issei and Nisei in English and Japanese on their attitudes regarding members of diverse other racial or ethnic groups. Rather than returning to Kansas, he enrolled at the University of Hawai'i, where he studied with Romanzo Adams. In 1930 he was hired by professor W. C. Coale to do interviews for a study sponsored by the US Office of Education, on teaching English to bilingual children in Hawai'i. The next year Masuoka took a job as secretary to Fred Hulse, a Harvard graduate student making an anthropological study on "racial hybridity."[1]

During this time, Masuoka met the renowned sociologist Robert E. Park, who was a visiting researcher at the University of Hawai'i (UH). His discussions with Park not only led him to modify his research questionnaire but also to adopt Park's approach to race relations. In 1931, after completing his thesis, Masuoka likewise met the sociologist Dr. Edward Byron Reuter, Park's former student, while he was visiting researcher at UH. Reuter invited Masuoka to study with him. Thus, in the fall of 1932 Masuoka moved to Iowa City to pursue his doctorate at the State University of Iowa. In addition to holding a graduate fellowship, he earned money by working in an off-campus restaurant.

In 1934 Masuoka completed his doctoral coursework and returned to Puunene. He spent three years in Hawai'i collecting material for his dissertation, "The Westernization of the Japanese Family in Hawai'i." Meanwhile, he began to disseminate his research—Masuoka was among the first Nikkei sociologists to publish scholarly articles about Japanese Americans in mainstream journals. His first publication was the cowritten article "Some Factors Influencing the Development of Language in Preschool Bilingual Children of Japanese Ancestry in Honolulu," which grew out of his UH research study and was published in 1935 in *Proceedings of the Hawaiian Academy of Science*. In 1936 "A Sociological Study of the Standard of Living," based on a research project Masuoka conducted for the Institute of Pacific Relations, appeared in *Social Forces*. He spun three further articles from his graduate research. In 1936 "Race Preference in Hawai'i" appeared in *American Sociological Review*, while "Changing Moral Bases of the Japanese Family in Hawai'i" was published in *Sociology and Social Research*. In 1938 he published "The Japanese Patriarch in Hawai'i" in *Social Forces*. That year he returned to Iowa to complete his dissertation, and in 1940 he received his PhD. Without prospects of professional employment, he remained in Iowa City an additional year, during which he attended journalism classes and pondered a career as a newspaperman.

Following the onset of World War II, Masuoka moved to Nashville to serve as chauffeur and personal assistant to the elderly Robert Park. Park had by then retired from the University of Chicago and was teaching at Fisk University. Masuoka would remain with Park until the sociologist's death in 1944. Meanwhile, in early 1943 he was hired by Fisk president Charles S. Johnson as teacher and researcher in the Department of Social Sciences. He served as coeditor with Johnson and with Ophelia Settle Egypt on the book *Unwritten History of Slavery* (1945), based on a collection of oral histories of formerly enslaved people conducted in 192–30. Masuoka edited the interview transcripts and prepared them for the publication. During this period he met the sociologist Edna Cooper, a graduate student at the University of North Carolina. The two married and in succeeding years had children.

While at Fisk, Masuoka resumed publishing. Within the five years following his arrival, he produced a half-dozen articles for the journal *Social*

Forces. His article "Race and Culture Contacts in the Emporium" (1944), which called for the study of race and culture from an ecological viewpoint, appeared in *American Journal of Sociology*. "The Hybrid and the Social Process" (1945), on the social status of mixed-race people, was published in the journal *Phylon*. "Changing Food Habits of the Japanese in Hawai'i," a study of the diets of one hundred Japanese families living in Hawai'i, was published in *American Sociological Review*. His article "Race Relations and Nisei Problems" (1946), appeared in *Sociology and Social Research*, while "Racial Symbiosis and Cultural Frontiers: A Frame of Reference" appeared in *Social Forces*. In 1946, in collaboration with Charles S. Johnson, he put out a book-length collection, *Racial Attitudes,* written and published under the auspices of the Fisk University Social Science Institute. He authored "Basic Problems of Asia and Democratic Education," which appeared in *Harvard Educational Review* in 1947, and also published multiple book reviews.

In 1948 Masuoka was promoted to associate professor of sociology at Fisk. Although he remained at Fisk for twenty-five years, his subsequent career there remains somewhat obscure. He spent a year as visiting professor at University of Michigan in 1950, following which he became Sociology Department chair at Fisk. He later taught stints at Luther College and Tennessee State University. In 1959 he won a Fulbright exchange grant and spent the year lecturing in Japan. After returning, he and his wife Edna Cooper Masuoka collaborated on the article "Role Conflicts in the Modern Japanese Family."

In contrast with his prodigious prewar and wartime output, he produced few original articles in later years. Instead, he devoted himself to preserving the memory of Robert Park. Masuoka served as a coeditor of the three-volume *Collected Papers of Robert Ezra Park*, and in 1961 he and his collaborator Preston Valien coedited a festschrift volume dedicated to Park, *Race Relations: Problems and Theory.*

Apart from a handful of book reviews, Masuoka had little to say publicly about Japanese Americans during these years. Rather, the writing he produced centered on African Americans in the South and was heavily informed by his presence at Fisk and by the civil rights movement. In 1956 Masuoka and Valien authored *A Memorandum on Social Consequences of*

Racial Residential Segregation for the Commission on Race and Housing. Masuoka's contribution to the *Race Relations* festschrift was a political study, "The Montgomery Bus Protest as a Social Movement." In 1970 Masuoka produced his final work, revising and introducing a new edition of Edward Reuter's classic book *The American Race Problem*. He died in 2004 at the age of one hundred.

The Adventures of T. Scott Miyakawa

T. Scott Miyakawa, a sociologist and historian, was an outstanding member of the first generation of Japanese American academics. His career exemplifies both the discrimination that Nisei were faced and the compromises that they made to succeed.

Born in Los Angeles on November 23, 1906, Tetsuo Scott Miyakawa was the eldest of three children of Yukio Miyakawa, a gardener, and his wife Rin. His brother, Tatsuo Arthur Miyakawa, was a graduate of Harvard University and the Boalt Hall law school at UC Berkeley. He taught at UCLA and Georgetown University during the 1930s. His sister, Maxine Kikuko Miyakawa, was a jewelry designer and writer, whose 1940 poetry volume *Starlight* was one of the earliest works of Nisei literature published by a mainstream press.

Scotty, as he was known, graduated from Los Angeles High School, then attended Cornell University, where he studied industrial and mechanical engineering. He was awarded a degree in mechanical engineering in 1931, in the depths of the Great Depression. Despite his Ivy League diploma, he was unable to secure a position with an American company after graduation. Instead, like many talented Nisei of the time, he went to work for a Japanese firm. Miyakawa was hired by the New York office of the Japanese-owned South Manchuria Railway to serve as English-speaking assistant to the office manager and to do economic research and public relations.

His assignment also turned out to include acting as a propagandist for Japan, defending Tokyo's invasion of Manchuria. In October 1931, a month after the "Mukden incident" (the sham event staged by the Japanese military to justify their intervention), Miyakawa published an article, "The Japanese Side," in the *New York Herald Tribune*. In it he blamed the crisis in Manchuria on "years of provocation and aggravation on the part of the Chinese," whom he charged with perpetrating or ignoring the murder of hundreds of Japanese, and insisted (without evidence) that Chinese authorities had called in Japanese troops for protection. He also denied that Japan aimed to separate Manchuria from China, asserting that Japanese authorities had forbidden any of their officials, civil or military, from even offering advice to anyone embarked on such an absurd scheme.

The following year, after the Japanese had indeed separated Manchuria from China and created the puppet state of Manchukuo, Miyakawa published a letter in the *New York Times* insisting that, despite evidence to the contrary, Japan depended indirectly on Manchuria for much of its food. Manchuria, he explained, produced the bean cake that served as fertilizer for Japanese farmers, as well as the millet that fed the farmers in Korea who in turn produced rice for Japan (he did not explain why Koreans should be relegated to an inferior diet). While the letter made no direct comment on Japanese control over Manchuria, Miyakawa's statements about Japan's needs implicitly justified it.

In January 1933 Miyakawa spoke at a Foreign Policy Association round table in Elmira, New York, where he was billed as a representative of the Japanese National Committee of the International Association of Commerce. His talk centered on the Lytton Commission (the League of Nations investigative team in Manchuria). He also gave a public lecture on Manchuria at Bennington College. In a public address in New York City in February 1933, Miyakawa criticized the Lytton Commission for ignoring Japan's "valid, vital" claims in Manchuria. He charged instead that the real aggressor in Manchuria was the Soviet Union, acting under "secret treaty" with China. That October, Miyakawa, billed as a representative of the "Japanese Chamber of Commerce," participated in a radio program with Chih Meng, director of the China Institute in America, a production titled

"What Is Happening in the Far East?" In July 1933 Scotty's brother Tatsuo was named assistant to Torao Kawasaki, the chief of the Information Bureau of Manchukuo, and joined in pro-Japan propaganda work.

Even as he worked for the Japanese railroad, Scotty enrolled in graduate study in sociology and statistics at Columbia University, studying under such professors as Robert Staughton Lynd and Robert M. MacIver, as well as working with the theologian Reinhold Niebuhr on religious studies. He remained at Columbia off and on for several years, receiving scholarships from the university in 1939–40 and 1940–41.

In 1934–35, Miyakawa travelled to Asia for several months, on what he later termed a "research trip," to study industrial development and trade. During his tour, he spent time in Japan, Korea, Manchuria, and China studying production and trade practices. In an interview with the *Literary Digest* upon his return, he spoke admiringly of standards of Japanese standards of quality in production. While American political leaders expressed fear that Japanese competition in the textile trade would lower standards for American workers, Miyakawa retorted, American mass-production techniques produced cheap but inferior goods and thereby threatened Japanese standards.

Miyakawa later stated that after his Asia sojourn he tried to secure employment in the US government or private industry but was unable to find a position at a salary sufficient to help support his parents. While he felt a loyalty to the South Manchuria Railway, which had allowed him time to pursue his studies, as an American he did not wish to accept a more senior position in Asia. In the end, he returned to New York, resumed his graduate work at Columbia, and continued working for the South Manchuria Railway, where in 1937 he became head of the research department. According to one source, when Prince Iyesato Tokugawa, descendant of the deposed shogun and president of the Japan's House of Peers, toured the United States, Miyakawa served as his press secretary. He performed similar duties when a Japanese economic mission toured the United States in 1937.

Scotty likewise continued his public expressions of support for Japan's foreign policy. In July 1937, a week after the Japanese army launched a full-scale invasion of China, Miyakawa (billed as the New York correspondent of the *Japan Times and Mail*) lectured on Japan's "perennial crisis" at a summer institute at University of Virginia. Defending Tokyo's actions, he stated that unless countries such as Japan could have freer access to raw materials and pay for them, international peace would remain an illusion.

Miyakawa was able to defend Japan's occupation of China, but as Japan and the United States moved toward confrontation at the dawn of the 1940s, he later claimed, he felt increasingly uneasy working for a Japanese firm. He insisted that he was pressed to remain at his job by friends in US intelligence services who sought sources of information. Sometime in 1941, the South Manchuria Railway closed its New York office. Miyakawa again refused to move to Asia. Instead, according to one source, he was hired to do marketing and public relations for a small company.

Meanwhile, along with his friend Larry Tajiri, who had moved to New York in mid-1940 to work for a Japanese news agency, Miyakawa faced off against the local Issei business community and its conservative pro-Tokyo orientation. Miyakawa and Tajiri joined others to form the New York Emergency Committee for Japanese Americans. After Pearl Harbor, the committee helped displaced Issei and Nisei find lodging and employment and advocated for their rights. Returning to his role as propagandist, this time for loyal Japanese Americans, Miyakawa issued positive public statements—for example, in January 1942 he noted that the Nisei had the largest per capita ratio of army enlistment among US minorities.

Scotty Miyakawa and his brother, sister, and mother (his father having died in 1940) were all living on the East Coast at the time of the mass removal of West Coast Japanese Americans in mid-1942. Scotty was nonetheless deeply touched by these events (he later stated that seven close relatives were confined). Operating through Freedom House, a New York organization, he used his contacts with outside sympathizers such as novelist Pearl S. Buck to gain support for Japanese Americans. In opposition to the Japanese American Committee for Democracy, which he considered too pro-Communist, he and his brother, Tatsuo, founded the short-lived Townshend Harris Association as an activist organization for liberal Nisei. (Tatsuo was hired soon after as an analyst by the Japan section of the Office of War Information in Washington, DC and ultimately went overseas to direct the OWI bureau at Hankow, China.) In 1942–43, Scotty began work with the JACL, although he did not become an official member. He used his outside contacts to act as an unofficial liaison in assisting the organization in securing national sponsors, and in mid-1943 he helped organize a JACL conference in New York on resettlement and postwar needs. During this period, he was in frequent contact with Alan Cranston, head of the Foreign Language Division of the OWI, and with ACLU director Roger Baldwin.

Despite his many contacts, Scotty Miyakawa had difficulty securing employment. He worked for a few months as a reports officer for the Coordinator of Information and for the OWI, but he was left behind when their Japan divisions moved to the West Coast. In the summer of 1942 he worked on a short-term assignment for the Military Intelligence Service, heading a team of Nisei compiling reports on Japan. Twice during these months he was offered a position as an economic analyst with the War Production Board (WPB), but both times his employment was vetoed without clear explanation by the WPB personnel department. According to one source, his previous work for the South Manchuria Railway led him to be placed on an FBI blacklist. Miyakawa himself stated that he was not only cleared by the FBI but also subjected to a rigorous check by army intelligence, and he suggested that racism toward Japanese Americans by personnel officers was responsible for his rejection. Whatever the case, after Miyakawa had waited several months, friends inside and outside government petitioned the Fair Employment Practices Commission (FEPC) to inquire into his WPB rejection. The FEPC offered Miyakawa a public hearing, but he was unable to afford an attorney to represent him, could not find free counsel, and thus regretfully declined the hearing.

In mid-1943 Miyakawa was finally able to secure a position, as physics instructor to air force cadets at the University of Missouri. He moved to Columbia, Missouri, to begin work. Although Miyakawa admitted that physics was far removed from his regular fields of study, he found that he enjoyed teaching. A year later he moved to University of Michigan, where he assisted the counselor in religious education on a survey of religious education in California universities. Once arrived in Ann Arbor, he contacted the ACLU to report the university administration's secret (and duplicitous) exclusion of Nisei students. Miyakawa charged that while

University of Michigan employed over two hundred Nisei resettlers in menial jobs, and dozens more served as Japanese instructors and students at the army language school on campus, the administration used national security as a pretext to exclude all but a handful of Nisei students. Even after the war ended and the university's ban on Nisei students was lifted, there were incidents of anti-Nisei prejudice in town. Miyakawa helped organize a local JACL chapter to assist resettlers in adjusting to life in the area and to encourage positive media coverage.

In June 1946 Scotty Miyakawa was invited by army headquarters in Tokyo to take a job as a statistician, as part of the US occupation of Japan. However, as with the WPB, the clearance process was protracted, and he finally lost patience and withdrew his agreement to take the job. Miyakawa was nearing his fortieth birthday and was frustrated by his inability to secure stable employment. It was then that he was offered a position as instructor in sociology at Boston University, where he would remain for twenty-five years.

Indeed, if the professional vicissitudes T. Scott Miyakawa encountered in his earlier years can be said to represent the trials of the Nisei generation, his later career in Boston encapsulates the rise of elite Nisei. During the postwar era, Miyakawa became a respected and much-traveled scholar. Like his exact contemporary S. I. Hayakawa, he refused to be pigeonholed simply as a specialist on Asian Americans, and he threw himself into studying a variety of topics. However, unlike Hayakawa, who kept his distance from Nikkei communities and opposed ethnic-based organizations, Miyakawa retained a community focus and devoted himself to working with the JACL and other organizations to document Japanese American history.

In the summer of 1946 Scotty moved to Boston University and took up the task of teaching Methods of Sociological Research and Social Theory in the Sociology Department. He undertook outside activities too—for example, he helped organize a Boston JACL chapter. In 1948 he lectured at the New England High School Institute of International Relations, an event organized at Harvard University.

During his first years in Boston, Miyakawa devoted the largest share of his time to researching and writing his long-delayed Columbia University doctoral dissertation, "American Frontier and Protestantism," which he completed in 1951. He would much later adapt the thesis into a book, *Protestants and Pioneers: Individualism and Conformity on the American Frontier* (University of Chicago Press, 1964). The work (Miyakawa's sole completed monograph) examines the relationship between community organization and frontier life in the Ohio Valley in the early nineteenth century. Taking aim at Frederick Jackson Turner's classic thesis about the "frontier" as a builder of individual character and self-reliance, Miyakawa made the point that the frontier was not always marked by lone individualism. Rather, the lives of American frontiersmen were constrained and regimented through the impact of Protestant churches, which acted as places of integration and brought conformity to newly settled western areas. While the book was widely reviewed and has been frequently cited since by historians of the frontier, Miyakawa seems not to have revisited the topic in later years.

After obtaining his PhD, Miyakawa embarked on a series of international residencies. First he received a Ford Foundation fellowship for 1951–52 that allowed him to travel to Europe to study labor and management relations in Scandinavia. He may have been inspired to turn his attention there by his sister Kikuko Miyakawa, who had settled in Copenhagen in the postwar years and married a Dane, Mogens Packness. In the end, however, Scotty spent most of the year studying conditions in Great Britain and Italy.

After returning from his European study trip, Miyakawa turned to work on Asia. In 1953–54, he served as a Fulbright professor at Doshisha University in Kyoto. He returned to Asia as visiting faculty member at the Center for Advanced Study and Training in Ceylon during 1957–58. (Scotty Miyakawa's connections with Asia were paralleled by those of his brother Tatsuo. After serving in China with the OWI during World War II, Tatsuo worked for US occupation authorities in Japan and later became the Japanese representative of the American Petroleum Export Company. In 1963 Tatsuo was hired by the US Commerce Department, and he spent the next two decades as director of the Japan desk and chief of the trade regulations section in the Far East division of the Office of International Regional Economics.) Curiously, while Scotty Miyakawa reviewed books on European industry, notably Sheila Patterson's *Immigrants in Industry*, as well as Asian studies, he did not write any articles or reports based on his research during his Asian residencies.

At the dawn of the 1960s, Miyakawa became involved in efforts to collect documentary materials related to the history of Japanese Americans and Japanese immigration. During this time, the JACL, under national president Frank Chuman, expressed interest in producing a definitive historical study of Japanese Americans. While there were existing histories by non-Japanese, notably Bradford Smith's 1948 work *Americans from Japan,* they did not make use of Japanese-language sources and oral histories. With the Issei generation aging and primary source materials in danger of disappearing, JACL leaders felt that immediate action was necessary. In 1960 the national JACL approved the formation of a committee under the direction of Shigeo Wakamatsu, to raise money for the preparation of a history of the Issei. The committee turned to Japanese American communities for financial support. The response was overwhelming. Hundreds of Nisei contributed sums, often in memory of their immigrant parents. In the end, the JACL raised some $200,000—an enormous sum in 1960 dollars—for the plan. Chuman contacted UCLA, his alma mater, and arranged with Chancellor Franklin Murphy to base the project there. In August 1962 the regents of the University of California approved the creation of the Japanese American Research Project (JARP).

The JACL turned to Miyakawa to direct the JARP. It was a natural choice. First, Miyakawa had long been connected to the organization. Furthermore, at least since his time working for the South Manchuria Railway, he had been interested in the history of Japanese Americans and in US–Japanese trade, and he had long been active in collecting historical material on these topics. In the fall of 1961 he produced a preliminary draft, "A Proposal for a Definitive History of the Japanese in the United States, 1860–1960," for review by the JACL committee and individual JACL chapters. His outline for the project contained a list of study objectives that included sociological surveys, the assembling of a documentary collection of oral histories and memorabilia, and production of a "definitive, scholarly volume" on the history of Japanese Americans. Originally Miyakawa's focus was the Issei, but on the advice of Harvard professor Edwin Reischauer he added the history of Nisei to the project.

Once he became JARP director, Miyakawa took a leave of absence from Boston University and moved to UCLA, where he was named visiting associate professor of sociology. In September 1963 he began preparatory work, with a staff of two research assistants. In 1964 the Carnegie Corporation of New York awarded the project a further $100,000 grant. Miyakawa expressed his intention to produce a historical study in several volumes, plus a trio of sociological monographs on the adjustment of immigrant Japanese, the postwar acceptance and integration of Japanese Americans, and the group's contributions to American culture. He meanwhile undertook the creation of the archive with primary sources. Miyakawa remained with JARP until 1965, when he returned to Boston University. Robert A. Wilson, a UCLA professor of Japanese history, succeeded him as director.

In the end, JARP was a mixed success in terms of results. A large archive of information was collected, including oral histories and numerous Japanese-language diaries, letters, and other primary sources. (Yuji Ichioka would supervise the addition of further material during the 1970s.) The ambitious multivolume history was never produced, though Bill Hosokawa's 1969 popular book *Nisei: The Quiet Americans* and Frank Chuman's 1976 legal history *The Bamboo People*, as well as some smaller studies, spun off from the project. Hosokawa later edited Wilson's manuscript to produce the monograph *East to America* (1980).

After leaving UCLA, Miyakawa seems to have largely withdrawn from involvement with JARP. Instead, he formed a separate study. Miyakawa called for large-scale research regarding Japanese Americans on the East Coast. Despite their small numbers, he asserted, they had been able to live free of the harsh anti-Japanese prejudice prevailing on the West Coast, and they had laid the foundation for the substantial trade between Japan and the United States. In 1970 Miyakawa produced a seventy-page preliminary report on Issei on the East Coast and US-Japanese trade in the late nineteenth century, "Early New York Issei Founders of Japanese-American Trade." Around the same time he also teamed up with historian Hilary Conroy to co-edit a pioneering anthology, *East Across the Pacific: Historical and Sociological Studies of Japanese Immigration and Assimilation*, which was published in 1972. Miyakawa included in the volume a scaled-down version of his manuscript on early New York Issei traders. Parallel to the Protestant ethic (famously described by Max Weber) that drove Western capitalists, he suggested, Japanese values promoted expansion of Japan's commerce on an international level in the nineteenth century. His work was later carried on by his assistant Yasuo Sakata.

In 1972, at age sixty-five, Miyakawa retired from Boston University (BU) and was named visiting professor of sociology at University of Massachusetts Boston. In 1975 he was promoted to full-time status and appointed chair of the department. During his time at UMass Boston he helped found an Asian studies program. In 1976 Miyakawa left UMass Boston and was named emeritus professor at BU. Sometime after, he grew ill. He was guarded about his condition (variously identified as cancer or leukemia), so his passing in August 1981 came as a surprise to many friends and colleagues. Following Miyakawa's death, the Department of Sociology at UMass Boston created a T. Scott Miyakawa Memorial Prize in his honor.

T. Scott Miyakawa's career and legacy are touched with irony. In spite of his elite education as an engineer, he was forced by anti-Nisei discrimination to enter the field of US-Japanese trade. Once World War II came, Miyakawa faced unemployment because of his past defense of Tokyo's international policy. Similarly, Miyakawa absorbed himself in studying the sociology of religion, which eventually became the theme of his doctoral thesis. However, by the time he issued his major publication in the area, he was nearing sixty years old and had returned to the study of US-Japanese trade. He organized a major scholarly research initiative in Japanese American history at UCLA, but his own interest in the study of New York's Japanese communities set him apart from West Coast–centric scholars.

Epilogue

NUNC PRO TUNC AND THE STORY BEHIND A PHRASE

IT WAS MORE THAN TEN YEARS AGO THAT MY FRIEND TETSUDEN Kashima told me of his dream project. Tetsu, a professor of sociology at University of Washington and an incisive scholar of wartime Japanese Americans, confided that he and some colleagues had hatched a plan to persuade the university administration to offer honorary degrees to those UW Nisei students of 1941–42 whose studies had been interrupted by their wartime removal, as a gesture of healing and reparation. At that time, no university had ever held such a diploma ceremony, but it seemed to me a particularly effective way of dramatizing the damage wrought by Executive Order 9066, not just to Nisei students but also to their universities.

Tetsu added that he was looking for a theme or slogan to pitch the project. I thought it over, and then said, "what about nunc pro tunc?" Tetsu's eyebrows shot up. "What is that?" he asked. I explained that it was a Latin term that literally means "now for then," used in law for rulings or decrees that were applied retroactively, as a way of correcting past errors. With that, Tetsu broke into a smile. We agreed that the diplomas should not only be offered honoris causa, in the usual manner of honorary degrees, but also nunc pro tunc. Tetsu added, "But I'm curious. You're not a lawyer,

Sanae Kawaguchi Moorehead, Toni Robinson, and Greg Robinson, New York, 2000. Photo by Heng Wee Tan. Author's personal collection.

and I know you've never studied Latin. How did you learn this phrase?" It was then that I revealed the path I took to becoming a historian of Japanese Americans, and the place of the late Toni Robinson in shaping it. Toni played multiple roles in my life, serving at different times as my employer, my editor, my attorney and literary agent, and my scholarly collaborator. Through it all, she was also—and above all else—my mother.

She was born Toni Sandler in New York in 1942. Toni's parents separated when she was a child, and she and her brother Bob were raised by their mother, Joyce, who worked outside to support the family. Toni was quite precocious: by the time she was fifteen years old she had finished high school, started college, and met Ed Robinson, who became her husband two years later. Ed and Toni Robinson would remain happily married for forty-three years. However, Toni never expected to be a stay-at-home wife. Beyond the examples of her mother and her cousin Judy Mackey, a distinguished economist, she was inspired by Eleanor Roosevelt. In later years Toni would often tell of a day when her school group visited Hyde Park and she met Mrs. Roosevelt, who spoke to them from the porch of the Roosevelt home.

After finishing college, the young bride took up various short-term jobs. One was as a writer for a children's encyclopedia. As part of her work, Toni was asked to prepare an article on the topic "concentration camps." Although it was 1962–63, a time when the WRA camps were little discussed in mainstream society, Toni's draft included a reference to Japanese Americans and Executive Order 9066. Her editor reprimanded her over the passage and insisted on removing all such references in the final article, leaving Toni with a burning sense of injustice.

This same feeling about justice meanwhile led Toni to become interested in the African American civil rights movement. She attended the 1963 March on Washington and helped plan demonstrations. It was while protesting discrimination at the 1963–64 World's Fair in New York that Toni was unexpectedly arrested and spent the night in the Women's House of Detention. The experience of seeing police lie in court and prisoners mistreated led Toni to resolve on becoming an attorney.

Before Toni continued on her career path, however, she and Ed decided to have children. Thus my elder brother Ian and I were born. Toni looked after us full-time during our first years. Once I started kindergarten, she went off to law school. In the succeeding years, she pursued her studies, graduated with honors, and was hired as an associate by a large law firm. She later moved to a smaller firm, where she made partner. While Toni handled occasional civil rights cases, much of her business was in litigation or in matrimonial law, representing clients in divorce and child custody cases. During these years, as I was growing up, Toni was a loving parent, and despite her heavy workload and long hours at the office she found ways to remain present in my life.

At the dawn of the 1990s, when I was in graduate school, Toni started her own solo practice. Soon after, she was diagnosed successively with Parkinson's disease and leukemia. In late 1994 she underwent a bone marrow transplant. It temporarily arrested the progress of the leukemia, but she remained frail from the Parkinson's disease. Still, Toni refused to give up her legal work. It was clear to the family that if she was forced to retire, her will to live would be affected. I had completed research on a PhD dissertation and started writing, but my progress was slow, and in any case I felt a higher duty to my family.

Thus it was that in 1996 I laid aside my dissertation, quit graduate school, and began work as my mother's legal assistant, first on a volunteer basis and then as a full-time salaried employee. While I had done office work before, I had no legal experience and had to learn from scratch. Luckily my training as a historian gave me a leg up in areas such as legal research and expository writing, and for the rest I could ask Toni for assistance. She reassured me that just having me around, since she could rely on me fully, was more valuable to her than any set of legal skills. Eventually I learned enough that I could take on tasks that would normally fall to a legal associate, such as drafting briefs and interviewing clients. This helped preserve Toni's energy and save her clients money. Because Toni was too weak to hold a briefcase, I also literally fetched and carried for her. In the process of my work, I learned legal concepts such as pro se and estoppel—and nunc pro tunc.

The law work was rigorous. If Toni needed to work late on her cases, I would stay with her at the office—sometimes we were there until midnight. All the same, it was a great treat for me to work together with my mother and see a side of her I might otherwise never have experienced. We became close collaborators, able to speak in shorthand and finish each other's sentences. Our writing styles complemented each other, and her edits improved my prose. I considered entering law school so that I could one day become my mother's law partner, but it was obvious that I could not simultaneously attend school and assist her. Toni's Parkinson's symptoms eventually progressed to the point that she could no longer handle her demanding caseload. She closed her office in late summer 1998 and spent the next months working from home to wind up her existing cases, with part-time help from me.

It was while I was working in Toni's law office that I became absorbed in studying Japanese American history. I was invited by a journal to write about Franklin Roosevelt and decided to contribute an article on FDR's pre-presidential writings. In the process of reading up for the article, I came across Roosevelt's articles and newspaper columns during the 1920s, in which he had called for exclusion of Asian immigrants and endorsed discriminatory laws against Japanese Americans on the grounds that they protected the "racial purity" of white Americans against interracial marriage. Horrified and fascinated, I pondered the relation of Roosevelt's racial attitudes toward Japanese Americans to his later signing of Executive Order 9066. The question grew from an article into an independent research project, until finally I decided to leave off work on my abandoned dissertation and concentrate on this new topic. Once my mother retired, I re-enrolled in graduate school and began writing a dissertation on FDR and Japanese Americans.

From the beginning, Toni shared my fascination with the subject. She let me do research in libraries and archives during slow periods at the office, and she encouraged me to present my initial findings at a conference. Gratified by her interest, and accustomed to working with her, I asked her to read and edit the drafts of my new dissertation once she retired. Thanks to her help, I was ultimately able to complete my research and write the body of the thesis—some five hundred pages—in less than nine months.

To help Toni edit my thesis, I shared with her the archival documents that I uncovered. I was intrigued by her analysis and proposed that we collaborate on a separate paper. Toni agreed but asked that our relationship not be specified, as she did not wish to feel like an interloper. We decided to focus on Toni's old hero, Eleanor Roosevelt, and her conflict with FDR over mass removal. In the fall of 1998, just after Toni retired, we traveled to Oregon and presented together at a conference. (My father, who had also taken an interest in my work, kindly attended the conference and drove us around.)

Once I completed my dissertation and had spare time, we began regular work together. It was an interesting education in the mechanics of collaboration. I acted as leg man, collecting research, and then wrote the first drafts. Toni studied the documents and did rewriting. Sometimes we disagreed and would have to find a compromise or give in—my friend Ken Feinour still loves to tease me about watching Toni and me screaming at each other over the placement of a comma.

Our new project traced the history of relations between blacks and Japanese Americans and their postwar alliance for racial equality. Ever since Toni's youthful involvement with civil rights protest, she had been fascinated by court struggles against discrimination. I came across information on postwar legal cases in the Supreme Court involving Japanese Americans, and Toni used her legal skill to dissect the arguments in the briefs (we were unusual in studying arguments in amicus briefs). After weeks of work, we produced an extended manuscript. We did a variation on the same theme when we wrote a paper about Nisei-Latino connections and the *Mendez v. Westminster* desegregation case and then presented our work together at a conference at Columbia University.

In 2001 I moved to Montreal. I continued to speak regularly with Toni, who maintained her close interest in my work. When my first book, *By Order of the President,* was published, she and my father threw me a big launch party. When I signed with another publisher to do a second book, Toni acted as my literary agent and taught me to look over the contract and request necessary changes. In the spring of 2002 we began work expanding our unpublished manuscript on black-Nisei connections into a full-length book. Unfortunately, Toni fell ill from leukemia, and she died soon after. Our two joint articles were eventually published (and later interpolated into my book *After Camp*)—the writings by "Robinson and Robinson" remain my most cited.

Tetsuden Kashima and his colleagues succeeded in their mission, and in May 2008 the University of Washington held a special event, "The Long Journey Home," to grant diplomas to the UW Nikkei students of 1941–42. As recommended, the degrees honoris causa were presented nunc pro tunc. Beyond my joy for the UW students—and later those at the dozen West Coast institutions that have since followed suit—I take special pride in this last part, as part of the legacy of Toni Robinson to Japanese American history.

ACKNOWLEDGMENTS

I close by thanking some key supporters. My chief thanks go to Larin McLaughlin of University of Washington Press, who commissioned the collection, and Chris Dodge for sensitive copyediting. I thank editor Kenji Taguma and the *Nichi Bei Weekly* staff, notably Heather Horiuchi and Tomo Hirai, for welcoming my columns. I likewise am obliged to Yoko Nishimura and June Magsaysay of *Discover Nikkei*, Russ Tremayne of College of Southern Idaho, Brian Niiya of the *Densho Encyclopedia*, and Duncan Ryuken Williams of the Hapa Japan Project for inviting my contributions. I offer thanks again to Matthieu Langlois, Valerie Matsumoto, Maxime Minne, Chris Suh, and Jonathan Van Harmelen, who collaborated with me on articles and then generously granted me permission to republish them. Frank Abe and Floyd Cheung, my collaborators on the book *John Okada*, consented to my putting our deliberations into print. Thanapat Porjit helped with initial research. During much of the period in which this book was written, Max Minne was a warm friend and associate. In its latter stages, Jonathan Van Harmelen offered vital support. Xiaolin Zhu and Heng Wee Tan encouraged me and put up with my zeal for Nikkei history. For help and friendship, I want to salute Konomi Ara, Jérôme Bosser and Marie-Natacha Papillon, Christopher Bram, Ben Carton, Gordon H. Chang, Connie Chiang, Hadrien Chino, Jean-Francis Clermont-Legros, Tom Coffman, Elena Tajima Creef, Mark Curry, Takako Day, Quentin de Becker,

Zhiyou Duan, Ken Feinour, Shelley Fisher Fishkin, Lynne Horiuchi, Satsuki Ina, Karen Inouye, Masumi Izumi, Seth Jacobowitz, Tetsuden Kashima, Saara Kekki, Junichiro Koji, Lon Kurashige, Catherine Ladnier, Zacharie Leclair, Lei Liu, Shirley Geok-Lin Lim, Marco Mariano, Michael Massing, Guillaume Marceau, Paul May, John Meehan, Jeremy Meyer, GerriLani Miyazaki, Takeya Mizuno, Sanae Kawaguchi Moorehead, Robert Moulton, Adron Nguyen, Phuong and Betty Nguyen, Maryka Omatsu, and Chizu Omori, Robert Schwartzwald, Ronn Seely and David Latulippe, Cathy Schlund-Vials, Gabriel Séguin, Charles Senay, David Tacium, Mayumi Takasaki, Dorothy Williams, Shirlette Wint, Frank Wu, and Carol Izumi, Eric Yamamoto, Alice Yang, Mitsu Yashima, and Dylan Yeats, and Junhan Yu. Finally, I thank my beloved Robinson-Postman-Sandler-Plotkin-Mackey-Rigel family for sustaining my interest in life and education.

NOTES

Chapter 1: Mixed-Race Japanese Americans

1 Ishikawa, "Study of the Intermarried Japanese Families in U.S.A.," *Cultural Nippon*, October 1935, 457–87, cited in Forrest L. LaViolette, *Americans of Japanese Ancestry: A Study of Assimilation in the American Community* (Toronto: Canadian Institute of International Affairs, 1945), 121.

Chapter 2: Literature

1 Note: I want to add a shout-out to historian Valerie Matsumoto and writer and artist Patricia Wakida, who inspired my work on Mary Oyama Mittwer. Some years ago Patricia was commissioned to contribute an article on Mary Oyama Mittwer for the new Densho encyclopedia (of which I was associate editor). In the process of her work on it, Patricia asked Valerie for information, and Valerie steered her my way. This inspired me to revisit and deepen my longstanding interest in Mittwer's career.

2 Kawakami, Kiyoshi Karl, *Asia at the Door: A Study of the Japanese Question in Continental United States, Hawaii, and Canada* (New York: Fleming H. Revell, 1914), 53.

Chapter 3: Wartime Confinement and Japanese Americans: Nikkei Stories

1 Edwin T. Layton, with Roger Pineau and John Costello, *"And I Was There": Pearl Harbor and Midway—Breaking the Secrets* (New York: Quill, 1985), 55, 74–75.

2 For an unofficial estimate, see Burt Takeuchi, "Pearl Harbor: Asian Americans Witness Historic Air Raid," *Nichi Bei Times*, May 25, 2001, 3, http://us_asians.tripod.com/articles-nihonmachi-outreach.html.

3   Hector Tobar, "A Journey Back to East L.A.," *Los Angeles Times*, April 9, 2010.

4   Daryl J. Maeda, *Chains of Babylon: The Rise of Asian America* (Minneapolis: University of Minnesota Press, 2009), 58.

5   Ironically, while the Hollywood films that made use of this device were all written and produced by whites (most often Jews), the use of such "passing" as a device for commentary on racism became a centerpiece of African American literature at least from the time of James Weldon Johnson's 1912 novel *The Autobiography of an Ex-Colored Man* (and arguably as early as the first novel by an African American, William Wells Brown's 1853 *Clotel: The President's Daughter*). Unlike Johnson's hero, however, in the Hollywood narrative the character who has previously been accepted as white must ultimately renounce that status.

6   A rare exception was the unsuccessful 1986 comedy *Soul Man*, in which a white student poses as black in order to take advantage of a minority scholarship and suffers racist attacks. Even then, in defiance of the model, he turns around at the end and says that his experience did not in fact teach him what it is like to be black, since he knew he could always change back.

7   Donald Bogle, *Toms, Coons, Mulattoes, Mammies, and Bucks; an Interpretive History of Blacks in American Films* (New York: Viking Press, 1973); Thomas Robert Cripps, *Slow Fade to Black: The Negro in American Film, 1900–1942* (New York: Oxford University Press, 1977).

8   Although many gay people do engage at some time in "passing" for straight, the passing narrative has not been widely used to illuminate anti-gay prejudice. Reverse-passing stories, such as the French film *The Closet* and the Hollywood film *I Now Pronounce You Chuck and Larry*, may play on the otherness of LGBT people, but these do not dramatize the dangers of homophobia—if anything, they make a spurious case for gay privilege.

9   Kaz, who is refused the chance to serve, is played by George Shibata, a Nisei from Utah who became the first Nisei West Pointer after the war.

10 Along with a pair of buddies (played by David Janssen and Vic Damone), he travels to Hawai'i, where the three date a blonde war correspondent and a pair of Nisei bar hosts (one of whom does a striptease). The movie does not make any commentary on martial law in Hawai'i. Finally Guy is sent into action on Saipan (though filming was done in Okinawa).

11 Robert Ito, the Nisei actor who portrays Mr. Kawashima, was himself placed in the Japanese Canadian confinement sites as a teenager. He resettled in Montreal, becoming a ballet dancer, before establishing a career in Hollywood, most notably as a laboratory assistant on the TV series *Quincy, M.E.*

12 Although the British Columbia Security Commission was dissolved at the end of 1942, and Japanese Canadians became subject to the decrees of the Ministry of

Labour, the government agency continues to be called the BCSC throughout the film.

13 Given that there were no fifth-generation Japanese Americans and few if any fourth-generation, it seems improbable that there would have been any inmates with only 1/16th Japanese ancestry.

14 Paul Spickard, "Injustice Compounded: Amerasians and Non-Japanese Americans in World War II Concentration Camps," *Journal of American Ethnic History* 5, no. 2 (Spring 1986), 5–23.

15 Esther Newman, "Yoshitaro Amano, Canal Zone Resident and Prisoner #203," *Discover Nikkei*, July 7, 2010, www.discovernikkei.org/en/journal/2010/7/7/yoshitaro -amano.

16 Testimony of Grace Shimizu, in "Treatment of Latin Americans of Japanese Descent, European Americans, and Jewish Refugees During World War II," Hearing before the Subcommittee on Immigration, Citizenship, Refugees, Border Security, and International Law of the Committee on the Judiciary, House of Representatives, 111th Cong., 1st sess., March 19, 2009.

17 Lisa C. Miyake, "Forsaken and Forgotten: The U.S. Internment of Japanese Peruvians during World War II," *Asian American Law Journal* 9 (2002): 163.

Chapter 4: Wartime Confinement and Japanese Americans: Friends and Foes

1 Dorothy Day, "Grave Injustice Done Japanese on West Coast," *Catholic Worker*, June 1942.

2 Dorothy Day, "Day after Day," *Catholic Worker*, July/August 1942.

3 Fabrice Robinet, "The Very Busy Life of an Immigrants' Rights Priest in 2018," *New York Times*.

4 "Brother Theophane Toasted Tomorrow," *Rafu Shimpo*, August 25, 1971

5 Larry Tajiri, "The Hearst Hand in Chicago," *Pacific Citizen*, August 12, 1944.

6 Letter from Brother Theophane Walsh to Mary Theresa Oishi, August 1944. Personal collection of Jonathan van Harmelen.

7 *Nichi Bei Times*, October 31, 1948.

8 Theophane Walsh, "A Few Words of Praise," *Kashu Mainichi*, February 21, 1959.

9 A 2016 MA thesis from the University of Paris explores Chinese-Japanese solidarity in the United States during this era. Léo Szwalberg, "Les luttes communes des Japonais-Américains et des Chinois-Américains de la Seconde Guerre mondiale à l'égalité des droits civiques: 1941–1988," https://rechercheisidore.fr/search /resource/?uri=10670/1.thp3u4.

10 Jane Hong, "Asian American Response to Incarceration," *Densho Encyclopedia*, https://encyclopedia.densho.org/Asian_American_response_to_incarceration.

11 *Pacific Citizen,* July 16, 1942. The *Pacific Citizen* had earlier reported that a Miyo Joan Kobuchi had been granted permission to leave Santa Anita to be married to Ernest Wong, a Chinese American from San Francisco. Later scholars repeated this premature (and garbled) version of the story as fact.

12 "Chinese American Blasts Persecutors of Japanese," *Topaz Times,* March 11, 1944.

Chapter 5: Political Activism and Civil Rights

1 Clifford Uyeda, "Rhetorics over Racial Discrimination," *Pacific Citizen,* November 10, 1961.

2 Clifford Uyeda, "This Is Our Voice," *Pacific Citizen,* July 26, 1963.

3 Clifford Uyeda, "Human Rights," *Pacific Citizen,* January 6, 1967.

4 Clifford Uyeda, "Less Partisan?," *Pacific Citizen,* February 17, 1967.

5 Ellen Endo, "Intermarriage Blast Surprises PSW CLers," *Pacific Citizen,* February 17, 1967.

6 Endo, "Intermarriage Blast Surprises PSW CLers."

7 "A Critic of McCarran-Walter Immigration Naturalization Act Regards Politics of the Day, and Statutory Provisions." *Pacific Citizen,* December 24, 1952.

Chapter 6: Arts and Sciences

1 Deborah Churchman, "It's Shark-Fin Rides—Not Soup—for This Ichthyologist," *Christian Science Monitor,* January 4, 1982.

Chapter 7: The Queer Heritage of Japanese Americans

1 I came across a 1940 census entry for one "Kimie Kawahara," but because she was listed as twenty-one years old and living in Maui she was unlikely to have been a college freshman in Oahu circa 1943.

Chapter 8: Other Places, Other Lives

1 Warwick Anderson, "Racial Hybridity, Physical Anthropology, and Human Biology in the Colonial Laboratories of the United States," *Current Anthropology* 53, no. S5 (April 1, 2012): S95–S107. Relations between the two seem to have been strained. Hulse complained that Masuoka was a straitlaced Christian convert who did not smoke, drink, or swear, saying, "That doesn't make life too easy for a sinner like myself."

SELECTED BIBLIOGRAPHY

Selected Archives

Bill Hosokawa Papers. Western History/Genealogy, Central Library, Denver Public Library.

Carey McWilliams Miscellaneous Papers. Hoover Institution Archives, Stanford University, Stanford, California.

Densho Archives (Densho Digital Repository). www.densho.org/archives.

Eleanor Roosevelt Papers. Franklin D. Roosevelt Library, Hyde Park, New York.

Isamu Noguchi Papers. Isamu Noguchi Foundation, Long Island City, New York.

Japanese American Research Project Interviews, 1966–1968. Bancroft Library, University of California, Berkeley.

Karl G. Yoneda Papers. Special Collections, Charles E. Young Research Library, UCLA, Los Angeles.

Mike Masaoka Papers. Special Collections, J. Willard Marriott Library, University of Utah, Salt Lake City.

Miné Okubo Collections, Riverside City College, Riverside, California.

Minoru Yasui Papers. Archives and Special Collections Department, Auraria Library, University of Colorado-Denver.

Norman Thomas Papers. Manuscripts and Archives Division, New York Public Library.

War Relocation Authority Files. Record Group 210, National Archives, College Park, Maryland, and Washington, DC.

Yuji Ichioka Papers. Special Collections, Charles E. Young Research Library, UCLA, Los Angeles.

Books and Articles

Abe, Frank, Greg Robinson, and Floyd Cheung, eds. *John Okada: The Life and Rediscovered Work of the Author of "No-No Boy."* Seattle: University of Washington Press, 2018.

Aizumi, Marsha, and Aiden Takeo Aizumi. *Two Spirits, One Heart: A Mother, Her Transgender Son, and Their Journey to Love and Acceptance.* Arcadia, CA: Peony Press, 2012.

Azuma, Eiichiro. *Between Two Empires: Race, History, and Transnationalism in Japanese America.* New York: Oxford University Press, 2005.

Black, Allida M. *Casting Her Own Shadow: Eleanor Roosevelt and the Shaping of Postwar Liberalism.* New York: Columbia University Press, 1996.

Bosworth, Allen R. *America's Concentration Camps.* New York: Norton, 1967.

Buck, Pearl S. *American Unity and Asia.* New York: John Day, 1942.

Butts, Ellen, and Joyce Schwartz. *Eugenie Clark: Adventures of a Shark Scientist.* North Haven, CT: Linnet Books, 2000.

Cayton, Horace R. *Long Old Road.* New York: Trident Press, 1965.

Chang, Gordon H., Mark Dean Johnson, and Paul J. Karlstrom, eds. *Asian American Art: A History, 1850–1970.* Stanford: Stanford University Press, 2008.

Chuman, Frank F. *The Bamboo People: The Law and Japanese Americans.* Del Ray, CA: Publisher's Inc., 1976.

Conn, Peter J. *Pearl S. Buck: A Cultural Biography.* New York: Cambridge University Press, 1996

Conroy, Hilary, and T. Scott Miyakawa, eds. *East across the Pacific: Historical and Sociological Studies of Japanese Immigration and Assimilation.* Santa Barbara: ABC-Clio Press, 1972.

Daniels, Roger, ed. *American Concentration Camps.* 9 vols. New York: Garland Press, 1989.

———. *Asian Americans: Chinese and Japanese in the United States since 1850.* Seattle: University of Washington Press, 1988.

———. *Prisoners without Trial: Japanese Americans in World War II.* New York: Hill and Wang, 1993.

Daniels, Roger, Sandra C. Taylor, and Harry Kitano, eds. *Japanese Americans: From Relocation to Redress.* Rev ed. Seattle: University of Washington Press, 1991.

De Genova, Nicholas, ed. *Racial (Trans)formations: Latinos and Asians Remaking the United States.* Durham, NC: Duke University Press, 2006

Eaton, Allen H. *Beauty behind Barbed Wire: The Arts of the Japanese in Our War Relocation Camps.* Foreword by Eleanor Roosevelt. New York: Harper & Brothers, 1952.

Fujino, Diane C. "Cold War Activism and Japanese American Exceptionalism: Contested Solidarities and Decolonial Alternatives to Freedom." *Pacific Historical Review* 87 (2018): 264–304.

Girdner, Audrie, and Anne Loftis. *The Great Betrayal.* New York: Macmillan, 1969.

Guthrie, Woody. *Bound for Glory*. New York: Plume, 1983.

Hansen, Arthur A., ed. *Japanese American World War II Evacuation Oral History Project*. 5 vols. Munich: K G Saur, 1991–95.

Hirasuna, Delphine. *The Art of Gaman: Arts and Crafts from the Japanese American Internment Camps, 1942–1946*. Berkeley: Ten Speed Press, 2005.

Hosokawa, Bill. *JACL in Quest of Justice*. New York: William Morrow, 1982.

———. *Nisei: The Quiet Americans*. New York: William Morrow, 1969.

Howard, John. *Concentration Camps on the Home Front: Japanese Americans in the House of Jim Crow*. Chicago: University of Chicago Press, 2008.

Ichioka, Yuji. *The Issei: The World of the First Generation Japanese Immigrants, 1885–1924*. New York: Free Press, 1988.

Irons, Peter. *Justice at War*. New York: Oxford University Press, 1983.

Ito, Kazuo. *Issei: A History of Japanese Immigrants in North America*. Translated by Shinichiro Nakamura and Jean S. Gerard. Seattle: Japanese Community Service, 1973.

Kashima, Tetsuden. *Judgment without Trial: Japanese American Imprisonment during World War II*. Seattle: University of Washington Press, 2003.

Kawaguchi, Sanae. *The Insect Concert*. Boston: Little Brown, 1958.

———. *Taro's Festival Day*. Boston: Little Brown, 1957.

Kawakami, Kiyoshi Karl. *Asia at the Door: A Study of the Japanese Question in Continental United States, Hawaii and Canada*. New York: Fleming H. Revell, 1914.

———. *Jokichi Takamine:. A Record of His American Achievements*. New York: W. E. Rudge, 1928.

———. *The Real Japanese Question*. New York: Macmillan, 1921.

Kikumura-Yano, Akemi, ed. *Encyclopedia of Japanese Descendants in the Americas: An Illustrated History of the Nikkei*. Walnut Creek, CA: AltaMira Press, 2002.

Kurashige, Scott. *The Shifting Grounds of Race: Blacks and Japanese Americans in the Making of Multiethnic Los Angeles*. Princeton, NJ: Princeton University Press, 2008.

La Violette, Forrest E. *Americans of Japanese Ancestry: A Study of Assimilation in the American Community*. Toronto: Canadian Institute of International Affairs, 1945.

———. *The Canadian Japanese and World War II: A Sociological and Psychological Account*. Toronto: University of Toronto Press, 1948.

Leong, Karen J. *The China Mystique: Pearl S. Buck, Anna May Wong, Mayling Soong, and the transformation of American Orientalism*. Berkeley: University of California Press, 2005.

Mackey, Mike, ed. *Guilt by Association: Essays in Japanese Settlement, Internment, and Relocation in the Rocky Mountain West*. Powell, WY: Western History Publications, 2001.

Maki, Mitchell T., Harry H. L. Kitano, and S. Megan Berthold. *Achieving the Impossible Dream: How Japanese Americans Obtained Redress*. Urbana: University of Illinois Press, 1999.

Martin, Ralph G. *Boy from Nebraska*. New York: Harper & Row Brothers, 1946.

Masuoka, Jitsuichi, and Preston Valien, eds. *Race Relations: Problems and Theory: Essays in Honor of Robert E. Park*. Chapel Hill: University of North Carolina Press, 1961.

Matsumoto, Toru. *The Seven Stars*. New York: Friendship Press, 1949.

Matsumoto, Toru, and Marion O. Lerrigo. *A Brother Is a Stranger*. New York: John Day, 1946.

McWilliams, Carey. *Prejudice: Japanese-Americans: Symbol of Racial Intolerance*. Boston: Little, Brown, 1944.

Miki, Roy. *Redress: Inside the Japanese Canadian Call for Justice*. Vancouver: Raincoast Books, 2004.

Minatoya, Lydia. *Talking to High Monks in the Snow: An Asian-American Odyssey*. New York: Harper Perennial, 1999.

Mittwer, Henry. *Zen Flowers: Chabana for the Tea Ceremony*. Rutland, VT: Charles Tuttle, 1992.

Miyakawa, Tetsuo Scott. *Protestants and Pioneers: Individualism and Conformity on the American Frontier*. Chicago: University of Chicago Press, 1964.

Mohl, Raymond A., John E. Van Sant, and Chizuru Saeki, eds. *Far East, Down South: Asians in the American South*. Tuscaloosa: University of Alabama Press, 2016.

Muller, Eric L. *American Inquisition: The Hunt for Japanese American Disloyalty during World War II*. Chapel Hill: University of North Carolina Press, 2007.

Myer, Dillon. *Uprooted Americans*. Tucson: University of Arizona Press, 1971.

Niiya, Brian, ed. *Japanese-American History: An A to Z from 1868 to the Present*. New York: Facts on File, 1983.

Okada, John. *No-No Boy*. Seattle: University of Washington Press, 1977.

Piehl, Mel. *Breaking Bread: The* Catholic Worker *and the Origin of Catholic Radicalism in America*. Philadelphia: Temple University Press, 1982.

Robinson, Greg. *After Camp: Portraits in Midcentury Japanese American Life and Politics*. Berkeley: University of California Press, 2012.

———. *By Order of the President: FDR and the Internment of Japanese Americans*. Cambridge: Harvard University Press, 2001.

———. *A Tragedy of Democracy: Japanese Confinement in North America*. New York: Columbia University Press, 2009.

Robinson, Greg, and Robert S. Chang, eds. *Minority Relations: Intergroup Conflict and Cooperation*. Oxford: University Press of Mississippi, 2016.

Robinson, Greg, and Toni Robinson. "*Korematsu* and Beyond: Japanese Americans and the Origins of Strict Scrutiny." *Law and Contemporary Problems* 68, no. 2 (Spring 2005): 29–55.

Seigel, Shizue. *In Good Conscience: Supporting Japanese Americans during the Internment*. San Francisco: Asian American Curriculum Project, 2006.

Shaffer, Robert. "Cracks in the Consensus: Defending the Rights of Japanese Americans during World War II." *Radical History Review* 72 (June 1998): 84–120.

Takahashi, Jere. *Nisei/Sansei: Shifting Japanese American Identities and Politics*. Philadelphia: Temple University Press, 1998.

Tateishi, John. *And Justice for All: An Oral History of the Japanese American Detention Camps*. New York: Random House, 1984.

Thomson, William T. *The World of Bamboo*. William T. Thomson, 1987.

Tremayne, Russell M., and Todd Shallat, eds. *Surviving Minidoka: The Legacy of WWII Japanese American Incarceration*. Boise, ID: Boise State University Publications Office, 2013.

US Commission on Wartime Relocation and Internment of Civilians. *Personal Justice Denied: Report of the Commission on Wartime Relocation and Internment of Civilians*. Seattle: University of Washington Press, 1997. First published 1982.

US Department of the Interior. War Agency Liquidation Unit. *People in Motion: The Postwar Adjustment of the Evacuated Japanese-Americans*. Washington, DC: Government Printing Office, 1947.

US Department of the Interior. War Relocation Authority. *WRA: A Story of Human Conservation*. New York: AMS Press, 1978. First published 1946.

Uyeda, Clifford I. *Suspended: Growing up Asian in America*. San Francisco: National Japanese American Historical Society, 2000.

Wat, Eric C. *The Making of a Gay Asian Community: An Oral History of Pre-AIDS Los Angeles*. Lanham, MD: Rowman & Littlefield, 2001.

Weglyn, Michi Nishiura. *Years of Infamy: The Untold Story of America's Concentration Camps*. Updated ed. Seattle: University of Washington Press, 1996. First published 1976.

Williams, Duncan Ryuken. *American Sutra: A Story of Faith and Freedom in the Second World War*. Cambridge: Harvard University Press, 2018.

Williams, Duncan Ryuken, ed. *Hapa Japan*. Los Angeles: Kaya Press, 2017. 2 vols.

Yashima, Taro. *Horizon Is Calling / Suiheisen wa maneku*. New York: Henry Holt, 1947.
———. *The New Sun*. New York: Henry Holt, 1943.

Yoneda, Karl G. *Ganbatte: Sixty-Year Struggle of a Kibei Worker*. Los Angeles: UCLA Asian American Studies Center, 1983.

Japanese American Press

Bandwagon (New York)
Chicago Shimpo
Continental Times (Toronto)
Crossroads (Los Angeles)
Doho (Los Angeles)

Gyo-Sho: A Magazine of Nisei Literature (English Club of Cornell College)

Hawaii Hochi (Honolulu)

Heart Mountain Sentinel (Wyoming)

Hokubei Mainichi (San Francisco)

Hokubei Shimpo / New York Nichibei (New York City)

JACD News Letter (Japanese American Committee for Democracy, New York City)

JACL Reporter (Japanese American Citizens League, Salt Lake City)

Japanese American Courier (Seattle)

Japanese American Mirror (Los Angeles)

Japanese American Review (New York City)

Kashu Mainichi (Los Angeles)

Manzanar Free Press (Manzanar, California)

New Canadian (Vancouver and Toronto)

New World Sun (Shin Sekai) (San Francisco)

Nichi Bei Shimbun (California Japanese-American News) (San Francisco)

Nichi Bei Times (San Francisco)

Nisei Weekender (New York City)

Northwest Times (Seattle)

Pacific Citizen (Salt Lake City and Los Angeles)

Rafu Shimpo (Los Angeles)

Scene (Chicago)

Trek (Topaz, Utah)

CREDITS

Chapter 1. Mixed-Race Japanese Americans: Family Stories

"*Hapa* Japanese America: An Overview," adapted from Greg Robinson, "The Early History of Mixed Race Japanese Americans," in *Hapa Japan: History*, vol. 1, edited by Duncan Ryuken Williams, 225–50 (Los Angeles: Kaya Press, 2017)

"Three Generations of the Takamine Family," *Nichi Bei Weekly*, October 17, 2013

"George and Arthur Hirose, "*Nichi Bei Weekly*, November 7, 2013 and March 6, 2014

"The Ohnick Family," *Hapajapan.com*, August 7, 2017

"The Thomson Family," *Hapajapan.com*, July 10, 16, 18, 2018

"The Osato Family: Sono Osato and Timothy Osato," *Nichi Bei Weekly*, September 23, 2013 and January 9, 2014

Chapter 2. Literature

"How *John Okada* Was Born," previously unpublished

"First Impressions: Early Reviews of *No-No Boy*," *Discover Nikkei*, June 7, 2018

"Sanae Kawaguchi and Mitsu Yamamoto: Nisei Women Writers," *Nichi Bei Weekly*, February 20, 2014

"Mary Oyama Mittwer and Henry Mittwer," *Nichi Bei Weekly*, December 20, 2012, and *Hapajapan.com*, October 31, 2017

"Nisei Poet Ambrose Amadeus Uchiyamada," *Nichi Bei Weekly*, September 5, 2013

"K. K. and Clarke Kawakami, Journalists" (with Chris Suh), *Discover Nikkei*, February 22, 2018, *and Nichi Bei Weekly*, January 1, 2017

Chapter 3: Wartime Confinement and Japanese Americans: Nikkei Stories

"Japanese Americans and Pearl Harbor: Another Sort of Infamy," Society for Historians
of Foreign Relations online forum, December 3, 2011

"Tsuyoshi Matsumoto: Teacher and Artist," *Discover Nikkei*, October 12, 2017

"Toru Matsumoto: Brother and Stranger," *Discover Nikkei*, December 13, 2017

"Parallel Wars: Comparing Early Japanese American and Japanese Canadian Internment
Films," *Discover Nikkei*, January 26–27, 2010

"The Unknown History of the Japanese American Committee for Democracy," *Discover
Nikkei*, January 11, 2018

"Mixing the Races," *Surviving Minidoka: The Legacy of WWII Japanese American Incarceration*, edited by Russell Mark Tremayne, Todd Shallat, and Melissa R. Lavitt,
27–39 (Boise, Idaho: Boise State University, 2013)

"The Unknown History of Japanese Internment in Panama" (with Maxime Minne),
Discover Nikkei, April 26, 2018

Chapter 4: Wartime Confinement and Japanese Americans: Friends and Foes

"Dorothy Day, the Catholic Worker and Executive Order 9066" (with Matthieu
Langlois), *Discover Nikkei*, August 14, 2018

"Brother Theophane Walsh, a Quiet Hero" (with Jonathan Van Harmelen), *Discover
Nikkei*, March 15, 2019

"Pearl S. Buck, Defender of the Nisei," *Densho Encyclopedia*, September 2015

"First Lady of the World? Reconsidering Eleanor Roosevelt and Japanese Americans,"
previously unpublished

"They've Come a Long Way: Chinese American Support for Japanese Americans in
World War II," *Discover Nikkei*, November 13, 2018

"Woody Guthrie and Japanese Americans," *Nichi Bei Weekly*, January 24, 2013

"Forrest LaViolette and the Paradoxes of Wartime Confinement," *Nichi Bei Times*,
November 1, 2007

Chapter 5. Political Activism and Civil Rights

"Clifford Uyeda and Ben Kuroki: Nisei Conservatives," *Discover Nikkei*, September 24, 2018

"Japanese-Americans and the McCarran-Walter Act," *Nichi Bei Weekly*, July 11, 2013

"Loren Miller: African American Defender of Japanese Americans," *Discover Nikkei*,
July 25, 2017

"Aiko Herzig-Yoshinaga, Godmother of Japanese American Redress Movement,"
Discover Nikkei, August 27, 2018, and *Nichi Bei Weekly*, August 16, 2018

"The Groundbreaking Political Career of Jean Sadako King," *Hapajapan.com*, March 15, 2018

"Diverging Paths: Redress in the United States and Canada," *Nikkei Voice*, September 2013

Chapter 6: Arts and Sciences

"Taro and Mitsu Yashima—War Heroes of Art" (with Valerie Matsumoto), *Discover Nikkei*, September 11, 2018

"Yoichi Okamoto: LBJ's White House Photographer," *Discover Nikkei*, October 11, 2018

"Prewar Nisei Films and Filmmakers," *Nichi Bei Weekly*, January 1, 2018

"Sueo Serisawa: A Life in the Arts," *Nichi Bei Weekly*, February 1, 2018

"Newton Wesley, Chicago Nisei Inventor of the Contact Lens," *Discover Nikkei*, November 21, 2017

"Eugenie Clark—the Shark Lady from Brooklyn," *Hapajapan.com*, July 6, 2018

Chapter 7: The Queer Heritage of Japanese Americans

"The Archeology of Queer *Nikkei* History," *Nichi Bei Weekly*, June 21, 2018

"The Evolution of Community Opinion and the Rise of Homophobia," *Nichi Bei Weekly*, June 25, 2015

"Japanese Americans Coming Out in the 1970s—The Community Forum," *Nichi Bei Weekly*, June 13, 2013

"Pioneering Nisei Lesbians," *Nichi Bei Weekly*, June 22, 2017

"Military Service and the Shift to Equal Rights," *Nichi Bei Weekly*, June 24, 2016

"Marsha Aizumi's *Two Spirits, One Heart*," *Nichi Bei Weekly*, January 1, 2013

Chapter 8. Other Places, Other Lives

"Japanese Americans in Mobile, Alabama," *Nichi Bei Weekly*, September 13, 2018

"Japanese Americans in Upstate New York," *Nichi Bei Weekly*, May 2, 2013; October 13, 2013

"Be a Good Sport about It: *Nikkei* Athletes in Louisiana," *Discover Nikkei*, September 5, 2017

"The Ito Sisters of Chicago," *Discover Nikkei*, October 30, 2018

"Jitsuichi Masuoka, Issei Sociologist at Fisk University," *Densho Encyclopedia*, December 2016

"The Adventures of T. Scott Miyakawa," *Discover Nikkei*, November 29–30, 2018

Epilogue

"*Nunc Pro Tunc*: The Story Behind a Phrase," *Discover Nikkei*, December 19, 2018

INDEX

Hoover, J. Edgar, 196
Hosokawa, Bill, 56, 138, 264

Iiyama, Chizu, 111*fig.*, 115
Iiyama, Ernest, 111*fig.*, 115
immigration, 95, 125, 130, 173, 183, 238, 245,
    263–64, 270; immigration restrictions,
    8, 81, 118, 163. *See* McCarran-Walter Act
    of 1952
Inukai, Kyohei, 9
Issei, 8, 56, 63, 92, 110, 137, 238, 259, 263–65;
    artists, 111; immigration of, 163, 168–69;
    internment of, 92, 119, 127; leaders, 112,
    115; laborers, 76, 137, 143, 198; photogra-
    phers, 193; sociologists, 252–56; writers,
    76–82, 135, 191
Ithaca, New York, 239–40
Ito, Eileen (Irene), 251
Ito, Elizabeth, 251
Ito, Josephine, 249–50
Ito, Tokumatsu, 248

Japanese American Citizens League (JACL),
    56, 99, 136, 141, 175, 182, 218, 260, 263; local
    chapters, 71, 115, 200, 205, 261; LGBT
    relations and, 226–30; civil rights activ-
    ism of, 158–69, 171–72, 183
Japanese American Committee for Democ-
    racy (JACD), 42, 110–15, 135, 150, 189
Japanese American Courier, 138, 154
Japanese American Research Project
    (JARP), 263–64
Japanese Canadians, 107–9, 155–56, 181,
    183–84
Johnson, Charles S., 254–55
Johnson, Lyndon B., 161, 193, 196
Jubilee (Catholic magazine), 55

Kashima, Tetsuden, 267, 272
Kashu Mainichi, 57, 75, 133, 218
Kawaguchi, Fuki Endow, 57, 62
Kawaguchi, Sanae, 57–59, 62, 268*fig.*
Kawahara, Kimei, 214–16

Kawakami, Clarke, 82–85
Kawakami, Kiyoshi Karl, 77–82, 77*fig.*
Kibei, 144, 199
King, Jean Sadako, 178–81
Kingman, Dong, 144
Kiyono Family, 235–37
Kobe Chronicle, 31
Korean Americans, 65, 171, 220
Korean War, 44, 159, 241
Korematsu, Fred, 175
Kuo, Helena, 144
Kuroki, Ben, 5, 158*fig.*, 160–62

LaViolette, Forrest, 152–56, 153*fig.*
LGBT activism, 213, 217, 220, 223, 230
Lippmann, Walter, 8
Long, Lotus, 9
Los Angeles, 14, 36, 57, 74. 93, 119, 126, 178,
    192, 256; African American community
    of, 143, 169–72, 182; art, 198–204; enter-
    tainment, 17, 27–28, 149–52, 251; Japanese
    American community of, 67–69, 94, 126,
    131–33, 215; LGBT community of, 220,
    222, 226
Los Angeles Times, 26, 65, 140, 162, 202, 227
Louisiana, 6, 193, 233, 243–48
Louisiana State University, 247
Loving v. Virginia (1967), 118, 162, 169

MacLeish, Archibald, 138, 250
Makino, Fred, 10
Manchuria, 81, 83, 258
Manzanar Free Press, 241
Marutani, William, 218–19
Maryknoll Mission, 74–75, 126–27, 131–33
Masaoka, Mike, 113, 163, 165–67
Mashino, Hiroshi "Herbie," 245–46
Masuoka, Jitsuichi, 252–56
Matsumoto, Toru, 97–101, 98*fig.*
Matsumoto, Tsuyoshi, 92 97
McCarran-Walter Act of 1952, 14, 96, 118,
    163–69
McCloy, John J., 91, 141

University of Chicago, 120, 152–53, 254
University of Hawai'i, 89, 96, 178–79, 253
University of Southern California, 64, 215
University of Washington, 49, 153, 223, 267, 272
University of Washington Press, 5, 50, 177
Uyeda, Clifford, 5, 157

Vancouver, British Columbia, 49, 103, 108
Ventura, Mamerto, 117
Ventura, Mary Asaba, 117–18
Vietnam War, 45, 192, 196–97, 229

Walsh, Theophane, 127, 130–33, 131*fig.*
The War Between Us (film), 105, 107–10
War Relocation Authority (WRA), 127, 140,
   144, 146, 154, 160, 233, 269; resettlement
   and, 100, 127, 241–43
War Relocation Authority camps: Gila
   River, 70, 137, 138*fig.*, 140, 241; Heart
   Mountain, 56, 66, 100, 132, 144, 154, 238;
   Jerome, 233; Manzanar, 69, 106, 107, 116,
   127, 132, 173; Minidoka, 100, 118, 127, 145;
   Poston, 242; Rohwer, 233; Topaz, 21,
   146–47, 242; Tule Lake, 53, 56, 70
Wartime Civilian Control Administration
   (WCCA). *See* assembly centers.

Washington, DC, 12, 119–20, 167–68, 184, 191,
   259; entertainment in, 26–27; journalism
   and, 81–85, 196; Japanese American
   activism and, 137, 141; resettlement in,
   174–76, 249
Washington (state), 8, 25, 76, 129, 158, 159, 193,
   238
Wesley, Newton, 6, 205–8
Wheaton College, 15
World War I, 28, 32–33, 108, 127
World War II, 62, 87, 116, 120, 135, 143, 148,
   158, 162, 181; Battle of Leyte Gulf, 85;
   draft resistance and, 52; military service
   in, 75, 238, 241, 262; film portrayals of,
   102

Yamada, Mitsuye, 227
Yamamoto, Hisaye, 57, 130
Yamamoto, Mitsu, 57, 60–62
Yamashita, Bruce, 229
Yashima, Taro, 187–92, 188*fig.*
Yashima, Mitsu, 187–92
Yasui, Minoru, 62–63, 159
Yin Kim v. California (1946), 171
Yoneda, Karl, 84, 105
Yonsei, 222

ABOUT THE AUTHOR

Courtesy of Émilie Tounevache, l'Université du Québec à Montréal

Greg Robinson is professor of history at l'Université du Québec à Montréal and the author of several books, including *After Camp: Portraits in Midcentury Japanese American Life and Politics* and *By the Order of the President: FDR and the Internment of Japanese Americans*. He also coedited *John Okada: The Life and Rediscovered Work of the Author of "No-No Boy,"* which won the 2019 American Book Award from the Before Columbus Foundation.

THE SCOTT AND LAURIE OKI SERIES IN ASIAN AMERICAN STUDIES